The Window Seat Pilot

D1739300

Robert "Russ" Singleton

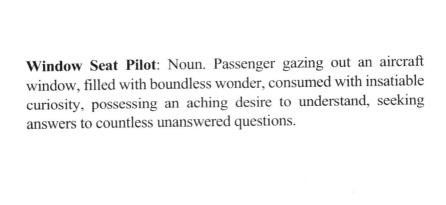

Window Seat Pilot: Noun. Passenger gazing out an aircraft window, filled with boundless wonder, consumed with insatiable curiosity, possessing an aching desire to understand, seeking answers to countless unanswered questions.

The Window Seat Pilot
Copyright 2023 © Robert "Russ" Singleton

The Flight Plan

Window Seat Pilots 1

The "Chair Fly" Drive 4

Showtime 6

Ramp Dance 17

Engines Spinning, Wheels Turning 41

Ground-Stop 52

We Slip The Surly Bonds 61

Hub and Spoke 68

A Venetian Canal 83

Rapid-D And Clear of Traffic 90

Oceanic Clearance 107

The Automation Tour 115

Feet Wet 122

Gustave And The Chip Log 135

"Break Time" 151

Reflections 163

Awake Amid The Bumps 183

Ears Popping 191

Sunrise, Clouds, Contrails 205

The Approach 217

Time To Earn The Pay Check 230

De-Brief, A Family Of Four 250

Epilogue 255

Final Words 256

Newark Liberty International Airport, Gate 126

Window Seat Pilots

Through the floor-to-ceiling windows before us; watchful, curious eyes track the jet as it rolls silently down the distant runway; accelerating from zero-to-rotate, twin rooster-tails of rainwater trailing in its wake. Smoothly and gracefully, the jet rotates and begins its silent, majestic, confident climb; corkscrew vortices spiraling off both wing-tips. A gentle thirty-degree bank, an effortless, climbing left turn. Cloud entry, and lost from sight.

The eyes sweep left, once again, to observe the silent progress, as yet another jet, having received its takeoff clearance, takes the active runway. The jet's strobe lights, wing lights and landing lights come alive; joining the brilliant reds, whites, blues, ambers and greens of the taxiway and runway lighting. An unseen hand advances the throttles, and the jet begins to roll. The nose-gear settles ever so slightly, as the jet accelerates from zero to just over 180 miles per hour. With a mile of runway to the rear, and a mile of runway ahead, the unseen hand pulls smoothly back on the yoke, at a ball-park rate of two degrees per second.

Yet another jet breaks free.

Tonight, to borrow the sublime words of a poet-aviator, *I will slip the surly bonds of earth, and dance the skies on laughter-silvered wings. I will join the tumbling mirth of sun-split clouds, and chase the shouting wind along. I will top the*

1

windswept heights with easy grace, where never lark or even eagle flew.

The words are those of John Gillespie Magee, from his poem High Flight, written at the age of nineteen, while flying Spitfires with the Royal Canadian Air Force, during World War Two's famous Battle of Britain.

Newark Liberty International Airport, Gate 126, Flight 28, Newark to London-Heathrow, Tail Number N95825, a Boeing 757-200. I am enjoying a few moments of relax-time before I embark upon the ninety minutes of pre-flight activity that precedes every departure. While I relax, I am taking time to connect with the one hundred and eighty passengers who will be sitting just aft of the flight-deck as we share our journey to London, thirty-five thousand feet above the frigid waters of the North Atlantic. Were it not for the passengers, there would be no flight tonight, there would be no slipping of the surly bonds. The passengers are Job One.

A family of four to my left; a mother, a father, two kids and a terrier in a kennel; have been fascinated by the silent airshow we have been observing together, through the rain-streaked windows. The children are asking the same questions that have been asked by both children and adults, all over the world, since Orville and Wilbur Wright first took to the air. Their parents, like parents all over the world, are doing their best to answer the questions breathlessly tossed their way. How does it fly? How fast does it fly? How do the pilots find the runway at night or in the fog? Where do clouds come from? The children and parents, the terrier too, will be five of our Window Seat Pilots for tonight's crossing of the North Atlantic.

As I listen to the eager questions, and the haltingly offered answers wrapped in love, the thought occurs to me: While many of my questions have been answered in the course of my forty-plus years in aviation, I still share the children's wonder and fascination with flight. Surprisingly, I still share many of their unanswered questions; for each answered question has led to yet another series of questions. I am reminded of my favorite Einstein quote: "As the circle of light increases, so too does the circumference of darkness." I have learned much through my years in aviation, yet there is still far more I have yet to learn. The humility implicit in that statement has kept me safe, alive and accident-free. I hope to keep it that way.

It is time to go to work, and it feels good.

The "Chair Fly" Drive

The city is heading home. I am heading to work. Traffic is moving along nicely, despite the heavy rain.

A dozen dog-eared index cards; frayed, rubber-banded and stained; lay in my lap. I have them committed to memory, inside and out, word for word. As the wipers sweep, and as the defrost works its magic; I am working my way through my pre-departure chair-fly routine, an expression first heard on the windswept plains of Enid, Oklahoma over four decades ago, while enrolled in Air Force flight training, at Vance Air Force Base, Class 81-07.

The chair-fly habit carried me safely through the intense and demanding years of military flight training, years marked by a fifty-percent wash-out rate and the loss of two classmates in fatal flight training accidents. It has likewise carried me safely through the four decades which have followed, here and abroad, through thick and thin.

Chair fly. *As I sit in my chair, I fly through the emergency procedures* summarized on the stained index cards laying in my lap: My eyes simulate darting from one flight instrument to the next; checking in with airspeed, altitude, heading, bank and pitch; as my fingers, hands and feet simulate their flow through each control movement. I am donning my oxygen mask, adding rudder, aileron and elevator. I am disengaging auto-pilot and/or auto-throttles. I am deploying or retracting speed-brakes, advancing or retarding thrust levers. I am punching the go-around switch, selecting maximum reverse thrust, or applying maximum manual braking.

Each chair-fly routine is reinforcing the muscle memory of Immediate Action items. As per the Flight Manual: *"Immediate Action items must be accomplished immediately; and, if delayed, would put crewmembers, passengers and aircraft in immediate jeopardy."*

I have been paid to fly, train and evaluate, in three different seat positions, in seventeen different models, of ten different aircraft. The chair-fly has been with me on every flight, every time; from first flight through this flight; and will remain with me through my retirement flight. It is a habit worth keeping.

I wrap up my review of the chair-fly scenarios, as I approach the airport exit. Comfortably seated in my chair, during the course of my drive, I have flown through a rapid decompression, an engine-failure on takeoff, an aborted/rejected takeoff, a two-engine flame-out, a single-engine go-around, a two-engine go-around, a terrain-avoidance maneuver, and a wind-shear escape.

If any of the scenarios were to occur on this evening's flight, my chair-fly drive ensures "I have *just* been there, I have *just* done that."

Newark Liberty International Airport, Flight Planning Area

Showtime

I have journeyed to the Crew Room and checked my mail-file for the latest flight publication updates. Tonight's updates include a change to the "Dual Hydraulic Failure" checklist, along with the latest Hong Kong, Quito and Stockholm arrival and departure changes. I have met Francis, the First Officer (FO); and Erica, the International Relief Officer (IRO). Handshakes all around.

There is a decades-old phrase associated with flying: "Kick the tires, and light the fires." Modern flight requires we first print the papers or download the data. Long before we step foot on the jet, we will work our way through fifty-seven pages of paperwork.

"Fit For Duty" Acknowledgement: Our first (arguably most important) pre-flight action, is the legally-driven FAA requirement, and the ethically-driven professional requirement, to affirmatively state we are mentally and emotionally, physically and medically, and in every other way, fit for duty. Every element of the flight-safety architecture is contingent upon self-monitoring one's fitness for duty. I check the box, hit the Send prompt, and the paperwork cascade commences. Francis and Erica do the same.

I have raised the red-flag on fitness-for-duty on one occasion. With an early evening show-time for a North Atlantic crossing to Glasgow, Scotland; we remained on the ground, in Newark, early the next morning, eleven hours later. We had suffered the endless delays associated with a massive East Coast snow-storm. We had taxied-out, and been de-iced, on two occasions. We had returned to the gate on both occasions, due to heavy snow and winds making for problematic visibility and impassable taxiways and runways. Despite the all-night delay, eleven hours later, in terms of both contract provisions and FAA regulations, we were still legal to fly.

There is a time to respectfully say "No Sir, No Ma'am." That episode was one such time. After eleven hours of all-night duty, with no time for rest, we were no longer fit to fly a seven-hour leg across the North Atlantic.

The Dispatch Release: The first pages off the printer, our *Dispatch Release,* grants us formal authority to take the jet from Newark to London-Heathrow. My signature on the Release, conveys my Pilot-In-Command acceptance of the conditions (weather, fuel load, maintenance status, cruise altitude and routing) under which our flight has been released.

Prior to my *Dispatch Release* signature, we (as a crew) will examine each of the fifty-seven pages with a fine-tooth comb; ensuring we are familiar with, and in agreement with, conditions laid out hours ago, in an office over a thousand miles away, by a team of dispatchers we have not met, utilizing a computer program we did not write. Our licenses, our lives and the lives of our Window Seat Pilots, are in play with each flight. The fine-tooth-comb review of the paperwork is a must.

One year prior to my entry into the flying profession, the crew of a Boeing 747 failed to use the fine-tooth-comb in the review of their flight papers; leading them to plan for an instrument approach, at their destination, that was listed, in their flight papers, as out-of-service. An unpleasant, tragic scenario ensued. We will use the fine-tooth-comb. Every time.

The "Minimum Equipment List" (MEL) is our first focus item. Our number seven brake (of eight brakes) has been deactivated and disconnected. A quick review of the MEL, confirms we are good-to-go. Under the Operations Considerations heading, we note the deactivated and disconnected brake will cost us a takeoff-weight penalty in Newark, and a landing-distance penalty upon our arrival in London-Heathrow; both due to reduced braking effectiveness.

The Minimum Equipment List (a joint effort of the FAA, the airline and the aircraft manufacturer) is, as the words suggest, a *list of the minimum equipment* required for dispatch, along with the required maintenance and operations considerations for any missing, inoperative, or degraded items. The MEL takes into account "the next critical failure" and provides an "acceptable level of safety" under "normal conditions."

The MEL is generally a solid and well-respected document. Having said that, a Captain (with flight-crew input) is expected to exercise her judgment in choosing to accept (or reject) an otherwise MEL-approved dispatch condition. I have opted to reject an MEL-approved aircraft on one occasion.

That one occasion constituted a flight between the Hawaiian Islands and the west coast of North America. At the time, it was the longest scheduled overwater segment, worldwide, without a suitable diversion option. Over the course of six hours, on four occasions, we had departed the Honolulu gate and begun our taxi to the departure runway. On each of those four taxi-outs, we experienced the failure, partial or total, of an onboard system. In each instance, we returned to the gate for corrective maintenance action. In each instance the system was MEL-able. In other words, we were good-to-go with the failed or compromised system.

Following the fourth taxi-out and the fourth gate-return, as we approached the six-hour delay, with a six-hour flight still ahead of us, following coordination with our Dispatch, I exercised Captain's Authority and cancelled the flight.

While each of the system failures had been MEL-able (accounting for the next "critical failure"); the cumulative impact of the failures, when coupled with a six-hour delay; on the longest scheduled overwater segment, worldwide, without a suitable diversion option; placed me out of my comfort zone. We were well beyond the "normal conditions" cited in the MEL preamble. Moreover, while the MEL accounted for the next "critical failure," it was unable to account for the next, and the next and the next critical failure. It was time to call it a day.

The Flight Plan contains twenty-eight flight segments, from Newark to London-Heathrow. Each segment is identified by latitude and longitude coordinates marking the segment start-point and segment end-point. Within each segment we have our planned altitude, ground-speed, true-airspeed, courses, wind-corrected headings, fuel-burn, forecast winds and segment enroute time.

A hard-copy of the company flight plan will accompany us, on the flight deck, as we cross the North Atlantic, allowing for real-time tracking of our actual performance. That actual performance, when compared to our planned performance, will allow for well-informed enroute adjustments and decision-making.

Upon arrival in London-Heathrow, we will likely hand the flight plan (as a souvenir) to a deplaning Window Seat Pilot, as we thank them for their business. Their souvenir will likely be covered with a jumble of hand-written notes (radio frequencies, fuel figures, pitch and power settings, winds and compass headings), reflecting the details of our Atlantic crossing.

This evening, our flight-plan calls for a takeoff weight of 236,600 pounds, on North Atlantic Track Whiskey, at Flight Level 350 (thirty-five thousand feet above mean sea level), with an enroute time of six hours and thirty-five minutes. While carrying 38,000 pounds of *pay*-load (*paying* passengers and cargo), we will burn 49,000 pounds of fuel as we cover the 3,089 miles to London. We are planned for fifty-nine minutes of taxi time between gate push-back and takeoff.

Reserve Fuel: We take a moment to make one simple, yet critical, calculation. While programming our Flight Management Computer (FMC) during the aircraft pre-flight, we will be prompted to enter an FAA-required Reserve Fuel figure.

That FAA-required Reserve Fuel is the sum of our Alternate Fuel and our 30-Minute Reserve fuel; allowing sufficient fuel for a divert to our planned Alternate (Manchester) plus thirty minutes of additional Reserve fuel. Put another way, the FAA-required Reserve Fuel will allow us to divert to our alternate, and land with thirty minutes of fuel remaining.

This evening, that calculation (often referred to as Bingo Fuel) is a very straightforward 4,900 pounds (Alternate Fuel) plus 3,400 pounds (30-Minute Reserve) for a total of 8,300 pounds.

Have I ever been short of fuel? Twice. In an earlier life, while conducting an overwater, night, low-level, air-refueling mission, off the Atlantic coast of Florida; my crew and I heard a "May-Day, May-Day, May-Day" call. We immediately terminated our air-refueling mission with a "Break Away, Break Away, Break Away" call, and responded to an ultimately fatal aircraft loss over the Gulf of Mexico.

Equipped with a robust communications suite, we remained on-scene, coordinating the search effort, until hitting our Bingo-Fuel (Alternate plus Reserve). Upon reaching Bingo, we returned to our home station; only to find, upon arrival, an impenetrable sea fog had rolled in, totally obscuring the airfield. We then diverted to our planned alternate (Alternate Fuel); only to discover, upon arrival, the printed guidance regarding the airfield operating hours were incorrect: The airfield was closed. Fortunately, we had sufficient play-time (Reserve Fuel) to divert to, and land at, a secondary alternate field.

More recently, overhead North Dakota, while enroute from Newark to San Francisco, the failure of our two on-board altitude-transponders (providing an altitude read-out to air traffic control), required an FAA-directed descent from 40,000 feet to 28,000 feet. The increased fuel burn at the lower altitude placed us well short of our San Francisco Bingo fuel (Alternate plus Reserve), forcing an enroute divert into Denver, for a fuel-upload, and our resumed journey onward to San Francisco.

Can you have too much fuel? Absolutely. On a recent flight from Munich to Newark, we lost two of our three hydraulic systems. Not wanting to cross the North Atlantic under those conditions, we opted to divert into London-Heathrow. Unfortunately, with a full fuel-load; appropriate for a nine-hour flight to Newark; a London-Heathrow landing would have placed our landing weight well in excess of the manufacturer's structural landing weight limitation. Of greater concern, we were simply too heavy to "fit" into either of the two London-Heathrow runways. With both concerns in mind, we declared an emergency, entered a holding pattern over the North Sea, and (in coordination with Air Traffic Control) dumped several thousand pounds of fuel (none of which reached the water's surface), allowing us to fit into the London-Heathrow runway. Following an overweight landing inspection and repairs to the hydraulic systems, we resumed our journey to Newark.

The North Atlantic Track (NAT) Message lists the latitude-longitude coordinates for eight pre-planned tracks across the North Atlantic. We cross-check our flight-planned latitude-longitude coordinates with the coordinates for our assigned NAT Track Whiskey. They are in agreement. So far, so good.

The Weather: First up, we review the forecast for our intended destination, and for our planned alternate. If, for any reason, we are unable to land at our intended destination (London-Heathrow), we will divert to our alternate airport (Manchester). The London forecast is calling for standard London weather: Scattered clouds, light winds and light rain. When going to London, always pack an umbrella. The Manchester forecast looks much the same. When going *anywhere* in the United Kingdom, always pack an umbrella.

Still focused on the weather, we turn our attention to our enroute alternates; Goose Bay, in Labrador, Canada; and Lajes, in the Portuguese Azores Islands. Here, our fine-tooth comb finds an issue. While the Goose Bay forecast looks good, the Lajes forecast is calling for low cloud ceilings at 600 feet, heavy rain, with crosswinds out of the east, gusting up to 40 miles per hour.

Not wanting to divert into Lajes under those conditions (a challenge), on one engine (an emergency), we make a quick call to our dispatcher. She agrees to amend our Dispatch Release to show Manchester as our second enroute alternate.

The Lajes weather (strong crosswinds on a wet/slippery runway) calls to mind a very pleasant memory, from an earlier life. While overnighting on the island of Shemya, at the far end of Alaska's chain of Aleutian Islands, we were called out of our crew-rest, at o-dark-thirty, and ordered to our aircraft.

Exceptionally strong winds were literally defying the wheel chocks, sliding our 175,000 pound aircraft over the sheet of ice that was the ramp. Our corrective action? Start the engines, turn into the wind, sit on the brakes and wait. With a cold box-lunch to keep us company. As an added bonus: The parking-brake was inoperative; hence, we took turns holding the brakes. For five hours. As we reveled beneath the wonder of the Northern Lights.

Wrapping up the weather, Newark has low overcast clouds, rain, reduced visibility and thunderstorms in the vicinity. Our enroute ride will be mostly smooth over North America, with pockets of light-to-moderate turbulence for the first half of our over-water segment. The descent into London-Heathrow should be smooth.

With the review complete, recognizing the ever-present threat of human error, I offer the paperwork to my flight-deck colleagues, asking each of them to conduct a thorough and independent examination.

As they do so, I turn my attention to one of the most important, and often under-rated, aspects of the job: Knowing the people with whom I will be working this evening.

With over fifteen thousand pilots, and over twenty-five thousand flight attendants, I am often working with eight crew members (two pilots, six flight attendants) whom I have never before met. Such is the case this evening.

In an effort to forge the all-important team-dynamic, I make it a point to know the names and the faces of each team-member, long before our first hand-shake. Accessing the company database, I am able to match faces and names. As we make our way to London-Heathrow, we will fill in the blanks; with the personal stories of hometowns, families, interests and hobbies.

Last task for the Flight Planning Area: Who is flying to London? Who is flying home? I win the coin toss. I will take us to London. Fran (his preferred form of address) will bring us home.

The near-universal tradition is for Captains and First Officers to alternate duties as the Pilot Flying and the Pilot Monitoring. The Pilot Flying will "actually fly" the jet. The Pilot Monitoring will "mentally fly" the jet; thinking through every decision, every application of the flight controls and every flip of a switch; from push-back in Newark, to gate arrival in London-Heathrow.

The term Pilot-Monitoring is the successor to the earlier term Pilot-Not-Flying. The change stems from the industry recognition that most aircraft accidents stem (by a wide margin) from human error. Substituting the word "Monitoring" for the earlier words "Not Flying" implies (compels) an active role (mentally fly the jet), versus the earlier passive role (not flying, along for the ride).

The change is far more than a mere case of semantics. Safety margins are substantially reduced for any pilot flying solo. The second set of eyes, calculations and judgments, is invaluable.

This evening, Fran and I are fortunate to have Erica (International Relief Officer) watching our every move, joining us in our every calculation, judgment and flight-control input.

We have one hour remaining prior to push-back. I take a moment to examine Erica's plotting chart. It looks good. I ask for, and receive, two thumbs-up. We are good-to-go. We gather our papers, I put the fine-tooth comb away, I sign the Dispatch Release, and we head out to the jet.

As we make our way through the terminal, we have with us our personal gear, and almost forty pounds of professional paperwork (Flight manuals and Jeppesen Charts). Twenty years ago, we carried the bags, one in each hand. Today, the bags are resting on wheels. We have evolved. We will continue to evolve. By the end of the year, our forty pounds of paperwork will be replaced by a single digital device. We will no longer manually update our paperwork with the latest change to the "Dual Hydraulic Failure" or the latest revisions to the Hong Kong, Quito, or Stockholm arrival charts. We will simply download and move on.

Show-time.

Reflection

With very few exceptions, virtually every aviation accident has featured an element of human error. To be human, is to commit error.

The remedy?

First: Check the ego. So long as our ego fails to account for our inevitable errors, we may (1) resist the creation of an environment that identifies threats, and allows for the timely identification of error, (2) we may resist acknowledging errors when (not if) they occur, (3) we may lose the opportunity to learn from our errors, and (4) we may lose the opportunity to share our errors with others, denying them a possible life-saving advantage in their merge with fate.

Second: Re-define "good." There was once a storyline that read as follows: Good pilots commit no errors. I am a good pilot. Therefore, I commit no errors.

Years ago, the aviation industry embarked on a full-court press to re-write that story line.

The new storyline reads as follows: Good pilots set tones and create environments, in which (1) the ubiquity of human error is acknowledged; (2) the threats that may lead to error are identified; (3) the identification of error is solicited, respected and validated; and (4) the inevitable errors are captured before they develop into unpleasant consequences.

Today, threat-and-error management plays a prominent role in flight training, flight evaluation and in every-day flight operations.

Today, every simulator check-ride, and every real-world check-ride, places an equal Pass-Fail emphasis on technical-flying skills and on threat-and-error management.

Today, a threat-and-error-management discussion is a required element of every pre-flight brief and every post-flight debrief, both real-world and simulator.

In life, as in flight: Humility, embrace it. Error, acknowledge it. Ego, check it. Good, re-define it.

Newark Liberty International Airport, Gate 126

Ramp Dance

As we approach the gate, I note the departure time displayed at the check-in desk shows a thirty-minute delay: Our 1925 push-back has been delayed to 1955.

Our first stop is with the Customer Service Agent. What has she told our Window Seat Pilots; the Mom, the Dad, the two kids, the terrier in a kennel, and the one hundred and eighty others who will be accompanying us this evening?

Her answer: Our aircraft was delayed on its inbound leg due to local weather conditions. With a glance at the weather out the window, I suspect the thirty-minute delay will be the first of many delays this evening. I render a sharp salute to the two kids, we flash our IDs to the Agent and we begin our journey down the jet-way.

Our flight attendants are already on board, conducting their pre-flight and security inspections. As we make our way up the aisle to the flight-deck, I make it a point to shake every hand and say "Hello" to every crewmember, first names all the way. We secure our bags on the flight-deck, and we begin our respective pre-flight duties.

Normally, the International Relief Officer (IRO), Erica, completes the exterior pre-flight, while the First Officer and Captain (Fran and I) complete the interior pre-flight. Tonight, despite the rain, I offer to trade duties with Erica. As I make my way through the galley, I stop for a moment to pour four cups of coffee and grab a handful of sugars and creams.

The ramp is busy this evening. The men and women who keep the jets healthy, well-fed and in the air, are hard at work. My "walk-around" is an exercise in teamwork, merely one element of the "ramp-dance" preceding each departure. While I will enjoy a dry and climate-controlled cabin for the next eight hours, the "rampers" endure the extremes of weather, twenty-four hours a day, three hundred and sixty-five days a year. I offer them cold drinks in the warmer months, and hot coffees in the cooler months. This evening, in view of the rain, I went with the coffees.

The maintenance team is conducting its own exterior inspection; correcting maintenance write-ups from the inbound crew; and servicing engine oil, hydraulic fluids and crew oxygen. The rampers are loading cargo and passenger baggage, securing the push-back tow-bar and clearing the ramp for aircraft movement. The cleaning team is disinfecting, carting out trash, cleaning seats, vacuuming carpets, mopping floors and scrubbing lavatories. The caterers are loading meals, drinks and the myriad requirements of our cabin service. Potable water is being loaded from the ramp. Lavatory waste is being trucked away. The fuelers are pumping the gas.

An unseen load-planning team is ensuring our weights (empty aircraft weight, passengers, cargo, baggage and fuel) are within limits and properly distributed (balanced) throughout the cabin, the cargo holds and the fuel tanks. Those weight limits vary by aircraft, airport elevation, outside air temperature, surface winds and the nature of our cargo. It can get complicated. It is vitally important. On smaller aircraft, those balance limits (which vary for take-off, cruise, and landing) often require passengers to switch seats prior to push-back from the departure gate.

Aviation literature is filled with instances in which load-planning errors have led to some unpleasant scenarios. Indeed, the literature is filled with instances in which every player on the team, both seen and unseen (air traffic control, aircraft fueling, maintenance, load planning, dispatching, marshaling, even aircraft washing), has played a role in unpleasant scenarios.

Cognizant of the wide range of flight-safety elements impacting every flight; seen and unseen, known and unknown, near and far; the flight-crew plays a key, indispensable, last-line of-defense role in catching those errors, thereby preventing unpleasant consequences. The fine-tooth comb is always with us.

With that in mind, the walk-around is an exercise in flight-safety. The landing gear is chocked. All antennas, probes and static-ports are in place, secure and free of debris. The steering bypass pin is installed. The gear down-lock pins are removed. Strut compression and brake wear indicators are within limits.

Tire pressure and tread-wear are normal. Flight-control surfaces, brakes and landing-gear are free of hydraulic leaks. The crew-oxygen blow-out disc is in place. Engine cowlings and access panels are secure with no evidence of oil leaks. Position lights and navigation lights are properly illuminated. Cabin over-pressure and under-pressure relief valves are secure. Engine and air-conditioning inlets are free of debris. Engine-reversers are stowed. Fuselage access panels and doors are flush and secure.

Aircraft have emerged from the wash-rack with duct tape (applied prior to the wash to protect sensors) remaining in place on various probes and ports; un-noticed by wash-rack personnel, by maintenance, or by flight-crew. Those aircraft have attempted to fly without the vital data those probes and ports provide. They have been unable to do so. Aircraft have been left unattended without wheel-chocks in place, without parking-brakes set. Those aircraft have followed Newton's Law of Gravity, and have rolled across ramps, over and through neighboring aircraft and hangars, before coming to rest in a ditch. Aircraft tire-pressure gages have not been examined. Those improperly inflated tires have blown at high speed while on takeoff roll. The debris from those blown tires has shredded adjacent tires. Those shredded tires have led to the collapse of landing-gear struts and punctured wing fuel tanks. Wrenches have been left within engine cowlings. Those wrenches have shredded engines while airborne. Flight-control actuator rods have been installed improperly, rendering aircraft unflyable. Unpleasant scenarios. All.

In each instance, the warning signs were there: Duct tape on sensors, no wheel-chocks, no internal or external parking-brake lights, low readings on tire-pressure gauges, tool boxes with missing wrenches, improper flight-control pre-flight checks. The walk-around is a task to be taken seriously. The last line of defense. Attention to detail. There are few other professions where inattention to detail has the potential to cost so many innocent lives.

There is an element of comfort in the routine of the walk-around. As always, it starts with the nose-cone and the nose-gear, moving on to the right-forward fuselage and the right engine; scanning the right wing's leading-edge, trailing-edge and underwing surface; pausing to examine the right main-gear; continuing along the right-aft fuselage to the tail assembly; and returning along the left side of the aircraft in reverse order. All is well.

The walk-around is an experience for the senses. Where many work-days begin with the sound of elevator music and the scent of coffee; my work-day begins with the sounds of the ground-power unit, its cousin the ground-air cart; and the ever-present scent of jet-fuel and jet exhaust; often accompanied by the seawater scents of Hawaii, Bermuda and the Caribbean; the tropical scents of Bali and Tahiti; or the Alpine scents of Munich and Zurich. I have felt the biting cold winds of an Oslo Winter, the furnace-hot winds of a Vegas Summer, the dripping humidity of the Amazon jungle and the blowing sands of the Middle East.

My hearing is treated to the sweet music of the high-pitched whine of an air-driven engine starter, the rise and fall of engine thrust settings as aircraft taxi and the distant thunder of full-power takeoffs and full-reverse landings. While my eyes remain focused on the walk-around, I cannot help but note the visual potpourri of movement as aircraft taxi in and taxi out, as distant aircraft rotate and lift-off, and as still others flare, touch-down and roll-out. All the while, I am dodging luggage carts, catering trucks, fuel tankers and cleaning vans.

There is, on occasion, the solitary walk-around of an early morning departure, the first launch of the day. The ramp is clear. The sounds are of silence. The lights are the breaking dawn of day, the jet's rotating beacon and the beam of my flashlight.

Why do I volunteer for the walk-around? I love the flood of visual, audible, tactile and olfactory memory-making moments that assault and besiege me with each ramp-dance. Oddly enough, given the tens of thousands of flight hours I will have accrued by the time of my retirement; of the many moments I will likely treasure, and dearly miss, following that retirement; the ramp-dance will rank near the top of the list. I treasure the dance.

My raincoat is soaked (but so is everyone else), we are running late, the walk-around is complete, and it is time to brief the crew. As I return to the jet-way, the aircraft fueler hands me her completed Fuel-Slip. She declines my offer for a cup of coffee. She is running behind. With an evening of anticipated weather-related delays, extra fuel will be in demand. She will be busy. With Fuel-Slip in hand, I climb the stairs of the jet-way, punch in the door access code and make my way to the forward cabin.

There are two versions of the FAA-required crew-brief: The two-word "Standard Brief" delivered to the lead flight attendant, with a relay to the full flight attendant team; or, the full crew-brief, delivered to the full crew. The former meets the regulatory requirement: The term "Standard Brief" is synonymous with "by the book." The latter, full crew-brief, serves as one part *introduction*, one part *set the tone*, one part *refresher* and one part *what is unique about this flight*. It is three minutes well-spent.

I advise our flight attendants of our flight-time, six hours and thirty-five minutes, along with our expected taxi-time of just under one hour. I review the weather, with the possibility of some bumps on our departure, a mostly smooth ride over North America, some light-to-moderate turbulence over the North Atlantic and possible weather-related delays into London-Heathrow. We review emergency procedures, with particular attention paid to the high-speed aborted/rejected takeoff. We cover methods of communication between the flight-deck and the cabin, enroute security issues and flight-deck entry procedures.

Despite the aluminum shell and the high-tech avionics, despite the behind-the-scenes computers generating flight-plans and reward-mile calculations, the airline business is a customer service business with wings. With that in mind, I see my primary role as a customer service agent, with the secondary role of flying airplanes.

Tone is all-important in developing a welcoming customer-service experience. Through-out my briefing, I make every effort to set an open tone, and remove the flight-deck door from the communication dynamic.

While security concerns mandate the flight-deck door will remain locked throughout the flight, it need not be a barrier to communication. I remind the flight-attendant team: If you see, hear, or sense something amiss, please give us a call. Aviation literature offers several lessons in this regard: Unpleasant scenarios have unfolded, in which critical, life-saving information was known in the cabin; information which was never relayed to, or solicited by, the flight-deck.

I remind the flight attendants that we are there to support them: "If there is anything we can do to help, please pick up the phone and give us a call." As a wrap, I invite them to visit the flight-deck any time they are in need of a comfortable seat, a quiet moment, or a fantastic view.

Stepping onto the flight-deck, we conduct a quick scan. All circuit breakers are in. The Halon fire extinguisher is onboard with pressure in the green. The smoke goggles and life vests are in good shape. The two window-escape-ropes are present and in good condition. The crash axe is onboard. The protective breathing mask (for fire-fighting protection) is onboard and sealed.

With a nod toward dry humor, I note the last two items: First, airport security prevents us from boarding the jet with a nail-clipper in our luggage, yet we have a crash axe on the flight-deck. Second, there are three of us on the flight-deck: If we were to experience a flight-deck fire, requiring us to discharge the halon fire extinguisher on the flight-deck; three sets of lungs, and three sets of eyes, would be subject to the hazards of smoke, fire and halon; yet, there is only one protective breathing mask on the flight-deck. How do we choose? Age, arm wrestle, coin toss, rank, seniority?

The Battery Switch is On. The Gear Handle is down. The Standby Power is in Auto. All fluid quantities are normal; with engine oil, hydraulic reservoirs and crew oxygen fully-serviced.

I drop into the left seat and reach for the Aircraft Maintenance Logbook. There are no open maintenance write-ups from previous crews. I review the closed write-ups of the last three days. Three are worth noting. Low pressure on the left hydraulic system: Maintenance has replaced a pressure sensor, pressure checks good, discrepancy has been signed off. Fuel flow for the right engine appeared high at cruise power settings: Maintenance has conducted an engine-run, discrepancy has been signed off. As per our earlier MEL discussion, brake number seven is inoperative: It has been disconnected and deactivated. The discrepancy has been signed off.

In addition to the standard maintenance pre-flight inspection; taking a two-engine aircraft across the North Atlantic, requires a maintenance inspection over and above that required for a similar two-engine flight across North America. Indeed, any two-engine aircraft that will be more than sixty minutes from an alternate airport requires an additional Extended Twin Operations (ETOPS) pre-departure service check (E-PDSC). In other words, "If we cannot put the jet on the ground in less than sixty minutes, it needs to be an especially healthy jet."

The E-PDSC has been signed off. Good to go.

As with any creature of habit, I make my nest. Crew bag stowed and open to my left, Taxi and Departure charts clipped to my chart holder, "will need" paperwork stapled and laying on the center pedestal, "may need" paperwork stapled and tossed to the left side.

My flight-deck preflight takes me on a tour of switches and displays. I ensure proper switch positions, instrument displays, warning displays and warning annunciations.

Along the way, I make some noise. The Traffic Collision Avoidance System (TCAS) calls out "TCAS System Checks OK." The weather radar calls out "Go Around, Windshear Ahead." Detection and warning systems for smoke, fire and overheat; monitoring our engines, cargo compartments and auxiliary power unit (APU); all check good with flashing red lights and alarm bells.

With my pre-flight complete, I access and print the latest Automatic Terminal Information Service (ATIS). The ATIS tells us Newark is utilizing Runway 22-Right for departures and Runway 22-Left for arrivals. The temperature is 49-degrees Fahrenheit. Winds are out of the southwest at 16 knots. The altimeter setting is 29.79 inches of mercury. Cloud ceilings are at 900 feet, visibility is roughly one mile, with rain and fog.

As we will discuss later this evening, air molecules passing over the upper surface of the wing, and beneath the lower surface of the wing, provide the key to Lift, the force enabling an aircraft to fly. Headwinds contribute more speed. More speed, gives us more air molecules. More air molecules, gives us more Lift. More Lift, gives us more "fly". Headwinds are a good thing.

While Navy aircraft carriers may tap into the benefits of headwinds, by simply turning themselves into the winds of the moment, fixed runways are unable to do so. With that in mind, runways are generally aligned to take advantage of wind's contribution to Lift. Newark's two main runways, 22-Left and 22-Right (and their reciprocal runways, 04-Right and 04-Left) are oriented along the 220-degree axis (and the reciprocal 040-degree axis). This runway alignment takes advantage of the two most prevailing wind patterns in the Newark area: Southwest winds from 220-degrees, and Northeast winds from 040-degrees. A third, less frequently used runway, aligned on the 110-degree and reciprocal 290-degree heading, accounts for occasional non-prevailing winds.

According to the ATIS, we will take off into a southwesterly headwind, gaining an extra sixteen knots of airspeed, an added dose of air molecules and an always welcome boost to our Lift.

While I make my nest and tour my half of the flight-deck, Fran likewise makes his nest and tours his half of the flight-deck. Our tours are rarely conducted without interruption. Cherie, our lead flight attendant, has a number of cabin issues, ranging from catering short-falls, to soiled seat cushions, to cabin temperature. The passengers are Job One. With that in mind, Cherie's cabin issues need to be addressed right now. With a few radio calls to Operations, they are dealt with.

The interruptions continue: Our gate agent informs us we will have on-board, undercover, security personnel, along with their assigned cabin seats. I make a mental note of those seat locations, and relay the information to Cherie, for relay to her team of flight attendants. The rampers have hazardous-material forms and live-animal forms, requiring my perusal and my signature. I peruse. I sign. I brief my colleagues. We have Hazmat in our forward cargo compartment and two live animals in our aft cargo compartment.

While Fran and I have been conducting our flight-deck tours, Erica has been conducting her cabin tour. She has checked to ensure the pneumatic-boost on all emergency doors and evacuation slides are properly charged. She has ensured megaphones, first aid kits, flashlights and the Electronic Locator Beacon (ELB) are on board and in their proper locations. She has confirmed a full load of potable water. She has confirmed the removal of lavatory waste.

Fran, Erica and I are human. As such, we will commit errors. Our task, for the next eight hours, is to catch those errors, thereby preventing any unpleasant scenarios. Our team effort in threat-and-error-management began in the Flight Planning Area, with independent reviews of the paperwork. Our team effort in threat-and-error-management will remain our constant focus, from those first moments in the Flight Planning Area, through to our London-Heathrow gate arrival. With that in mind, Fran and I are both heads-down over the Flight Management Computer (FMC) as we ensure entries are properly loaded. With Erica looking on, Fran conducts his independent check, I conduct my independent check, and together, we conduct a third check as a team.

Our North Atlantic flight will take us well beyond the range of ground-based radios and navigation aids. With that in mind, Fran conducts an operational check of our two long-range, high-frequency (HF) radios and an accuracy check of our on-board navigation systems. We have good HF radio reception. Likewise, our present-position agrees across all on-board navigation systems: Three independent Inertial Navigation Systems (INS), two independent Global Positioning Systems (GPS) and our Flight Management (FMC) system. All is well.

While tedious and redundant, pre-flight checks are key to avoiding unpleasant scenarios. The industry literature is replete with instances in which aircraft have attempted to fly with incorrect Flight Management Computer (FMC) programming.

On 20 March 2009, an Airbus A340 departing from Melbourne, Australia, was "as close as we have ever come to a major aviation disaster in Australia" (Australian Transport Safety Bureau). On its takeoff roll, the aircraft was unable to become airborne until 486-feet *beyond the departure end of the runway,* hitting a six-foot antenna 1,148-feet *beyond the departure end of the runway,* barely clearing a seven-foot perimeter fence 1,630-feet *beyond the departure end of the runway.*

The First Officer had erroneously entered a takeoff weight of 525,800 pounds rather than the correct 725,800 pounds (a 200,000-pound error); prompting the Flight Management Computer to calculate a lower-than-required takeoff thrust setting, resulting in a slower-than-required rate of acceleration, consuming the entire 12,000-foot runway length, plus an extra 486-feet *beyond the departure end of the runway.* It was their very good fortune, that their departure path took them over water, clear of any terrain or obstructions. The Captain's words: "I thought we were going to die. It was that close."

On 22 May 2015, the flight-crew of a Boeing 777 departing from Paris, committed the same error, with the First Officer's FMC entry off by 200,000 pounds. Moments later, the Captain independently committed the same 200,000-pound error. Amazingly, the First Officer completed his calculations a second time, with the same erroneous entry, off by 200,000 pounds. A frightening scenario ensued.

On 21 July 2017, a Boeing 737 departed Belfast, Northern Ireland. The industry standard minimum height for crossing the departure end of a runway is 35-feet. It was not until they were *1500-feet beyond the departure end of the runway,* that they attained the 35-foot height.

Their Flight Management Computer (FMC) required an entry for the Outside Air Temperature (OAT). The OAT at the time was 16 degrees Celsius. The flight-crew erroneously entered an incorrect OAT figure of minus 47 degrees Celsius. The incorrect OAT entry led to an erroneous, under-powered takeoff thrust calculation, a slower rate of acceleration, a much longer takeoff ground roll and an abysmally slow rate of climb. As was the case with the Melbourne departure; it was their good fortune, that the terrain sloped downhill, away from the runway, with no significant terrain or obstructions in their departure path.

On 3 September 1989, a Boeing 737 departed Sao Paulo, Brazil. Three hours and twenty minutes later, both engines flamed-out due to fuel starvation, leading to a crash-landing in the Amazon jungle. While conducting his flight-deck preflight, the Captain had erroneously entered a heading of 270 degrees, rather than the required 027 degrees. Rather than conducting his own (required) pre-flight check, the First Officer had simply copied the Captain's erroneous 270 degree heading.

There are few other professions where a single uncaught error can cost so many lives. An uncaught error in this business will not lead to the game-losing touchdown, it will not lead to a drop in the quarterly earnings report, it will not lead to an improperly sized piece of sheet-rock. While each of those errors is no doubt a matter for concern; an uncaught error in the aviation business can make for a deadly serious business.

Tedious, redundant, obsessive, compulsive, meticulous. It comes with the job. We will check. We will check again. We will do so independently. We will do so as a team. With Erica watching our every move.

Recalling the white-glove room-inspections of an earlier life, a USAF Thunderbird lead-pilot once explained the inspection rationale to an assembly of young minds: The attention-to-detail in a room-inspection (no dust to be found on the white glove) would build an attention-to-detail mindset that might, one day, save lives in the serious business of aviation. Lesson learned, sir.

It is time for the flight-deck brief. We close the flight-deck door. There will be no interruptions. "I left my ego in the parking lot. I hope you did the same. There is no room for ego on the flight-deck. Let's respect standard operating procedures, checklists and limitations. I try to do it standard every time. If you see me doing something non-standard, I am doing it by accident. Please call me on it. I will do the same for you. If I say something, brief something, or do something that does not sound right, or does not look right, please call me on it. I will do the same for you.

"Let's respect comfort zones. If anyone is uncomfortable, please speak up. The pilot flying will bring us back into the comfort zone, no questions asked. If I am not hearing what you are telling me, please keep telling me until I do hear you. If it looks like we are going to bend metal or break bones, please do whatever it takes to keep that from happening. When the smoke clears, I will thank you.

"Let's verbalize, verify and monitor the Mode Control Panel, the FMC [Flight Management Computer] and all our clearances. Let's not hit an 'Execute' button until we all know what we are executing. While 'On-Time' is important, we will not rush for any one, at any time, for any reason. If anyone is feeling rushed, please speak up: We will throttle-back, enter a holding pattern, or set a parking brake, no questions asked.

"We have some threats this evening. Departure weather and delays out of Newark: We will not rush. Fatigue on an all-night flight: We will watch each other like hawks. Two engines over the North Atlantic: We will always know our nearest alternate and how we intend to get there. International procedures into London-Heathrow: We will have a thorough briefing prior to descent. Arrival weather into London-Heathrow: We have calculated our Bingo-Fuel and we will stick with it.

"Let's have our taxi charts out during all ground operations. We do not move the jet until we all agree on where we are going. If, at any time, anyone is unsure where we are, or where we are going, please speak up. We will stop the jet, set the parking-brake and let Ground-Control yell at us. Let's minimize heads-down time while the wheels are turning on the concrete.

"If we have a broken bird, we will come back around and land. We will not keep a broken bird in the air. If we need a longer runway, we can go to JFK.

"For rejected takeoffs, please call out whatever pops up on our EICAS [Engine Indicating and Crew Alert System] display. I will call out 'Reject' or 'Continue'. If I freeze up and say nothing, please use your best judgment and execute. If I opt to 'Reject', please back me up on the engine-reversers and wing spoilers. As we come to a stop, please call Tower and hit the PA with 'Remain Seated, Remain Seated'.

"We have a good runway. We have a good jet. We have a normal takeoff weight. We have some crosswind, reduced visibility and low ceilings. We have hazardous materials in the forward compartment and pets in the rear compartment. We have a deactivated brake.

"The Newark-Eight Standard Instrument Departure (SID) for Runway 22-Right has us climbing to 400-feet on the runway heading, followed by a left turn to a heading of 190-degrees. At 2.3 miles, we will turn right to a heading of 220-degrees. The turns will come quickly. Please back me up on compliance. We will level at 5000-feet. I will hand-fly through ten thousand feet, unless things get crazy.

"In the event of an engine failure after V1, we will climb out on runway heading until 1.8 miles, followed by a right turn to a heading of 250-degrees. We will begin our flap retraction at 820-feet."

Turning to Erica, sitting in the jump-seat, I remind her: "You have the best seat in the house. You have the big picture. You are our last line of defense. Please watch us like a hawk.

"Any questions, comments, suggestions?"

With the briefing complete, I call for the Receiving Aircraft checklist. This checklist captures the critical items accomplished on our respective pre-flight tours of switches, indications and warnings. It is a challenge-and-response "check" list. Fran will call out each checklist challenge. I will visually "check" for proper switch position and/or display. I will then reply with the applicable checklist response.

"Receiving Aircraft Checklist Complete."

Checklists play a critical role in flight safety. If respected, and properly utilized, they can catch many an error, and may prevent many an unpleasant scenario. If not respected, or not properly utilized, they are worthless. The key determinant is the individual pilot. She is either a believer, or she is a non-believer.

The believer is marked with a healthy dose of humility, recognizes her potential for human error and will employ any and all tools to catch those errors, increasing the likelihood of a safe flight. I want my family on that pilot's jet.

The non-believer is marked with an overly developed ego, perceives himself as free of error, is generally dismissive of checklists, and presents a threat to all aboard. I do *not* want my family on that pilot's jet. Fortunately, the non-believers are a small and vanishing breed.

I have walked off one flight-deck in my aviation career. On the first leg of a three-day, multiple-leg trip, the Captain had refused to conduct a Receiving Aircraft Checklist. I was not about to start a three-day, multiple-leg trip with a non-believer. I grabbed my bags, I put on my hat and I walked. Based on the eye-witness account of the flight-deck jump-seater, that Captain was replaced.

Not every checklist oversight constitutes a deliberate disregard. A former flight instructor, in my earliest days of aviation, shared his checklist experience on the eve of my "initial solo." He and his back-seater (weapon systems operator) were conducting a night strike-mission. As they rolled in on their target, they were both taken aback by the uncanny ability of the ground-based air defenses to "lead" their flight-path through the entire course of their bomb-run, as evidenced by their uncomfortably close encounters with "tracer" rounds of 30mm and 40mm anti-aircraft artillery. As they later approached their aerial-refueling tanker, for a fuel top-off, my instructor reached out to flip the switches to restore his red, green and white wing-tip strobe lights, only to find they had not been turned off, as called for in the "Combat Entry Checklist," a checklist they had failed to complete.

Distraction, fear, adrenaline, task-saturation, or (in his case) a combination of all four, can conspire to wreak havoc on the best practices of checklist-discipline. Error. Humanity.

We are all caught up. Passenger boarding is nearing completion. I take a final stroll through the cabin. On my return journey, I encounter Hannah, of Anchorage, Alaska. Hannah will be this evening's nervous Window Seat Pilot. I have tried many different tacks with the nervous flyer. I have tried "You are safer on this airplane than you were on your drive to the airport." I have tried "I have been flying for forty years, and I still have all my fingers, and all my toes." I have tried "The only injury I have ever suffered was on my son's skate-board." I have tried "There are SO many redundancies built into modern aircraft, no worries."

This evening, Hannah remains unconvinced: She remains nervous. Given her nervous state, I opt to forgo the dry humor:

"When your time is up, your time is up; when my time is up, your time is up as well" and "If we do impact, I will arrive at the scene of the accident moments before you, thereby cushioning your impact."

Rather than dry humor, I invite her to join us on the flight-deck as we complete our pre-departure activity. She accepts my invitation. I suggest she bring her camera or cell-phone. Together, we make the stroll to the flight-deck, pausing in the First Class galley, where I introduce her to Cherie, our Lead Flight Attendant. With her acceptance of Cherie's kind offer of coffee or tea, we step into the flight-deck. The introductions continue: Fran and Erica.

At my urging Hannah sets herself down in the Captain's Seat, while I set myself down in the second jump-seat, across from Erica. Setting her coffee to the side, with one hand on the yoke, with the other hand on the throttles, and my Captain's hat resting atop her abundant auburn curls; Hannah flashes a warm smile as Erica captures the moment on Hannah's cell-phone camera.

Three pre-departure items remain: Our pre-departure clearance (PDC) from air traffic control, our "takeoff numbers" from load-planning, and our push-back clearance from ramp control.

First item off the printer is our PDC. With my assurance that all is well, Hannah removes the PDC clearance from the printer. Utilizing our filed flight plan, air traffic control has cleared us "as filed" from Newark to London-Heathrow. After takeoff, we are cleared for the Newark-Eight standard instrument departure (SID) with the Merit-Transition. Our transponder code is 4411. With Fran's assist, Hannah sets the 4411 transponder code. This transponder code will identify our flight to air traffic controllers from Newark push-back to London-Heathrow arrival.

With the PDC in hand, Fran, Erica and I are once again heads-down as we ensure the assigned Newark-Eight SID and the Merit Transition are properly loaded in the Flight Management

Computer (FMC). The SID checks good. The Merit Transition makes for a nice merge with our flight-planned route. We are good-to-go. I ask Hannah to confirm: With a nervous smile, she gives us two thumbs-up.

Standard Instrument Departures (SIDs) minimize air traffic controller workload, allow for flight-crew route-familiarization, and minimize radio transmissions in a congested radio environment. Having been assigned the Newark-Eight SID, with the Merit Transition, we can familiarize ourselves, ahead of time, with the expected route of flight. We can program our Flight Management Computer (FMC) and our on-board navigation aids to provide proper flight guidance. We have done so. Lastly, we can save several radio transmissions (heading 190-degrees, heading 220-degrees, altitude of 5000-feet) and an equal number of required radio read-backs, by simply accepting the SID and the transition.

The SIDs are often designed to avoid terrain surrounding an airport, assist with air-traffic separation, or respect local noise-abatement concerns. Air-traffic separation is of particular concern in the New York metropolitan area. On an average day, Newark, JFK and LaGuardia airports each have over 1100 daily flights, while Teterboro (one of the nation's busiest corporate jet airports) has over 500 daily flights; for a total of roughly 3800 daily flights. Those 3800 daily flights operate to/from four closely-spaced airports, making for a challenging air traffic control scenario. The SIDs go a long way toward assisting with aircraft separation.

Second item off the printer are our "takeoff-numbers." Again, with my assurance that all is well, Hannah removes the takeoff-numbers from the printer. Our empty weight is 135,300 pounds. We are carrying 38,000 pounds of payload, for a zero-fuel-weight of 173,300 pounds. We are carrying 63,300 pounds of fuel, for a total gross weight of 236,600 pounds. Our V1

Speed will be 142 knots. Our Vr Speed will be 148 knots. Our V2 Speed will be 154 knots. We will retract our wing flaps at 188 knots, 208 knots and 228 knots.

The V1 speed of 142 knots, will be our "Go-No-Go" speed. As we transition through 142 knots, on the takeoff roll, Fran will call out "V-1." We will be committed to the takeoff. Should an emergency occur following V1, we will treat it as an airborne emergency: We will "Go." Should an emergency occur prior to V1, we will treat it as a ground emergency: We will "No-Go."

The Vr speed of 148 knots, will be our "Rotate" speed. Fran will call "Rotate" as we pass through 148 knots. The 148 knots will provide sufficient Lift to overcome our 236,600-pound weight. Upon hearing the "Rotate" call, I will smoothly pull back on the yoke, at a ball-park rate of two degrees per second, stabilizing at roughly fifteen degrees nose-up.

The V2 speed of 154 knots, is our "Takeoff Safety Speed." It is the minimum airspeed at which our aircraft can remain airborne, with directional control, with one engine inoperative. In the event we lose an engine after V1, our target airspeed will be V2 or greater.

As the "numbers" spit off the printer, as I run my fingers through my once-red, now-grey and receding hairline, I smile at the memory of ancient history. Twenty-five years ago, pre-computer, pre-satellite-communication, pre-digital-download; while serving as a Second Officer, in the now-obsolete Flight Engineer position; calculating the takeoff-numbers was my responsibility. That task entailed flipping through a thirty-pound "performance manual" incorporating takeoff weights, airport elevation, outside air temperature, headwinds and tailwinds, runway lengths, runway slope and runway condition (dry, wet, snow depth).

Three very powerful and enduring lessons were learned through that experience. First, there are SO many opportunities for error in the calculations. Second, as was the case with our earlier-discussed Melbourne, Paris, Belfast and Sao Paulo scenarios, an error in any one of those seemingly mundane calculations, can mean the difference between walking away to a waiting limousine, or being carried off to a waiting ambulance. Third, attention to detail is a life-saver. Inattention to detail is an unforgiving threat.

I likewise recall the distinct discomfort I felt, as no one was "checking my work." While three sets of eyes, three sets of ears, three brains and an air traffic controller would be attentive to the actual flying of the airplane; my eyes and my brain were alone in my take-off data calculations. It made for a very humbling experience.

From the cabin we overhear the final cabin command: "Flight attendants, arm doors for departure, cross-check, stand-by for all-call." With push-back imminent, the flight attendants will "arm" the cabin doors and escape slides, ensuring a powerful pneumatic-boost to both, in the event an emergency evacuation becomes necessary. Once armed, they will "cross-check." Following the cross-check, they will then stand-by for an "all-call" to report "doors and slides armed."

With warm hand-shakes all around, and my politely asking her to return my Captain's hat, it is time to bid Hannah a farewell. We do so, with a promise from each of us, to stop by for a visit, at some point along our journey.

Back in the seat. The rudder pedals are adjusted for my height. I check for full rudder and full brake application, left and right. Fran does the same. Headset and microphone are in place. We have started the auxiliary power unit (APU). We have set the parking-brake. The rampers have pulled the external electric power cable and have removed the wheel chocks. We are on ship's power. I have my Seltzer, my cup of ice, my slice of lemon, my apple and my raisins. Fran and Erica have their cups of coffee.

We are ready. The ramp is ready. However, we will not move the jet until Cherie gives us a face-to-face thumbs-up, and her "Cabin Ready" statement; indicating all cabin checklists are complete, all passengers are seated, all baggage is stowed and all exit doors and slides are armed. She gives us her thumbs-up and her "Cabin Ready." The flight-deck door is closed and locked.

We secure our seat-belts and our shoulder harnesses, as our Window Seat Pilots stow their tray tables and bring their seatbacks to the full upright position. They have stowed their carry-on luggage beneath the seats in front of them and they have unplugged their personal-electronic-device charging cords. The FAA requires they do so.

Why do so? Before an aircraft can be certified for flight, it must pass a battery of tests; to include one test in which the entire aircraft, with every seat occupied, is evacuated in less than 90 seconds, utilizing only half the available exits, under night-time conditions, with nothing more than emergency cabin lighting to illuminate exit paths and emergency exits. Tray tables, seat backs, charging cords and carry-on luggage may serve as obstacles during an emergency evacuation; tripping passengers, delaying evacuation and putting lives at risk. As such, they need to be upright, stowed and unplugged.

Likewise: Cherie's pre-departure reminder to leave all carry-on luggage behind in the event of an emergency evacuation. The moment one passenger spends saving their carry-on luggage, may be the moment another passenger succumbs to smoke inhalation. Not a fair trade.

Seatbelts, while fastened, likewise constitute obstructions in an evacuation. Hence, the FAA-mandated requirement: The pilot-in-command must ensure every passenger knows how to fasten and unfasten their seatbelt, a lesson included in Cherie's pre-departure passenger briefing.

It is time to "push." I call for the "Before Push" checklist.

Fran's flow takes him through six fuel pumps and six hydraulic pumps. He hits the Seat Belt sign, activates our transponder and turns on our rotating beacon. With the flip of the rotating beacon switch, all ground traffic in the vicinity of our aircraft comes to a halt. Getting us off the gate, and on our way, is the number one priority.

With the checklist complete, Fran keys his mic-switch for the first of the many "command and control" calls required to get us from our Newark gate to our London-Heathrow gate. His first call is to Ramp-Control for push-back clearance. They reply: "Flight 28, you are cleared to push, tail to gate one-twenty."

On cue, the rampers check in with their "Ramp to flight-deck, walk around complete, all doors and access panels secure, ready for push-back."

I turn to Fran and Erica. "Are we good? Are we set?"

They reply: We are good. We are set.

I release the parking-brake, and stick with the script: "Flight-deck to ramp, parking-brake is released. Cleared to push. Tail to gate one-twenty."

With the release of the parking brake, I am conscious of a notion that virtually every retired Captain has shared with me. Once the parking brake is released, the Captain is in complete control of, and fully responsible for, the conduct of the flight. No Captain has ever referred to this moment as an Ego moment. Rather, every Captain has referred to this moment as one in which the responsibility is keenly felt, and comfortably shouldered.

The Captain is responsible for building and maintaining a healthy team dynamic; ensuring adherence to every standard operating procedure and aircraft limitation; meeting every air traffic control routing, airspeed and altitude restriction; ensuring a proper focus on the Window Seat Pilot; calmly dealing with every situation and/or emergency that may arise; and, above all else, ensuring the safe conduct of the flight, and the lives of every person aboard the aircraft.

While a wise Captain will seek inputs from all crewmembers, the ultimate responsibility for every action, choice and decision rests with the Captain. End of statement. Should something go wrong, the Captain will receive the "come see me" phone call. Following the safe landing of an emergency aircraft on the Hudson; the Hollywood movie documenting the event, was titled with but one word: The Captain's name.

While there are other professions in which singular responsibility is present, there are few others in which the responsibility is so consequential, for the lives of so many, and in which the responsibility is exercised without any level of supervision looking over one's shoulder. There is no one present, at thirty-five thousand feet over the North Atlantic, to override, and re-direct, an action.

The upshot sentiment from the retired Captains? They have been to the proverbial mountaintop. There is no other job, no other calling, that matches the responsibility and the freedom, that is experienced and exercised, as an airline Captain. None. No close second.

<u>Reflection</u>

From Day One in flight training, aspiring pilots are schooled in perhaps the greatest challenge in aviation, and perhaps one of the greatest challenges in life: The attainment and retention of situational-awareness. Though many have tried, any effort to catalog the elements of situational-awareness would be futile. No pilot has ever had, or ever will have, total situational-awareness.

The great pilots are, at all times, consciously and deliberately striving to expand their situational-awareness, while remaining ever-mindful of the limits of their situational-awareness.

Virtually every aviation accident, certainly every unpleasant scenario to be discussed during the course of our journey this evening, has stemmed from a gap in situational-awareness.

Roughly eighty-five percent of pilot-submitted flight-safety reports, include a reference to "loss of situational awareness."

The ever-present potential for a situational-awareness gap, keeps the smart pilot humble, and on the safe side of risk.

In life, as in flight: Situational awareness, seek it, retain it, and be ever-mindful of the unknowns.

Newark Liberty International Airport, Gate 126

Engines Spinning, Wheels Turning

The alley-ways between terminal concourses can often get quite busy and quite crowded. Given multiple push-backs and arrivals, given the varying aircraft wingspans, proper push-back instructions, and compliance with those instructions, is key to avoiding collisions. Our push-back team has done their job well: Our tail is indeed at Gate 120. No collisions.

"Ramp to flight-deck, push-back complete, set parking-brake, cleared to start both engines."

With the push-back complete, the rampers have visually cleared the area to the fore and aft of our engines. We will not suck anything through our engine intakes during engine start, nor will our engine thrust (hurricane force) disturb anything to our rear as we throttle up. Both unpleasant scenarios have occurred.

I set the parking-brake. Fran closes the air-conditioning packs, and shifts our APU (auxiliary power unit) pneumatic pressure from cabin air-conditioning systems to the engines' air-driven starters. In an earlier day, ground-crew shoulder muscles spun a propeller through its start cycle. Today, pneumatic muscles will do the job. Our Window Seat Pilots will experience a few moments without the comfort of conditioned air as we complete the engine start sequence.

"Flight-deck to ramp, parking-brake is set, we are spinning number one engine." With a flick of my thumb, I flip the left engine's Start Switch.

41

Within moments, we have left engine rotation, indicated on our rpm gages, followed shortly thereafter by oil pressure. With the engine accelerating through twenty-five percent rpm, I hit the fuel control lever, energizing the engine igniters and allowing fuel flow into the engine's burn-chamber.

Within moments, we have "light-off." All eyes are on the exhaust gas temperature (EGT) gage as it rises at a steady pace, and stabilizes just short of 500-degrees Celsius. A quick scan of the engine instruments tells us we have a good start.

"Flight-deck to ramp, we are spinning number two engine."

Once again, three sets of eyes track the start sequence: Rotation, fuel flow, light-off, EGT, good indications. Two good starts. With both engines up and running, our rampers give us their final call: "Ramp to flight-deck, thank you for the coffees, steering bypass pin removed, tow-bar disconnected."

On script, I reply "Flight-deck to ramp, you are quite welcome. Cleared to disconnect headset. Thank you for a nice push-back. We will look for you on the left side for the salute."

I call for the After Start Checklist.

Fran and I run through our respective "After Start" flows, as Erica monitors both of us. We restore pneumatic pressure to the cabin's air-conditioning system. Our Window Seat Pilots are once again comfortable. We confirm our engine-driven generators have picked up the electrical load. Assured of pneumatics and electrics, we kill our Auxiliary Power Unit (APU). We set our auto-brake system to the RTO (Rejected Take Off) setting. In the event of a high-speed aborted/rejected takeoff, our brakes will automatically engage at the maximum setting. Lastly, we select Engine Anti-Ice to the ON position.

Referring to our loading-planning "numbers" printout, we set our takeoff flap setting to fifteen degrees. Given the critical importance of a proper takeoff flap setting, three sets of eyes confirm the flap/slat handle position, the flap/slat indicator position and the flap/slat setting annotated on the "numbers" printout. The Window Seat Pilots seated over our wings take note as hydraulic motors drive our trailing-edge flaps, and our leading-edge slats, to their takeoff positions. Proper flap/slat positions are key to Lift; hence, they are key to life. As we noted earlier, checklists are key to error management; hence, they are likewise key to life. On 16 August 1987, the flight-crew of a McDonnell Douglas DC-9 attempted to takeoff from Detroit, Michigan, with their flaps and slats fully retracted, an error they failed to catch, due to their failure to run the "After Start Checklist." Rocketing down the runway, without flaps and slats, rapidly running out of runway, they lacked sufficient Lift. They never got airborne. An unpleasant, tragic scenario. Checklist discipline.

Focused on flight-controls, I work the yoke to the full-aft and full-forward position, and to the full-right and full-left position, checking for unrestricted elevator and aileron movement. I do the same with the rudder pedals, full-left and full-right, again checking for unrestricted rudder movement. While I work the flight-controls through their full range of movement, our three sets of eyes are glued to the flight-control schematic, displayed on the flight-deck's lower-center display screen. We take note as our ailerons, elevators and rudders display proper response. With my check complete, Fran works his yoke and rudder pedals through the same routine, as three sets of eyes again track the schematic display.

Recall the earlier-mentioned unpleasant, tragic scenario in which flight-control *actuator-rods* and *control-rods* had been improperly installed. The up-down axis *actuator-rod* had been improperly connected to the left-right axis *control-rod*. On takeoff, the pilot had pulled back (up-down axis) on the yoke, expecting a nose-up response. Instead, his aircraft rolled rapidly to the left (left-right axis). The aircraft was un-flyable.

Our control-rods and our actuator-rods have been properly installed. Had any element of our flight-controls not operated properly, this flight-control check, our three sets of eyes, and the visual depiction on our display screen, was our opportunity to catch the error. All is well.

"After Start Checklist is Complete." Our push-back crew is off to our left side. They have scanned fore and aft, and they have given us the "Good-To-Go" salute. We are cleared to throttle-up. I return the salute and flash our taxi light. We are on our way.

In 1903, in Kitty Hawk, North Carolina, Orville and Wilbur Wright utilized a cast-iron, four-cylinder piston engine, weighing approximately 180 pounds, producing twelve horse-power at 1025 rpm, with a bicycle chain turning the engine's cam shaft. By contrast, today's largest turbo-fan engine, utilizing carbon-fiber fan blades, weighs in at 18,260 pounds, and tops out at 127,900 pounds of thrust. We have evolved.

"Flight 28, taxi via Romeo-Lima and Bravo. Hold Short of Kilo. Contact Ground Control, on Bravo short of Kilo." With the parking-brake set, three sets of eyes review our airfield diagrams. Taxiway Romeo-Lima leads to taxiway Bravo, with a right turn on taxiway Bravo. Taxiway Bravo leads to taxiway Kilo. While on Bravo, we will "hold short" of taxiway Kilo. We are in agreement.

This is a good thing. A surprisingly high percentage of unpleasant scenarios occur on the ground. There are often too many aircraft, moving in too many directions, at night or in low-visibility conditions (similar to this evening), on unfamiliar airfields, lacking standardized airfield marking, on the backside of the clock, after sixteen hours of duty-time. A threat. A recipe for error.

The deadliest aircraft accident to date, involved a collision of two jumbo aircraft while on the ground. The industry literature is rife with instances in which aircraft have attempted to takeoff on closed runways, takeoff on runways under construction, and take-off on runways of insufficient length. Taxiing aircraft have collided while taxiing. Departing aircraft have taxied into the path of arriving aircraft. We will discuss several of those incidents, during the course of our flight, this evening.

In the span of the last two years, I have experienced two ground incidents. In the first incident, while following a ground marshaller's guidance, my right main gear "departed the prepared surface," taxiing over roughly thirty feet of turf before returning to the "prepared surface" of the ramp. Fortunately, we were light-weight and the ground was frozen. In the second incident, while parked in the alley-way, short of our arrival gate, with our engines shut-down, with our parking-brake set, while awaiting a tow-in to our gate; we were struck, at our six o'clock, by an aircraft maneuvering for taxi-out. As noted earlier, the alley-ways between concourses are often busy and crowded, a recipe for collisions.

The lesson? There are no zero-threat environments. There are no zero-threat situations. True in flight. True in life.

Roughly sixty feet aft of the flight-deck, the two "high bypass ratio" turbo-fan engines slung beneath our wings are humming smoothly. Working from front to rear, the "fan" portion of our engines is a spinning blur. The spinning fan-blades operate much like a conventional propeller. The bulk of the fan-produced air-flow (roughly eighty-five percent) will "bypass" the engine core and exit to the rear as thrust. That eighty-five percent of bypassed fan-air earns the engine the "high-bypass-ratio" label.

The remaining (roughly fifteen percent) of the fan-air will pass through the engine core and into the engine's burn-chamber wherein it will join forces with fuel and ignition. The energy produced in the mix of fuel, air and ignition, will pass through the turbine section, mounted just aft of the burn-chamber. That burn-chamber energy will cause our turbines to spin. The power output of the spinning turbines will then be translated forward, along a spinning shaft, to drive the fan-blades.

I scan to the left, and call "Clear Left." Fran scans to the right, and calls "Clear Right." We make a final scan of our instrument panels. No amber warning lights. Again, I turn to Fran and Erica. "Are we good? Are we set?"

We are good. We are set. I release our parking-brake, Fran hits the taxi light, and I throttle-up.

We are moving, and we are "sterile." Between now and our climb through ten thousand feet, our only discussion will be flight-related. A spirited discussion of the New York Yankee playoff chances will have to wait. The seltzer, the cup of ice, the slice of lemon, the apple and the raisins will have to wait.

If details kill, so too distractions kill. The industry literature is filled with instances in which distraction has led to unpleasant scenarios. Those distractions have been captured on cockpit voice recorders. Eventually, those voice recordings and/or transcripts have been released to the media. Window Seat Pilots and industry professionals alike have asked, time and again: "How could they have been paying so little attention? How could they have missed their airspeed, their altitude, their heading, their low fuel state?"

Many stories compete for the poster-child of distraction. High on the list: On 21 October 2009, a flight-crew, with auto-pilot and auto-throttles engaged, overflew their planned destination by roughly 150 miles, while being out of radio contact with air traffic control for seventy-eight minutes. Five minutes prior to their estimated time of arrival at destination, puzzled that no descent had been initiated, puzzled that no announcements had been made, a flight attendant called the flight-deck. That call captured both pilots distracted by their laptop computers amid a lengthy discussion of crew-scheduling. No one was flying the jet.

In their case, there was no engine flame-out due to fuel starvation, there was no impact with terrain due to inattention.

Nonetheless, the potentially deadly threat of distraction was on display for all to see. Saved by a flight-attendant's call to the flight-deck.

We will be "sterile" because it is the smart thing to do. We will be "sterile" because the FAA mandates a "sterile" cockpit for all operations below ten thousand feet. We will be "sterile" because we do not want to be a "breaking-news" head-line. Between now and our climb through ten thousand feet, our only discussion will be flight-related.

There are many reasons to keep to the straight and narrow path in the flying business. Two reasons come to mind: Survival and professionalism. However, never far behind, there is one additional, very powerful motivation to do the right thing, every time. That reason, put simply, is the desire to avoid any situation in which a pilot's family may have to read a transcript, hear a voice-recording, or watch a re-enactment of the failure of their mother, father, son, or daughter to do the right-thing, with one-hundred and eighty-four lives on board. Losing a loved one will be painful enough. Losing a loved one because he failed to do the right-thing will be doubly painful. Knowing the loved one took the lives of one-hundred and eighty-four innocent Window Seat Pilots, because he failed to do the right-thing, is not a legacy any pilot wishes to leave with his family. Do the right-thing. Every time. We will be sterile.

As we have been conducting our pre-flight and our push-back; six Air Traffic Control (ATC) jurisdictions, Domestic (USA and Canada), Oceanic (Gander and Shanwick) and Domestic (Shannon and London); have been utilizing our scheduled takeoff time, along with our planned courses, altitudes and airspeeds; to proactively plan for enroute traffic de-confliction and ATC workload management. Any takeoff delays, such as those we are experiencing this evening, will be used by ATC to adjust those traffic de-confliction and workload management plans.

From an ATC perspective, our flight plan serves two additional functions. In the event of a loss of radio contact, the six ATC jurisdictions will utilize our flight plan (when will we turn, to what courses; when will we climb or descend, to what altitudes; when will we accelerate or decelerate, to what airspeeds) to ensure traffic de-confliction. Lastly, in the event we were to fall off the grid, for whatever reason, ATC would utilize our flight plan, along with any radar data, as a start-point for any search-and-rescue operations.

The search-and-rescue start-point calls to mind my early days in the Air Rescue business, in the unforgiving environment of the Arctic and Alaskan wilderness. Time, and time again, our Pre-Search briefing would include the sad news that no flight plan had been filed with ATC, greatly complicating the search challenge, and frequently making for an unpleasant outcome. The no-flight-plan feature frequently went hand-in-hand with no ELT (Electronic Locator Transmitter), no fuel reserve, no survival gear, an overweight aircraft and the lack of an Instrument Rating; all in the interest of increased payload, increased revenue, increased profit and, sadly, increased risk. The early lesson for this newly-minted aviator? Do the right-thing. Every time.

Reflection

In life, as in flight, we never fly solo. In life, as in flight, we interface with others. Trust them. Do not depend upon them.

On 28 September 1992, an Airbus A300, was cleared for an approach into Kathmandu. The approach included seven step-down segments, each segment defined by a minimum descent altitude. Each of those minimum descent altitudes was based on ensuring terrain clearance. While flying in the weather, with limited visibility, the flight-crew erroneously initiated each of those step-downs, one segment early, descending up to 1300-feet below the minimum (terrain-clearing) descent altitudes. Upon initiating each step-down, the pilots accurately reported, to air traffic control, their present position and their actual altitude.

The air traffic controllers did nothing to alert the flight-crew of their inappropriate altitudes. The accident report noted the controllers were too timid and reluctant to intervene, deferring to the flight-crew in matters of terrain avoidance. A tragic consequence ensued. Air traffic control. Trust. Do not depend.

On 29 April 2013, a Boeing 747-400 (freighter version) departed Bagram Airfield, Afghanistan, loaded with five heavily-armored vehicles (roughly 80 tons of weight). Shortly following takeoff, roughly 1200-feet above ground level, an improperly secured armored vehicle (16-tons) broke free of its restraints, rolled to the back of the cargo hold, and crashed through the rear pressure bulkhead; crippling key hydraulic systems, severely damaging tail-mounted flight controls and rendering the aircraft uncontrollable. A tragic consequence ensued.

The National Transportation Safety Board determined the probable causes included "improper restraint of the cargo." Aircraft loading. Trust. Do not depend.

On 28 October 2008, an Airbus A330 flight-crew departing Montego Bay, Jamaica arrived at their aircraft, only to find the Aircraft Performance Manual was missing. Unable to calculate their takeoff data, the flight-crew turned to their Flight Dispatch department. The Captain relayed all relevant data to the dispatcher, for input into the flight operations computer system. As an error-management technique, the dispatcher then repeated all relevant data back to the Captain. As an added error-management technique, the process was repeated with the First Officer relaying all relevant data to the dispatcher, with the dispatcher again repeating all relevant data back to the First Officer.

Foremost among the relevant data points was the takeoff gross weight of 462,000 pounds, correctly relayed by both the Captain and the First Officer, twice correctly repeated by the dispatcher.

Despite the redundancy of the double relay of relevant data, the takeoff numbers provided to the flight-crew reflected a takeoff gross weight of 266,000 pounds, a 196,000 pound error from their actual takeoff gross weight of 462,000 pounds. A frightening consequence ensued. Flight dispatchers. Trust. Do not depend.

As discussed earlier, on 30 May 1995, an Air Force F-15 attempted a takeoff from Spangdahlem Air Force Base, Germany. Immediately after becoming airborne, the aircraft rolled sharply to the left and crashed a short distance from the runway. Examination of the wreckage revealed the up-down and left-right flight-control inputs had been improperly installed. When the pilot commanded up (takeoff) the jet rolled left (impact). The aircraft had just completed a twenty-day maintenance overhaul. The jet was un-flyable from the moment it exited the maintenance hangar. Aircraft maintenance. Trust. Do not depend.

In life, as in flight: Trust. Do not depend.

Ground-Stop

As we enter the Bravo taxiway, the wipers, silent and steady, conduct their sweep. In the intervals between wiper passage; arriving raindrops impact, vaporize and merge with the ambient fog; as they encounter and suffer the 28-volt, 115-degree windshield heat.

Why windshield heat? Bird-strike protection. A heated (and therefore more supple) windshield is more likely to survive a bird-strike, than a frozen and brittle windshield. We do not want a shattered windshield while airborne. Nor do we want pilot eyes, ears and vital organs perforated with glass shards and bird residue. Lastly, we do not want the hefty dry-cleaning bill that would likely accompany a bird residue-splattered uniform. Why windshield heat? Prevent restrictions to visibility, due to windshield icing (exterior) or windshield fogging (interior).

We make our call, "Newark Ground, Flight 28, we are on Bravo, holding short of Kilo." Ground Control gives us the bad news: "Flight 28, you are number twenty-three for departure, we have a 'Ground Stop' on all departures. Monitor this frequency."

My premonition as we walked down the jet-way was on target. Our thirty-minute delay at the gate will not be our last delay this evening. Our first call is to Cherie, and her flight attendant team. Our second call is to the Window Seat Pilots, for they are Job One. The airport is under a "Ground Stop." All departures have been halted. We have not been given an estimated "off time." We hack the stop-watch, and promise an update every fifteen minutes. The Window Seat Pilots will know what we know. There will be no secrets. It may not always be good news, but they will always have the latest news.

We have asked for, and received, permission to shut down our engines as a fuel-saving measure. With our engines shut down, we will not be moving, we will be blocking traffic. The upshot? When an aircraft is granted permission to shut down engines on an active taxiway, there is clearly no rush. No one is moving. We will be here for a while. We have re-started our auxiliary power unit (APU). We have electrical power and we have air conditioning. We sit. We wait. We monitor the radio.

Far too often, while riding in the cabin, while experiencing a delay, I have shared the Window Seat Pilot frustration of no information, no announcements, no updates, no explanations. We are not delivering boxes to a sorting facility, to be loaded on delivery trucks. We are carrying mothers and fathers, sons and daughters, sisters and brothers. They want to get where they are going. They may be returning from a war zone. They may be attending a wedding. They may be a bit nervous about getting there (as is our Hannah of Anchorage). They deserve answers. With that in mind, I release my lap-belt and my shoulder-harness, I step out of my seat, I open the flight-deck door, and I go for a stroll.

As I stroll, I answer the Window Seat Pilot questions. I offer my "best guess." On occasion, I suggest it is "anybody's guess." Either way, I walk the full length of the cabin, and I face the music. Why do so? Two reasons, both rooted in respect. First reason: Respect for our Window Seat Pilots. Second reason: Respect for Cherie and her flight-attendant team. By strolling the cabin, by addressing the concerns and answering the questions, I hope to ease and absorb any Window Seat Pilot displeasure, thereby shielding Cherie and her flight-attendant team from expressions of displeasure. It is time well spent. As I conduct my stroll, I note Hannah is sound asleep: Our pre-departure flight-deck tour must have done the trick, and eased our nervous-flyer's concerns.

Delays are a fact of life in the flying business. Ironically, while no passenger would prefer a delay, passenger preference plays a large role in those delays. Where an airline may have once flown four larger aircraft between any two cities, with flights departing every four hours; today, due to passenger preference, that airline may now serve the same city-pair with sixteen smaller aircraft, departing every hour, on the hour. Each of those twelve additional aircraft occupies a gate, ties up a takeoff-departure slot, an approach-landing slot and claims a slice of enroute airspace. Four jets have morphed to sixteen jets, frequently carrying the same number of passengers.

There is no doubt "enough room" to accommodate the growth in traffic between any city-pairing. It is indeed a big sky. However, all traffic must converge, in time and space, during the departure and arrival phases of flight. Basic physics poses a problem: No two objects can occupy the same point in space at the same point in time. There is simply not enough room on the arrival routes into, and the departure routes out of, our major airports.

As an added passenger preference, air traffic must converge when the paying passenger wants his or her flight to arrive or depart: Before the business conference starts and after the business conference wraps up, before the amusement park opens and after the amusement park closes. For those making connections, passenger preference further dictates the inbound flight and the outbound flight connect within a reasonably-brief time frame.

As such, passenger preference does not allow for a metered traffic flow over twelve, sixteen, or twenty-four hours. The 3800-plus daily flights from the four major New York area airports are not metered over a twenty-four hour period: With 160 flights per hour, spread between four airports, at a rate of forty flights per hour, per airport. On the contrary, those 3800-plus daily flights arrive and depart as "banks," enabling the desired reasonably-brief connect times. Daily airport visuals provide ample evidence: Gates and ramps are vacant one hour, and packed to the gills two hours later. Hence, the terms "volume, congestion, delay."

Airborne delays may take the form of "holding," or airspeed reductions, or "delaying vectors," or a combination of all three. It is not uncommon to hear the following air traffic control directive: "Flight 28, reduce to slowest practical airspeed, turn ninety degrees right of course, vectors for spacing, expect holding overhead Sparta." Airborne delays may be encountered at great distance from the destination airport. On a recent flight from Seattle, Washington to Newark, New Jersey, air traffic control directed us to enter a holding pattern overhead Omaha, Nebraska, due to "volume" into Newark. As air traffic converged on Newark, a ripple effect forced us into our holding pattern, twelve hundred miles, and three hours flight time, to the west.

Following touch-down at destination, having endured one or more forms of airborne delays, the Window Seat Pilot must often deal with the consequences of concrete congestion: His or her arrival gate is occupied, with no other gates available.

The entire system is predicated on aircraft arriving and departing on time: Departing aircraft push-back on-time, thereby vacating a gate, allowing arriving aircraft to park on-time at the newly-vacated gate. If departing flights are not vacating gates on schedule, their counterpart arriving flights cannot arrive on schedule. The term "slack" is not built into the system. A willingness to pour concrete and expand gate space is the only answer to "concrete congestion."

Particularly frustrating for the Window Seat Pilot, is the apparent inconsistency between the Captain's announcement "There are no available gates," and the sight of open, vacant, unused gates viewed through the cabin window. Explanation: Not all gates are created equal. Given the wide range of aircraft lengths and wingspans, not every gate can accommodate every aircraft. Wingtip clearance must be accounted for when matching arriving aircraft with available gates. As an analogy, imagine a parking lot with a dozen "Compact-Car Only" slots available, as you pass by in your oversized sport utility vehicle. Frustrating. But reality.

Given the choice between an airborne delay or a ground delay, a ground delay is the industry's preferred choice. While on the ground, passengers are free to move about the cabin, alter plans via cell phone and enjoy a drink or a bite to eat. Ideally, ground delays are encountered prior to passenger boarding, allowing passengers to enjoy the relative comforts of the terminal.

By contrast, an airborne delay burns fuel, puts time on the engines (both of which "burn" money) and makes for a far less comfortable passenger experience (tray tables stowed, seatbacks fully upright, personal electronic devices stowed).

Air traffic control likewise prefers a ground delay, as it minimizes controller workload, allows them to focus on arriving aircraft, and reduces the safety issue of multiple aircraft, circling in close proximity, while stacked in holding patterns.

While traveling as a passenger, in the cabin, I have often overheard cell-phone conversations in which the Captain's announcement regarding a departure delay due to "destination weather," is at odds with a family member, at the destination airport, reporting destination weather as "blue sky and sunshine."

The answer may rest in how one defines "destination weather." While the destination airfield may indeed be "blue sky and sunshine," adverse weather conditions may be impacting flight operations along the arrival corridors (Standard Terminal Arrival Routes), often extending up to one hundred and fifty miles (a three-hour drive) from the destination airport.

Regarding delays, Air traffic Control workload is the system circuit breaker. Controllers can handle only so many aircraft before safety margins are threatened. Just as my flight-deck brief included the explicit statement "We will not rush for anyone, at any time, for any reason," controllers cannot allow themselves to be overloaded by anyone, at any time, for any reason. Under adverse weather conditions, the workload is substantially increased, as time-saving "visual approaches" are not possible, and the safety element of "see and avoid" for aircraft separation is compromised.

A controller's priority is heavily weighted toward accommodating arriving aircraft, at the expense of departing aircraft. Arriving aircraft have likely encountered multiple airborne delays (holding patterns and/or delaying vectors), are likely low on fuel as a result of those delays, and are candidates for a potential diversion due to low fuel. Consequently, in the midst of our ground-stop this evening, our Window Seat Pilots are likely to see several arriving aircraft, while seeing few, if any, departing aircraft.

Occasionally, air traffic control may institute a ground-stop for a select set of departures, while allowing other departures to progress unimpeded. If weather is impacting Standard Instrument Departures (SIDs) to the west of an airport, the ground-stop may apply only to those aircraft utilizing the western SIDs. Departures utilizing northern, eastern, or southern SIDs may be permitted to proceed as scheduled. As the weather proceeds west-to-east, passing to the north of the airport, western departures may be permitted to proceed, while northern departures are shutdown. As the weather continues to the east, northern departures may receive a green light, while eastern departures are shutdown.

A ground-stop may come with an "Estimated Departure Clearance Time" (EDCT), often referred to as a "Wheels Up Time." The EDCT is air traffic control's best estimate of when an aircraft can anticipate entering the traffic flow. As with any estimate, particularly one contingent upon the whims of weather, some EDCTs are on target, some are not, and some are ever-changing as the scenario evolves.

Initial delays can often lead to a cascading series of subsequent delays. On a recent two-day, round-trip between Newark and Los Angeles, we were delayed for over four hours on the Newark departure, due to Newark weather. Arriving in Los Angeles four hours late, our FAA-required "minimum crew-rest" led to a two-hour departure delay the following morning, from Los Angeles back to Newark. Despite shaving thirty minutes off the return flight from Los Angeles (fly faster, burn more fuel), we arrived ninety minutes late in Newark, leading to a one-hour delay on the subsequent outbound flight, a full twenty-four hours following our original weather delay.

The Newark–Los Angeles experience highlights yet another reason for delays: Flight-crew legality. The FAA has strict limits regarding both Duty Time and Flight Time. Those limits apply to rolling twenty-four hour periods, as well as rolling seven-day and thirty-day periods. Two hard limits: One hundred hours in thirty days, one thousand hours in three hundred and sixty-five days.

The FAA limits may be applied at any point in a trip sequence. Inflight delays (holding patterns and/or delaying vectors) leading to additional duty/flight time, may render a flight-crew illegal for their next scheduled flight.

An extended ground delay (such as ours) plus planned flight-time, may render a flight-crew illegal prior to departure from the gate. More frustrating for The Window Seat Pilot, an extended ground delay, following push-back from the gate (such as ours), may require the flight-crew to return to the gate, and de-plane the aircraft. If another flight-crew is available, the delay may be a matter of hours. If no other flight-crew is available, the delay may be a good bit longer, reflecting the requirement for the original flight-crew to enter the FAA-required Crew Rest.

Either way, we are delayed. As we sip our caffeine of choice, we are filling in the blanks in our life stories. Fran is married with two children. His wife is a pediatric nutritionist, his daughter is a softball star, his son is a tennis star. Together, they spend a bit of every Summer visiting with his Sicilian family. Erica, married to a fellow (competing airline) pilot, has just purchased a few acres of Pennsylvania countryside. Together, she and her husband enjoy the silent country serenity, and the company of their two pure-bred Labradors.

Every fifteen minutes, we provide our Window Seat Pilots with an update. They will know what we know, when we know it. No secrets.

Reflection

Formation flying typically involves a Flight-Leader (Lead) and a Wingman (Two). A Wingman's job is simple. Be there.

What a flight-leader wants to hear, more than anything else, are three simple words: "Two is in." Upon hearing those comforting words, the flight-leader knows his wingman is in position, providing mutual support, in an often hostile, challenging and demanding environment.

In life, as in flight; the people with whom we share our lives, are counting on you and I to be there. They take comfort in knowing we are there. As flight leader and wingman, as parent and child, as sister and brother, as wife and husband, as friend and partner; we are providing mutual support in an often hostile, challenging and demanding environment.

In life, as in flight: Be there. Two is in.

We are not paid to be right. We are paid to make the mission happen. If our insistence on being right degrades the team dynamic, if a degraded team dynamic imperils making the mission happen, then we are wrong.

In life, as in flight, we are always part of a formation, always part of a team: Be it a marriage, a family, a business, or a flight-crew. Many a spouse, many a parent, many a manager and many a Captain; may take false comfort in having been right, as their marriage, their family, their business, or their flight-crew fails to make the mission happen. With often tragic consequence. Make the mission happen.

Newark Liberty International Airport, Runway 22-Right

We Slip The Surly Bonds

We have been sitting for just over ninety minutes. On my recommendation, Cherie's flight attendant team has not offered a courtesy cabin service. With no firm "wheels up" time, we wish to avoid a scenario in which air traffic control issues us a taxi clearance while our flight attendants are in the midst of a cabin service. If we are unable to return our cabin to "taxi status" in a timely manner, we may run the risk of "losing our place in line."

I have taken two strolls through the cabin. I have answered the delay questions, allayed the thunderstorm fears, and calmed the nerves of a handful of Window Seat Pilots. Hannah of Anchorage, our nervous flyer, remains comfortably asleep.

I return to my seat just as the flight-deck speakers issue the welcome words: "Flight 28, we have a re-route for you, advise when ready to copy." With three pens and three slips of paper at the ready, we reply "Flight 28, ready to copy re-route."

The line of thunderstorms has stalled to the northeast of the airport, sitting astride the major routes between New York and Boston, impacting flights (including our own) destined for the North Atlantic. As a consequence, air traffic control has re-routed those flights (including our own) to the northwest, with a later turn to the northeast, once clear of the weather. We are heads-down as we re-program the Flight Management Computer (FMC) to reflect

61

our new routing. We conduct three independent checks, and top it off with a final check as a team.

To allow for real-time tracking of our flight performance, reflecting our northwestern re-route; we request, and receive, an updated flight-plan with adjusted enroute times and fuel figures. Mindful of our ninety-minute delay, we likewise pull up the latest weather forecast for London-Heathrow, Manchester and Goose Bay. All remains well.

Once again, we run through the engine start sequence: Rotation, fuel flow, light-off, EGT. Two good starts. With the After Start Checklist complete, and a "Cabin-Ready" call from Cherie, we throttle up and resume our taxi.

The rain is torrential. Amid the swirling, wind-whipped mist and rain; the taxiway lights, runway lights and approach lights have been set to their full intensity. For the last ninety minutes, we have enjoyed a front-row seat to the air-show, as aircraft have emerged from the ragged bottoms of the cloud base, at roughly two-minute intervals. With our informed, professional eyes, we have tracked the path of each jet: On-speed and on glide-path, as they flare and touch down on centerline, disappearing on their landing roll-out, cloaked by the night, the mist and the rain.

We hear our cue to join the air-show, with the long-awaited words: "Flight 28, you are cleared for takeoff, Runway 22-Right. After takeoff contact departure control on frequency 119.2." Sticking to the script, Fran replies "Flight 28 is cleared for takeoff on Runway 22-Right."

I activate all exterior lights as we approach our final turn to the active runway. Doing so conveys the following message to every other aircraft: We have been cleared for takeoff, do *not* enter or cross Runway 22-Right.

Noting the lighted 22-R signs posted on either side of the taxiway, as per script, Fran and I call out "Runway 22-Right." As we roll out on the runway centerline, noting our compass heading of 220 degrees, as per script, we both call out "runway heading verified." Two simple, and obvious calls: We are entering the correct runway, and our aircraft heading agrees with our assigned runway heading. Yet, far too many aircraft have attempted takeoffs on the wrong runway, often with tragic consequence.

On 27 August 2006, an aircraft departing Lexington, Kentucky, was cleared for takeoff on Runway 22, a runway 7,000-feet in length. However, the flight-crew erroneously lined up on Runway 26, a runway of only 3,500-feet in length. Too short. An unpleasant, tragic scenario ensued.

On 31 October 2000, on a night very similar to this evening, with heavy rain and reduced visibility, a Boeing 747 was cleared for takeoff on Taipei's Runway 05-Left. Unfortunately, the flight-crew lined up on the parallel Runway 05-Right, which was closed due to construction. Forty-one seconds after the start of their takeoff roll, the aircraft collided with concrete barriers and heavy construction equipment. An unpleasant, tragic scenario ensued.

The two accident reports explicitly noted that a mere glance at their flight displays, prior to their takeoff roll, would have revealed their error. Fran and I, along with Erica, have taken that glance; we have confirmed our runway.

We take a final glance at the weather radar: There are no weather buildups along our intended departure flight-path, or along the published engine-failure flight-path. Had there been any weather astride either of the two flight-paths, we would have coordinated with air traffic control for revised departure routing. We do not want to fly through a thunderstorm.

To the front, through our rain-streaked windshields, steady white lights mark the runway centerline. To the left and right, additional steady white lights mark the runway edges. Further to the left and right, blue and green lights mark taxiway edges (blue) and taxiway centerlines (green), while flashing red, green and white strobes mark the position of taxiing aircraft.

I ask the question: "Are we set?" I note the "Good to go" replies. I hit the wipers, I advance the throttles to an intermediate thrust setting, I settle in my seat, I take a deep breath, and I call for auto-throttle engagement.

With Fran's flip of a switch, the auto-throttles engage, and we are on our way. My right hand rides the throttles as they advance to full takeoff thrust setting. As per script: I call "Check Thrust." Fran confirms proper takeoff thrust setting, and replies, as per script "Thrust Set."

Holding firm nose-down pressure on the yoke, I apply right aileron into our right crosswind, while applying opposite left rudder, keeping our rapidly accelerating jet aligned with the runway centerline lights at our twelve o'clock. I take comfort in the accelerating rhythmic cadence as the nose-gear, twenty feet below us, rises and falls over each of those raised centerline lights.

My mind is primed for the high-speed reject procedure (the aborted takeoff), reviewed hours ago on the chair-fly drive to the airport.

"Rudder, Stop Drift, Track Centerline, Thrust Levers Idle, Auto-Throttles Off, Speed Brakes, Maximum Reverse Thrust."

As the jet accelerates, as the airspeed increases, and as the flight controls become more effective, I slowly relax my aileron and rudder inputs. As per script, Fran calls out "one hundred knots." A quick glance at my airspeed indicator confirms our airspeeds are in agreement. Given the critical role played by airspeed, a variation of ten knots would have required a rejected takeoff. Fran's call is my cue to relax the nose-down pressure on the yoke, easing to the neutral position.

Over the course of our six hour and thirty-five-minute flight, the roughly one minute devoted to the takeoff roll is perhaps the most demanding segment, in terms of the required level of mental alertness. There is no margin for complacency, distraction, or casual regard. One must be at the top of one's game.

The mind must be laser-focused on the "Reject." Fingers prepared to disengage auto-throttles, feet prepared to add rudder, hands prepared to retard throttles, deploy speed-brakes and activate thrust reversers; all amid a potentially challenging asymmetric thrust scenario (full thrust on one engine, zero thrust on the other) while on a slippery runway. At a speed of 250 feet-per-second, a mere one-third of one second separates us from the runway edge.

Beyond the mechanics of a rejected takeoff, the mind must be prepared to make the proper decision: Do we reject for this condition, or do we continue? The calculation must be made in the first heart-beat. The decision must be made in the second heart-beat. Proper execution must be implemented in the third heart-beat.

Having said all of that, there are few life thrills that match sitting at the pointy-end of one hundred and twenty tons of jet, and eighty-eight thousand pounds of thrust, while rocketing along at 250 feet-per-second, with nothing but rain-streaked window and rain-flooded concrete at your twelve o'clock, knowing a mere twist of the wrist will have us airborne, flying, and *breaking the surly bonds of earth.*

With Fran's "V-1" call at 142 knots, we are now a "Go." We are committed to fly. The mind must instantly switch gears, and focus upon an entirely different scenario: From the high-speed reject, to the first steps of the engine-failure, likewise reviewed hours ago on the chair-fly drive to the airport:

"Rudder, Stop Drift, Rotate, Add Rudder, V-Bar, Do Not Over-Rotate, Positive Rate, Gear Up."

The feet must be prepared for immediate rudder application amid the asymmetric thrust; the hands must ensure a reduced angle of climb while wings level on runway heading; the eyes must be focused on the instruments for proper rotation, climb angle, heading and airspeed.

With Fran's "Rotate" call at 148 knots, I smoothly pull back on the yoke, at a ball-park rate of two degrees per second. We smoothly and effortlessly break ground. As the windshield view progresses from runway lighting to the darkness of night, I hold a pitch angle of roughly fifteen-degrees nose-up, maintaining a target airspeed roughly fifteen knots above our V-2 (take-off safety) speed of 154 knots.

The eyes are inside-outside, inside-outside, alternating between the artificial-horizon on my Primary Flight Display (PFD), and the runway centerline lights disappearing beneath the nose. We enter the overcast at four hundred feet. There is no more "outside." There is only "inside." We are on the instruments. We are airborne with two good engines.

Reflection

One of the single-most important flight lessons an aspiring pilot can learn: You do not strap yourself into a jet, and go for a ride.

You strap the jet onto your back, and you take the jet for a ride.

The statement conveys a fundamental distinction: The former passive version, the latter active version.

The pilot is in command. The pilot puts the jet where she wants it to be.

The 240,000-pound jet is not in command. The auto-flight system is not in command. The 90,000 pounds of thrust are not in command.

The pilot is not along for the ride.

True with flight. True with life. Do not strap into life. Rather, strap life onto your back. And fly.

Position: Four Hundred Feet, Departure End, Runway 22-Right

Hub and Spoke

With a quick glance at the altimeter and the vertical velocity indicator, I confirm "two climbing" indications. I make the call. "Gear Up." Fran reaches forward and raises the Landing Gear handle.

Our left hydraulic system, the workhorse of our three independent hydraulic systems, kicks into gear. Our mid-cabin Window Seat Pilots note the muffled rumble as hydraulic motors smoothly re-position our left and right landing gear beneath our center fuselage. They likewise note the muffled snap, as the gear doors are secured in the closed, locked and streamlined position.

Noting 400 feet on the altimeter, and referencing the artificial horizon, I gently roll into a thirty-degree left bank, rolling out on a heading of 190-degrees. Fran switches our VHF radio over to frequency 119.2 and checks in with New York Departure Control, "Good evening, New York, Flight 28, passing 1500 feet for 5000 feet, on the Newark Eight Departure."

"Flight 28, New York Departure Control: Negative radar contact. Check transponder."

Fran flips the switch from Left Transponder to Right Transponder. We hear the comforting words: "Flight 28, New York Departure Control: You are radar contact, comply with the Newark Eight Departure, climb to and maintain five thousand feet."

With an eye on the airspeed indicator, as we accelerate through 168 knots, I call for flaps five. Noting our Distance Measuring Equipment (DME) readout at 2.3 miles, I gently roll into a thirty-degree right bank, rolling out on a heading of 220-degrees. With eyes on the airspeed indicator, accelerating through 188 knots, I call for flaps one. As we pass through 208 knots, I call for flaps up. Our left hydraulic system once again goes to work, as it completes the flap/slat retraction sequence, leaving us with a "clean-wing" as we slice smoothly through the air. With each step of the retraction sequence, our Window Seat Pilots are treated to the sounds of the left hydraulic motors, and the sight of our wing leading-edge slats, and our wing trailing-edge flaps, retracting.

Approaching our initial level-off at 5000-feet, with my right hand riding the throttles, I confirm proper auto-throttle response, as the engines "throttle back" from climb power, to an intermediate cruise power setting. I make the call for a 250-knot air-speed. Fran spins 250 knots into the "Airspeed Select Window." With my right hand once again riding the throttles, I confirm proper auto-throttle response, as the engines "throttle up" for the targeted 250 knot airspeed.

I smile as I fondly recall two noteworthy take-offs. The first occurred while in Air Force flight training: My first takeoff in the venerable T-38, a twin-engine, supersonic trainer (nicknamed the White Rocket). The target level-off altitude, following takeoff, was roughly 1500-feet above the airfield elevation. When my instructor called "Rotate," I did so. Within the blink of an eye, we had busted through the 1500-foot level-off, and were well on our way to busting through 3000-feet, before he calmly stated "I have the aircraft." It was indeed a white rocket. I was not the first. My instructor had been there, and had seen that trick, many times.

The second memorable takeoff occurred fifteen years later, as I transitioned from the now-obsolete Second Officer (Flight Engineer) position, to the First Officer (Co-Pilot) position. To that point in time, my only flying experience had been military, an environment where passenger comfort was not an issue, an environment where aggressive maneuvering was smiled upon. Immediately following rotation in the Boeing 737, my muscle memory kicked in, as I rolled into a very aggressive sixty-degrees of right bank, while pulling a handful of "g" forces, making for a very nice, tight turn. Rather than the calmly-worded "I have the aircraft" of my T-38 episode; I heard my instructor's soft chuckle, and a mild "That was fun, but let us not do that again." The sixty-degree bank angle was roughly triple the standard airline bank angle of twenty-degrees. The "three-g" force was likewise roughly triple the "one-g" airline standard. Bank angles and g-forces tend to spill the coffee and drive up the dry-cleaning bills. Fun. But, wrong place, wrong time.

Countless times, over these many years, I have longed to once again aggressively rotate, wrap in the bank, crank in the g-forces, and pull the jet around. Yank, bank and crank. I have behaved. I have not spilled the coffee.

I have chosen to hand-fly the departure. Hand-flying an instrument-departure while "in the soup," absent the comforting visual cues of the horizon; at four-miles-per-minute ground-speed, with a six thousand foot-per-minute rate of climb, in a congested air-traffic environment; leaves little room for error, and little forgiveness for slow mental processing. It is all about the "instrument cross-check."

The "hub and spoke" concept forms the basis for the instrument cross-check. The artificial horizon on the Primary Flight Display (PFD) serves as the "hub" of that cross-check, the "go to" for situational awareness. The artificial-horizon provides a graphic display of degrees nose-up (climb) and degrees nose-down (descent), along with degrees of left bank (left turns) and right bank (right turns). It is intuitive: Blue sky above, brown earth below, a white horizon separating the two, a fluorescent orange airplane superimposed upon it all. A mere glance provides instant situational-awareness: Level, up, down, left, right.

From the artificial-horizon hub, the eyes travel out along a "spoke" to check-in with the airspeed indicator: Not too fast, not too slow. We do not want to exceed a flap's structural airspeed limitation with a late flap retraction call, nor do we want to lose our required Lift with an early flap retraction call. We must nail the flap retraction sequence at 168, 188 and 208 knots. With the "clean-wing" (no flaps, no slats), we must avoid violating the FAA-mandated airspeed limit of 250 knots below ten thousand feet.

From the airspeed indicator, our eyes travel back to the artificial-horizon at the hub of our cross-check; once again confirming pitch angle (up/down) and bank angle (left/right). Having done so, we head out along yet another spoke to our compass heading. We must track the runway heading of 220-degrees to 400-feet, we must then turn left to a heading of 190-degrees, and maintain that heading until 2.3 miles, at which point we must turn right to a heading of 220-degrees.

Failure to make the required turns on time, may take us out of "protected airspace" and into a potential "traffic conflict" with one of the other 3,800 aircraft transiting our four local airports. While in a high-terrain environment, failure to make required turns on time, may lead to an unpleasant scenario with a label all its own: Controlled Flight Into Terrain (CFIT). Lastly, failure to make the required turns on time, may lead to "certificate action" (loss or suspension of license), followed by the loss of a pay-check, followed by the need to find a "real job."

Back to the artificial-horizon, confirm pitch angle (up/down) and bank angle (left/right); and a trip along yet another spoke to the altimeter (indicating our altitude): The turn at 400-feet and the level-off at 5000-feet. Back to the artificial-horizon, and out yet another spoke, again and again.

While working the standard hub-and-spoke pattern, the cross-check must include side-trips to our flap indicator to confirm flap retraction (avoid structural overspeed), to our landing gear indicator to ensure gear retraction (avoid structural overspeed), to our weather radar to confirm we are clear of thunderstorms, to our Distance-Measuring-Equipment (DME) for our 2.3 mile turn-point, and to our TCAS (Traffic Collision Avoidance System) to ensure we are clear of traffic. All the while, a good portion of the grey matter must be devoted to monitoring radio transmissions: Listening for our call-sign, and mentally tracking instructions given to other aircraft. Our minds are busy.

The artificial-horizon is key. It is everything. It is life. Aviation literature is replete with instances, both obscure and famous, in which a failure to respect the artificial-horizon has led to unpleasant, often tragic, scenarios. To emphasize the point, in the earliest days of flight training, instructors routinely placed duct tape over all other flight-deck instruments except the artificial-horizon. Students performed just fine in "instrument conditions" with sole reference to the artificial-horizon. When those same instructors reversed the drill, and placed duct tape over the artificial-horizon while leaving all other flight-deck instruments available, students struggled. To repeat: The artificial-horizon is key. It is everything. It is life.

While "in the soup," absent a visual horizon, the intuitive cues of the artificial-horizon are life-savers. Again: Blue sky above, brown earth below, white horizon bisecting, fluorescent orange aircraft super-imposed. Intuitive. Countless lives would have been saved, had pilots simply trusted their artificial-horizon. Countless lives would have been saved, had pilots adhered to the simple mantra: "Trust your instruments." Put another way, "Do not trust your senses."

For good reason: Spatial disorientation. Our "balance" apparatus resides within our inner ears: Semi-circular canals filled with fluid, and lined with small hairs (cilia). As the fluid within the canals sways back and forth across the hairs, movement and balance signals are sent to our brain.

In rapid accelerations, the fluid moves backwards over the hairs (just as we are frequently slammed back into our seats in rapid automotive accelerations). The hairs interpret this backward movement as "we are in a climb." In rapid decelerations, the fluid moves forward over the hairs (just as we are frequently thrown forward in rapid automotive decelerations). The hairs interpret this forward movement as "we are in a descent."

While our brains may perceive a need to "correct for the climb" by descending, or "correct for the descent" by climbing, a brief glance at our instruments would indicate we remain in level flight: No climb, no descent, no need to correct.

An inadvertent, imperceptibly slow, gentle roll to the left or right, properly displayed on the artificial-horizon as a left or right turn, may have the opposite effect. Due to the gentle nature of the roll, the inner ear fluids may pass too slowly over the hairs lining the semi-circular canals, thereby failing to trigger the "we are in a turn" perception.

Unlike the accelerate/decelerate scenario; in this instance, there *is* a definite need to correct, as we do *not* want to be in an uncorrected, inadvertent roll to the left or right. However, our brains (having *not* been triggered by fluid passing over the hairs) will tell us to disregard the "erroneous" instrument indications. Our brains will tell us "We are in level flight, the instruments are incorrect, no correction is required." Spatial disorientation. Trust your instruments. Do not trust your senses.

The visual sense, standing alone and independent of the inner ear's semi-circular canals, can likewise lead to an episode of spatial disorientation. One common scenario comes to mind: A sloping cloud deck at the twelve o'clock position, with a roughly twenty-degree downslope from right to left. The pilot perceives the right-to-left downslope, not for what it is, a sloping cloud deck; rather she perceives "I am in a right turn," and rolls into left bank, to be "level" (parallel) with the perceived horizon (the sloping cloud deck). Spatial disorientation. Do not trust your senses. Trust your instruments.

While a discussion of spatial disorientation may entail a handful of paragraphs; it's threat to aviation can be demonstrated in less than fifty seconds. In December 2016, an aircraft departing Cleveland Lakefront airport was cleared for takeoff, with instructions to level at 2000-feet. Seconds after takeoff, having entered "the soup," with no visual horizon, the jet was climbing at 6000 feet per minute, quickly busting through the assigned 2000-foot level-off. The bank angle increased to over sixty-degrees (triple the normal bank angle) while pitch transitioned to fifteen-degrees *nose-down* (triple the normal nose-down pitch). Airspeed increased to 300-knots with a descent rate of 6000 feet per minute (a 12,000-foot per minute reversal from the moments-earlier 6000 feet per minute climb). Total flight time: Takeoff to impact, was fifty seconds. Probable cause, as cited by the NTSB: Controlled flight into terrain (CFIT) *due to pilot spatial disorientation.* In a perfectly good airplane.

"Flight 28, climb to and maintain ten thousand feet, proceed direct Syracuse, altimeter setting two-nine-seven-nine."

Fran sets ten thousand feet in the "Altitude Select Window." We both point to, and visually *verify*, the ten-thousand-foot setting. We both *verbalize* "Set, ten thousand feet." We both set 29.79 in our altimeters. We both glance across the flight-deck to visually *verify* the other has done so, while *verbalizing* "Set, Two Nine

Seven Nine." Lastly, we both *verbalize* the unit of measurement, "Inches of Mercury."

Fran punches a few keys, and brings Syracuse to the top of the Flight Management Computer (FMC) Legs-Page. Before punching the "Execute" key, he *verbalizes* "How does this look to you?" I *verify* Syracuse at the top of the Legs Page. I *verify* the Navigation-Display depicts a dashed white line (depicting our desired modified course) from our present position direct to Syracuse. Having *verified* both those displays, I *verbalize* "Looks good to me." Fran punches the "Execute" key.

We both *monitor* as the dashed white line on our Navigation-Displays morphs into a solid magenta line (depicting our new active course). Lastly, we *monitor* as the flight director's "command bars" direct a pitch-up for our climb to ten thousand feet, and a roll to the left reflecting our course change to Syracuse.

Still hand-flying, I gently pull back on the yoke for the climb to 10,000-feet, and I gently roll left for the Syracuse course. My right hand rides the throttles as they throttle-up to climb-power. Fran and I have both *verbalized, verified* and *monitored.*

We both verbalized and verified the correct altitude setting, of ten thousand feet. Why do so? Altitude deviations constitute, by an exceptionally wide margin, the vast bulk of in-flight errors. Working the math, with a mere one thousand feet of vertical separation between aircraft, with aircraft climbing and descending at closure rates of ten thousand feet per minute, it will take a mere six seconds to close the minimal-allowable thousand-foot vertical gap between aircraft. Altitude deviations place lives in danger.

We both verbalized and verified the local altimeter setting of 29.79. Local altimeter settings, provided by air traffic control, and utilized for all flights below 18,000-feet, ensure a common baseline for all aircraft operating within a local area. Incorrect altimeter settings may lead to improper altitude readings. Improper altitude readings, in turn, may lead to a CFIT (controlled flight into terrain) scenario, or a midair-collision scenario.

We both verbalized and verified "Inches of mercury" as our applicable unit of measurement. Why do so? While our unit of measurement over North America is inches of mercury, the unit of measurement as we descend over the United Kingdom, for our arrival into London-Heathrow, will be millibars (or hectopascals) of mercury. Just as pounds do not equal kilograms; so too, inches of mercury do not equal millibars of mercury. An incorrect unit of measurement may place lives in jeopardy. Indeed, both scenarios, incorrect altimeter settings and incorrect units of measurement, have contributed to unpleasant scenarios.

As an example, an altimeter setting of 29.92 inches of mercury, set as 992 millibars, would place an aircraft (and all Window Seat Pilots) at an actual altitude 630-feet below the altitude displayed on the aircraft altimeter. Given that most "instrument approach minimums" direct an aircraft to level-off 200-feet above the ground, a 630-foot altitude error would likely lead to an unpleasant scenario. *Verbalize, verify and monitor. Textbook.*

In the lateral plane, prior to punching the "Execute" key, we both verified Syracuse at the top of our FMC Legs-Page, we both scanned our Navigation-Displays, and we both verified a dashed white line (depicting our desired modified course) proceeding from our present position direct to Syracuse.

Why do so? The advanced automation features, ubiquitous in modern aircraft, have often led to an unhealthy sense of security, complacency and inattention. A "plug it in and go" mindset can be a killer.

Not long ago, a fully-loaded Boeing 757, identical to ours, impacted a mountainside in Columbia. That unpleasant scenario of controlled flight into terrain may have been avoided with a mere glance, by either pilot, at the Navigation-Display, prior to executing a route change very much like our route change to Syracuse.

In the Columbia incident, prior to punching the "Execute" key; the Navigation-Display likely indicated a dashed white line (depicting an *erroneously* modified course) pointing in a direction *opposite* to the desired/intended direction of flight: A 180-degree course-reversal over the captain's left shoulder, rather than the desired/intended straight-ahead course. The "Execute" key was punched, the dashed white line (depicting the erroneous modified course) morphed into a solid magenta line (depicting the new active course). The auto-flight system turned the aircraft left. Shortly thereafter, terrain was impacted.

Three thoughts regarding the Colombia experience. First, the flight-crew was overloaded, operating in mountainous terrain, at night, with a last-minute air traffic control re-route.

Second, recall our flight-crew brief prior to our departure: "We will not rush for anyone, at any time, for any reason. If anyone is feeling rushed, speak up. We will throttle back, set the parking-brake, or enter a holding pattern." A holding pattern may have saved lives in Colombia.

Third, the Columbia scenario could have been my scenario, Fran's scenario, Erica's scenario, or any other pilot's scenario. By nature, we, as pilots, are driven to *make-it-fit*. We are *mission hackers*. We try to *make it happen*. We are *can-do*. We articulate *good-to-go*. We are drawn to the challenge. We are often one with the adrenaline rush. The edge is often our sweet spot. It takes a conscious effort, some might say a monumental effort, to fight the *make-it-fit* mindset. Hence, my opening comments: "I left my ego in the parking lot, I hope you did the same, no egos on the flight-deck."

A clear example of the *make-it-fit* mindset? Industry-wide, only four percent of unstable approaches (too fast, too high) prompt flight-crews to execute the mandatory FAA-required go-around. Put another way, ninety-six percent of the time, flight-crews continue to fly an unstable approach in an attempt to shoe-horn a too-high, too-fast approach into the runway, despite an explicit FAA requirement to execute a go-around.

Additional evidence of the *make-it-fit* mindset? One study of flight-crew behavior regarding thunderstorms found that in 1,310 of 1,952 thunderstorm encounters, flight-crews knowingly flew into thunderstorms during landing attempts, rather than executing the mandatory FAA-required go-around.

The *make-it-fit* factor was present in the Cali scenario. Air traffic control had offered the flight-crew a choice between continuing with the original, more leisurely route to the airfield; or the much shorter, much tighter route. The flight-crew opted for the shorter/tighter route, with the Cockpit Voice Recorder capturing: *"We'll have to scramble"* and *"We can do it."*

Back to our flight. Our Syracuse routing takes us wide to the west, avoiding the weather off our right wing. Our weather radar is a kaleidoscope of reds and yellows; ample confirmation of the need for our Syracuse re-route. The Window Seat Pilots seated along the right side of our aircraft have an incredible view of nature's light-show as bolts of lightning illuminate the towering cumulonimbus clouds hammering the earth below with torrential rain. The "rampers" are having a tough night.

Climbing through 10,000-feet, I conclude it is "time to grow up." The fun (hand-flying) has to end sometime. Ten thousand feet is my "sometime." I engage one of our three auto-pilots. I release my shoulder harness, adjust the tilt on the weather radar, cycle the No-Smoking sign, and turn off the Sterile Cockpit Light.

Cycling the No-Smoking sign is our cue to Cherie, and her flight-attendant team, that we have passed through ten thousand feet, and "personal electronic devices are now permitted." Turning off the Sterile Cockpit Light, cues them that we are no longer "Sterile." Non-security and non-safety calls to the flight-deck are now permitted.

Passing through 12,000-feet, we break out of the clouds. We are "on top." Welcome to heaven. I punch the "Vertical Speed" button, and select a 100 foot-per-minute climb-rate. Fran advises Air Traffic Control of our reduced climb-rate. We want a few moments to enjoy the cloud-surfing experience. The nose drops for our much-reduced climb-rate; and, for a few moments, we cruise along the cloud tops, at roughly 400 feet per second.

Bathed in moonlight, they offer a vision of peace and serenity. Forty years on the flight-deck, roughly five flights per week. Working the math, that comes to over ten thousand flights. Yet, breaking out, on top, reducing the rate of climb, and skimming along the cloud-tops for a few moments of cloud-surfing, still brings me an emotion I have yet to experience in any other setting.

While seated at the pointy-end of the jet, there is nothing else quite like it. Cruising in silence, along the top of an endless, horizon-spanning blanket of pure white clouds, bathed in the brilliance of sunlight or the soft touch of moonlight, is an experience to behold and treasure. The moments of cloud-surfing will cost us a bit of fuel. It will, however, be an insignificant amount. The moments are worth the fuel burn, not merely for the three of us, seated on the flight-deck; but, for our Window Seat Pilots as well.

With the "peace and serenity fix" satisfied, I punch the "V-NAV" button and we resume our 6,000 foot-per-minute rate of climb. Once again, Fran advises Air Traffic Control. As we climb through 18,000-feet, we turn off our taxi lights, wing lights and landing lights. Above 18,000-feet, we dispense with local altimeter settings, opting to share (along with every other aircraft above 18,000-feet) the global standard altimeter setting of 29.92 inches of mercury. With that in mind, Fran and I set, verbalize and verify 29.92 inches of mercury.

Our "Altitude Select Window" reads 31000. Our "Airspeed Select Window" reads 290. Our Legs-Page has Syracuse at the top of the screen, followed by Boston. Our Navigation-Display has a solid magenta line from our present position, direct to Syracuse, and onward to Boston. The left auto-pilot is controlling our lateral path (Syracuse, Boston) along with our vertical path (climbing to FL 310). The auto-throttle system, engaged at the start of our takeoff roll, is controlling our engine thrust setting for a 290-knot airspeed while in the climb.

The weather radar indicates continued activity to our right-rear quadrant. The view out the front window has a blanket of stars above, and a cloud deck below, sloping from left to right with a twenty-degree tilt. We are free of weather. We are in the clear. I secure the engine anti-icing. All is well.

Reflection

On a recent late-night drive home from the airport, while conversing with my son, via phone, I noted I was low on fuel. Fearing I might not find an open gas station at the late hour, I asked my son to do some quick research for me: Where was the nearest, open gas station?

My son's first words to me: "Dad, keep flying the airplane." The student had become the teacher. He had heard that phrase, from my lips, for most of his twenty-plus years.

Keep flying the airplane. Never, for any reason, stop flying the airplane.

Whether it be a dual-engine-failure, an engine fire, or an uncontrolled cargo fire; whether it be a family crisis, a financial crisis, or a health crisis; whether it be low-fuel on a late-night drive; keep flying the airplane, keep making "it" happen.

Simulator check-rides provide ample opportunity to put this truism into play. Drenched in sweat, after four hours in the seat, after handling one emergency after another, as the simulator session comes to a close; while on final approach, with a catastrophic engine-failure; we never stop flying the airplane, we never stop trying to put the jet on the runway, we never stop wrestling the beast, we never let go of the yoke.

On 3 September 2010, a UPS Boeing 747 departed Dubai. Twenty-one minutes into the flight, six miles above the earth, the flight-crew was alerted to a fire in their cargo compartment. Four minutes later, the intensity of the fire had burned through

81

a portion of their flight-control cables, rendering controlled flight problematic. Moreover, their flight-deck had filled with smoke; so much so, that neither pilot could see out their window, nor could either pilot clearly see their flight instruments.

Two minutes later, the Captain lost all oxygen. Three minutes later, the First Officer informed air traffic control "I need immediate vectors, I cannot see, I am flying blind."

For an additional twenty minutes, having lost his Captain, while flying solo, without any reference to his flight instruments, without any view through his flight-deck window, with compromised flight-controls, on a flight-deck swirling with blinding and toxic smoke and fumes, employing relay aircraft for air traffic control communications, that First Officer never stopped flying the airplane.

Keep flying the airplane.

What are you telling yourself, what are you telling the passengers in your life, when you step away from the flight controls and walk off the flight deck?

The passengers in your life; be they spouses, children, partners, teammates, or co-workers; placed their faith in you, when they boarded your jet.

In life, as in flight, never stop flying the airplane.

A Venetian Canal

It is time to transition from the "departure-and-climb" mindset, to the "cruise" mindset. It is time for my seltzer with a slice of lemon. It is time for my apple and my raisins. It is time to marvel, once again, at the wonder and magic of flight. Thirty rows aft of the flight-deck door, a Window Seat Pilot, with a terrier in her lap, is pondering the question: How does something so big stay in the air?

The answer to that question can be traced to a stroll taken centuries ago, along the Grand Canal in Venice, Italy. Among the many men and women strolling along the Canal, was a Dutch-Swiss mathematician by the name of Daniel Bernoulli.

Daniel holds few equals in the sciences of today. The breadth and depth of his knowledge was truly remarkable. He researched, wrote and taught in the fields of logic and mathematics, physiology and medicine, biology and philosophy, mechanics and physics, astronomy and oceanography. He earned an MD degree, a position with the prestigious Academy of Sciences of St Petersburg, ten awards from the equally prestigious Paris Academy of Sciences, and professorship positions at Switzerland's Basel University, in Anatomy, Botany, Physiology and Physics.

As he strolled in the year 1738, he attempted to keep pace with a discarded wine bottle floating with the Canal's current. Observant gentleman that he was, he noted the bottle accelerated around the curved foundations of the footbridges spanning the Canal, emerging downstream from beneath each bridge a few steps ahead of him. On each occasion, he would quicken his pace, and catch up with the bottle, only to once again fall behind as the bottle accelerated around the curved foundation of the next bridge, once again emerging several steps ahead of his pace. Like the water's acceleration around the curved foundation of the Venetian bridges, so too, airflow accelerates over the curved upper surface of our wing.

While our wing curvature is not as pronounced as the foundations of a centuries-old bridge spanning a Venetian canal, it is nonetheless curved. Airflow approaching the leading edge of our wing thus has further to "run" over the curved upper surface of our wing than does airflow passing beneath the flat underside of our wing. Having to run a greater distance, the airflow along the upper surface must run at a faster speed. Therefore, airflow passing over the upper surface of our wing is "running" faster than airflow passing beneath the lower surface of our wing.

That, in and of itself, is not the end of the story. Mr. Bernoulli's real contribution to this evening's flight was his discovery that faster air constitutes lower pressure air. The faster airflow over the upper surface of our wing is at a lower pressure than the slower airflow passing beneath the lower surface of our wing. The same phenomenon explains why your boarding pass will be sucked out your open car window (into faster, lower pressure air) as you make your drive to the airport.

Our wing experiences "Lift" due to the pressure differential between the lower air pressure above our wing (faster air), and the higher air pressure beneath our wing (slower air). Mr. Bernoulli put it all together in his book Hydrodynamica, published in 1738.

There is a bit more to the "Lift" dynamic. Beyond wing curvature, four additional pilot-controlled factors come into play: *Angle of attack, coefficient of lift, wing surface area* and *airspeed.* All four, like wing curvature, are directly related to Lift. If we increase any of the four, we increase Lift.

We begin with angle-of-attack. In rough terms, angle-of-attack is the angle between our wing and the relative wind. As we increase our angle-of-attack, we increase our coefficient of lift. As we increase our coefficient of lift, we increase Lift. As we were accelerating down Newark's Runway 22-Right earlier this evening, Fran called "Rotate" at 148 knots. We had sufficient airspeed to break free the surly bonds of Earth. Yet, we were not flying. Something was missing. We needed "something more." My response to Fran's "Rotate" call, was to smoothly pull back on the yoke at a ball-park rate of two degrees per second, stabilizing at an angle of roughly fifteen degrees nose-up. Doing so increased our angle-of-attack. The increased angle-of-attack boosted our coefficient of lift. The increased coefficient of lift boosted our Lift. We had our "something more." We were flying. *Angle-of-attack, coefficient of Lift.*

Long before we lined up for takeoff, we extended our wing's leading-edge slats and our wing's trailing-edge flaps. Doing so increased the surface area and curvature of our wing. Both actions increased our Lift. Flaps and slats. *Surface area and curvature.*

As we accelerated on our climb-out, passing through 168 knots, we retracted our wing flaps and slats from 15-degrees to 5-degrees. As we continued to accelerate, passing through 188 knots, we retracted them from 5-degrees to 1-degree. As we passed through 208 knots, we completed the transition from 1-degree to a clean-wing with the "Flaps Up" call.

Why did we do so? As we accelerated, as our airspeed increased, we no longer needed the additive properties (increased curvature and increased surface area) provided by flap and slat extension. Our higher airspeed "clean-wing" (flaps/slats retracted) could do for us what our slower airspeed "dirty-wing" (flaps/slats extended) had done for us as we rolled down the runway.

Six hours from now, as we decelerate for our approach and landing into London-Heathrow, losing the additive property of airspeed, we will once again extend our wing flaps and slats (increasing wing curvature and surface area) in an incremental manner to compensate for each successive airspeed reduction. *Airspeed.*

Of the four pilot-controlled elements of the Lift equation (angle-of-attack, coefficient of lift, wing curvature-surface area, and airspeed), airspeed is the only element that is "squared." Any increase or decrease in airspeed has an outsize impact on Lift. Hence, the aviation expression "speed is life." Or the Hollywood version, "I have a need for speed."

The Window Seat Pilot might ask, "If flaps and slats are a good thing, why do we retract them?" While flaps and slats do, indeed, boost Lift through increased wing curvature and surface area, they also increase drag. When we require increased curvature and surface area (at low airspeed, during takeoff and landing), we accept the increased drag. When we do not require increased curvature and surface area (high airspeed, cruise flight), we prefer to do without the increased drag (increased fuel burn). Hence, our clean-wing as we pass overhead Boston, leveling at thirty-one thousand feet.

While the increased angle-of-attack on takeoff gave us the "something more" required to lift us off the Newark runway, too much angle-of-attack is not a good thing. The coefficient of lift increases with angle-of-attack. However, it does so only to a point. Beyond that point, a further increase in angle-of-attack will create turbulence over the upper surface of the wing, thereby "killing" Lift, eventually leading to an aerodynamic "stall." The airplane will stop flying. Hence, my takeoff rotation stabilized at an angle of fifteen degrees nose-up.

The only solution to an aerodynamic stall is to relax back-pressure on the yoke, allowing the nose to drop, thereby reducing the angle-of-attack, and allowing airflow to once again pass smoothly over the upper surface of the wing.

The "relaxation of back-pressure" and allowing the nose to drop, entails a trade-off, in which we trade altitude for airspeed: Drop the nose, lose altitude, gain airspeed, kill the stall, regain Lift. Unfortunately, on takeoff and landing, in close proximity to the ground, there is often insufficient altitude available to manage an altitude-for-airspeed trade. Two flight-training classmates experienced such a scenario: An aerodynamic stall while in the landing phase, with insufficient altitude available to manage an altitude-for-airspeed trade.

Every nine months, while in the simulator, every pilot trades altitude-for-airspeed, while practicing their "stall recovery." Shortly thereafter, every pilot executes the "upset recovery" procedure. First step in both recoveries? Push the yoke forward, reduce the angle of attack, restore the lift, resume flying, and live.

In an effort to prevent an aerodynamic stall, many modern aircraft display a "Pitch Limit Indicator" on the artificial horizon. Increasing pitch (angle-of-attack) up to this pitch limit is permissible. Increasing pitch (angle-of-attack) beyond this limit is not advisable. Modern aircraft may also be equipped with a "stick-pusher" that automatically pushes the yoke forward, lowering the nose, reducing the angle-of-attack, thereby preventing a stall. Lastly, aircraft such as our Boeing 757, also incorporate an "auto-slat extend" feature that automatically extends wing slats as the angle-of-attack approaches the stall-angle, increasing wing curvature and surface area, thereby increasing Lift, precluding onset of an actual stall.

A pleasant angle-of-attack memory from an earlier life: "Riding the tickle" in the T-38, affectionately referred to as the White Rocket. Coming off the "perch," fifteen hundred feet above the touchdown zone, with the runway located aft of my right shoulder (roughly at my five o'clock position), fully configured for landing, I rolled in the right bank, retarded the throttles, looked back over my right shoulder, fixed my eyes on the runway threshold, and "pulled" the jet down and around the descending turn for a super-smooth (smile) touchdown. Aside from a handful of glances at my airspeed indicator; for the most part, my eyes were not in the cockpit. Rather, they were on the touchdown zone, as I pulled the jet down and around.

How did I know "all was well?" I rode the "tickle." I flew by the seat of my pants, with my wing on the knife's edge of an aerodynamic stall. The tickle in the seat of my pants, was the low-amplitude, high-frequency tickle, suggesting an approach to a stall, as the air passing over the upper surface of the wing struggled to remain smooth.

Had I relaxed my pull on the yoke, thereby reducing the angle-of-attack, I would have traded the "tickle" for "smooth", and rolled out wide, overshooting the runway. Had I pulled back, just a hair too much, I would have morphed from "tickle" to "buffet." The higher amplitude buffet would have indicated turbulence over the wing, a loss of Lift, and an impending aerodynamic stall.

While on the knife's edge, residing between the smooth and the buffet, between the overshoot and the stall, the "tickle" constituted the "sweet spot." I would gladly suffer the fleas of a thousand camels in exchange for another opportunity to "ride the tickle."

Reflection

Prioritize. In aviation, the twin mantras are "Aviate, Navigate, Communicate" and (while in the midst of an emergency) "Maintain aircraft control, analyze the situation, take proper corrective action."

Emergencies are a given. If one loses sight of the over-arching need to "Aviate" and "Maintain aircraft control"; all too often, an initially manageable situation, can spiral into an unmanageable crisis and an unpleasant scenario. Lacking those two critical focus elements (Aviate, Maintain aircraft control), all subsequent elements are often for naught.

In the late-night hours of December 29, 1972, a wide-body aircraft approaching Miami, experienced an indicator malfunction for their nose-mounted landing gear. While trouble-shooting the malfunction, the three flight-crew members failed to monitor their flight path, thereby failing to note their descent, until moments prior to impact with the Everglades. An unpleasant, tragic scenario ensued. Aviate. Maintain aircraft control.

On the evening of December 28, 1978, a McDonnell Douglas DC-8 approaching Portland, Oregon, likewise experienced a landing gear indicator malfunction. For over an hour, the three flight-crew members focused on the malfunction, while not monitoring the aircraft's fuel status, leading to fuel-starvation and flame-out of all four engines. An unpleasant, tragic scenario ensued. Aviate. Maintain aircraft control.

In life, as in flight; be ever-mindful of your priorities, never more so, than while in the midst of life's emergencies.

Position: Overhead Boston

Rapid-D And Clear of Traffic

We are level at our initial cruise altitude. Air traffic control has advised us we can anticipate a smooth ride. With that in mind, we have turned off the Fasten Seat Belt sign. While the passengers are free to move about the cabin, we will keep our seat belts fastened on the flight-deck, in the event we encounter any unexpected bumps along the way.

We have cross-checked my altimeter reading of 31,000 feet, Fran's altimeter reading of 31,060 feet and the standby altimeter reading of 31,100 feet. Our three altimeter read-outs are within the 200-foot limits required for "Reduced Vertical Separation Minima" (RVSM), a prerequisite for operations on the North Atlantic Track system. The RVSM altimetry accuracy allows for one-thousand foot vertical separation between aircraft in a non-radar environment.

To enter RVSM airspace, we must have three independent, operating altimeters, within limits; an operative autopilot system; and an operative altitude-alert system (the system will trigger an audible flight-deck alert if we depart our planned altitude by greater than three hundred feet).

We have scanned all displays, all switches and all buttons. We have requested, and received, the latest forecast for the winds along our route of flight. We have re-confirmed our cruise speeds and altitudes, our estimated time of arrival for London-Heathrow and our estimated Fuel Overhead Destination (FOD). All is well.

During the course of our flight, our FMC will continuously monitor the projected FOD. If, at any point, the FOD falls below our earlier-calculated Bingo Fuel (Alternate Fuel plus Thirty-Minutes), the FMC will trigger an *Insufficient-Fuel* message, indicating that if we were required to divert to our planned Alternate, we would land at the Alternate with less than thirty minutes of fuel-remaining.

By explicit FAA definition, less than thirty minutes of fuel-remaining constitutes an Emergency; as such, it will require a decision. Something will have to change. We will either reduce our fuel-burn (by altering our airspeed, our altitude, or our routing) thereby boosting our FOD, to once again exceed our Bingo, allowing us to continue to our planned destination; or, we will be forced to land short of our destination (with an enroute divert).

Next up, our crew-rest schedule. Until recently, Federal Air Regulations required flights scheduled to exceed eight hours, to be staffed by three pilots; while flights scheduled to exceed twelve hours, required four pilots. The additional pilots, referred to as "International Relief Officers" (IROs), are fully trained and qualified in all respects; indeed, they carry the same Type Rating certificates as Captains. More recently, given the findings of research into the nature, causes and effects of fatigue; those Regulations have evolved into a more complex matrix factoring in a number of fatigue-related factors. Either way, Erica, our International Relief Officer, is required to be on the flight-deck during all "critical phases of flight" from departure gate push-back through level-off at our initial cruise altitude; and from top-of-descent through gate-arrival at destination. Erica has worked the crew-rest math. Each of us will enjoy an hour and fifty-minute crew-rest. Erica gets the first break. I will take the second break. Fran will get the third break.

"Flight 28, climb to and maintain Flight Level 350."

Before accepting the ATC clearance, Fran and I are heads-down over our Flight Management Computer (FMC). Accounting for our current weight, outside air temperature and actual winds; the FMC informs us our Maximum altitude is 35,000-feet, our Optimum altitude is 32,000-feet and our Recommended altitude is 33,000-feet. With that in mind, we request an amended clearance to our Recommended altitude of 33,000 thousand feet.

"Flight 28, you are cleared as requested. Climb to and maintain Flight Level 330." We set, *verbalize* and *verify* 33,000-feet in the "Altitude Select Window." We *monitor* as aircraft pitch and power adjusts for our climb to Flight Level 330 (nose up, power up). *Verbalize, verify, monitor.*

The FMC-generated "Maximum" altitude is the lowest of three possible values: The aircraft manufacturer's certified maximum altitude, the stall-margin altitude, or the thrust-limited altitude.

The manufacturer's certified-maximum altitude is based on the structural integrity of the cabin when placed under pressure. Just as a submarine has a certified-maximum depth before the external sea-pressure (pressing inward) leads to structural damage; so too an aircraft has a certified-maximum altitude before internal air pressure (pressing outward) leads to structural damage. The higher our altitude, the greater the differential pressure upon our aircraft structure. Our structural limit is a differential pressure of 9.1 pounds per square inch. Thirty-five thousand feet may be the altitude at which we reach 9.1 inches of differential pressure. Hence, our "Maximum."

As we climb in altitude, the air becomes thinner, with fewer air molecules available to provide Lift. When we lose Lift, we run the risk of an aerodynamic stall. Thirty-five thousand feet may be the altitude at which we have just enough Lift to support our weight. Hence, our "Maximum."

The third possible FMC-generated "Maximum" altitude is the "thrust-limit altitude." As we climb in altitude (higher/thinner air), our engines generate less thrust. As an example, the thrust available at FL370 is a mere one-fourth the thrust available at sea-level. The "thrust-limit altitude" ensures sufficient thrust for a 300 foot-per-minute rate of climb, at twenty-two degrees of bank, at maximum continuous thrust. Thirty-five thousand feet may be the altitude at which those climb performance criteria are met. Hence, our "Maximum."

In view of the above discussion of structural limits, stall limits and climb limits, we prefer not to fly at our Maximum altitude. Hence, while air traffic control cleared us to Flight Level 350 (thirty-five thousand feet), and while our FMC has indicated FL350 as our Maximum, we nonetheless requested an amended clearance for FL330. As a general rule, most flight-crews choose to remain at least 1000-feet below the FMC-generated Maximum altitude.

The FMC-generated "Optimum" altitude is the optimal "fuel efficient" altitude, not accounting for actual winds and actual outside air temperature.

The FMC-generated "Recommended" altitude is the "Optimum" altitude, corrected for actual winds and actual outside air temperature. As a general rule, both the Optimum altitude and the Recommended altitude will increase as we reduce our weight due to fuel-burn. Hence, the "step-climb" profiles present in most flight plans. All other factors being equal; as we burn gas, as we reduce our total weight, we will climb; gaining better fuel-economy and benefiting from stronger tailwinds at the higher altitudes.

Prior to the advent of the Flight Management Computer, while serving in the now-extinct Second Officer (Flight Engineer) position; each of those cruise altitude calculations (and so many more), required tedious reference to the earlier-mentioned thirty-pound Planning and Performance Manual. The FMC is a welcome addition to the team.

Time now, to tend to matters of health. Every hour, I will step out of the seat, drink a good bit of water, and work my way through a flight-deck stretching routine. At the flight's halfway point, I will take a stroll to the aft galley to stretch my legs, and prepare myself a cup of tea.

Federal Air Regulations (FARs), state we may leave the flight-deck for "physiological reasons." While some of my colleagues interpret "physiological reasons" rather narrowly, as in "restroom break," I choose to interpret it rather broadly, as in "stretch the legs, take a walk, get the blood flowing, clear the mind."

As with every career, an aviation career has its upsides and its downsides. One downside is the threat to one's health. Maintaining a healthy diet is a challenge. Keeping oneself fit is a challenge. Restful sleep is always a challenge in a daylight hotel room, overhead a traffic-filled street, having crossed up to twelve time zones, on a sixteen-hour, backside-of-the-clock flight.

Amid the security environment in which we operate, keeping oneself adequately hydrated can pose an additional challenge. With a focus on flight-deck security, passage between the flight-deck and the cabin, for a "restroom break," has become a time-consuming, service-interrupting exercise. Consequently, many pilots are reluctant to engage in "the hassle." Hence, water intake is down, and kidney stones are up. As a rule of thumb, the Window Seat Pilot does not want the pilot to pass a kidney stone, over the North Atlantic. Nor does the pilot wish to do so.

My in-flight routine of two liters of water, hourly stretching, and my mid-flight, full-length stroll, is but one element in my effort to mitigate the health risks. While on the London layover, I will avoid caffeine and alcohol. I will get a full aerobic workout, a few hours of fresh air, a solid meal and I will hope for eight to ten hours of sleep. Recalling the advice offered to me, decades ago, on my very first flight, as a new-hire airline pilot, (coincidentally to London); if I wake, during my attempts at sleep, I will abide by two hard and fast rules: I will not look at the clock, nor will I turn on a light.

Having shared my layover plans, Fran has likely already labeled me as boring. Having said that, Fran is twenty years younger and still has the strength of a bull. He played Division One baseball, and has coached his local high school baseball team to three Pennsylvania state championships.

As I step out of the seat, Fran dons his oxygen mask and confirms his oxygen regulator is set to one-hundred percent oxygen. Federal Air Regulations (FARs) dictate he do so. Should we experience a "rapid-decompression" while I am out of the seat, the "Time of Useful Consciousness" would be roughly fifteen seconds, leaving little time to find and don the oxygen mask, prior to losing consciousness. The "find and don" task, undertaken in the midst of a rapid-decompression, would likely be handicapped by a handful of alarm bells, the paralyzing cold, the deafening sound of winds whipping through the aircraft, and a whirlwind of debris flying about the flight-deck.

The rapid-decompression scenario is but one of two possible decompression scenarios. An equally dangerous (some might argue more dangerous) scenario is a gradual loss of pressurization, with a commensurate gradual climb in "cabin-altitude." The gradual climb in cabin-altitude would lead to an equally gradual oxygen-starvation of the brain, with eventual loss of consciousness.

In our earlier lives, Fran and I both experienced physiological-training trips to an "altitude chamber." While seated in the chamber, on two simulated, fully-pressurized, high-altitude flights, we were exposed to both decompression scenarios: A rapid-decompression scenario and a slow-decompression scenario. During the course of both scenarios, we were asked to conduct the simplest of tasks: Count backwards from ten to one, write our name on a sheet of paper, make church steeples with the fingers of both hands, play a simple game of tic-tac-toe with a partner. We were video-recorded while attempting to complete the simple tasks. Following the simulated flights, we observed those video recordings. Oxygen starvation is not pretty.

Recognizing the danger posed by both the rapid scenario and the slow scenario, aircraft manufacturers have incorporated a number of safety features: Triple-redundancy in aircraft pressurization systems, a flight-deck alarm as the cabin-altitude passes through ten thousand feet, and the auto-deployment of passenger oxygen masks as the cabin-altitude passes through fourteen thousand feet. Aircraft operators have likewise developed standard operating procedures and training programs, focused on depressurization scenarios.

Nonetheless, despite the system redundancies and the safety features, despite the procedures and the training, decompression has claimed lives. As but one example, In August of 2005, a Boeing 737 departed Cyprus, enroute to Athens, Greece, with a pressurization switch in the incorrect position. The incorrect switch position was missed during the Pre-Flight checklist. It was missed again during the After-Start checklist. It was missed yet a third time during the After-Takeoff checklist. During the subsequent climb-out from Cyprus, several aircraft pressurization warnings were properly triggered, but were improperly interpreted by the flight-crew. Unaware of their oxygen-starvation peril, the flight-crew lapsed into unconsciousness; while the aircraft leveled at thirty-four thousand feet, flew from Cyprus to Athens, entered a holding pattern overhead Athens, suffered a dual-engine-flameout due to fuel-starvation, and impacted terrain in the vicinity of Marathon, Greece; all while on autopilot. Oxygen starvation. Checklist discipline.

The fifteen-second "Time of Useful Consciousness" is the reasoning behind that portion of Cherie's pre-departure passenger-safety briefing, in which adult passengers are urged to secure an oxygen mask over their own nose and mouth prior to assisting a child. Reversing the sequence over those critical fifteen seconds, may lead to a situation in which an adult has placed a mask upon their child, and has subsequently lost consciousness, leaving the clueless child wondering why Mommy/Daddy will not wake up.

"Flight 28, you are cleared from present position, direct to the Bradd intersection. Report when ready for flight level three-five-zero."

Once again, prior to execution, Fran and I *verify* the Bradd intersection at the top of our Flight Management Computer (FMC) Legs-Page, we *verify* a dashed white line direct Bradd on our Navigation Display. It looks good. We execute. We *monitor* as the dashed white line morphs to solid magenta, and as the aircraft banks gently to the right.

The re-route has shaved four minutes off our flight time, and upped our London-Heathrow Fuel Overhead Destination (FOD) by a few hundred pounds.

Having spent a career on the airborne side of the air traffic control dynamic, I recently paid a visit to "New York Center," one of twenty-one Air Route Traffic Control Centers scattered across the country, each charged with controlling the traffic within their slice of airspace.

My guide for the day was Ryan, a 32-year veteran of military and civil air traffic control. Looking across the rows of radar screens, manned by their respective controllers, each responsible for his/her slice of airspace, Ryan began his lesson. "The bottom-line is safety. Safety requires aircraft separation. Aircraft separation requires controller vigilance. Controller vigilance requires reasonable workload. Reasonable workload requires flow control. Put another way: Impair flow control, overload a controller, imperil vigilance, threaten aircraft separation, compromise flight safety." It was crystal clear, and in keeping with our earlier discussion of air-traffic delays.

He continued: "There are many types of aircraft; however, from the air traffic controller's perspective, there are only two types: Those flying in accordance with Instrument Flight Rules (IFR), and those flying in accordance with Visual Flight Rules (VFR).

"While a full chapter could be devoted to the distinctions between IFR and VFR, for the purpose of our discussion we need only note that aircraft flying in accordance with IFR are generally required to maintain radio contact with, and are under the control of, air traffic controllers. Those operating in accordance with VFR are generally not required to maintain radio contact with, or submit to the control of, air traffic controllers.

"Just as aircraft are distinguished by flight rules, airspace is distinguished by access requirements. Certain airspace segments require no communication, navigation, or transponder equipment. Other airspace segments, due to traffic congestion or proximity to airports, require some combination of communication and/or transponder equipment."

Ryan led me to an operating radar scope. "There are two types of radar-returns on this scope: Two altitude-transponder squawks, and one raw-data radar-return." He placed his pointer on one of the read-outs, tracing over a series of luminescent numbers. "This is an altitude-transponder squawk. It provides the controller with aircraft call-sign and type, along with airspeed and altitude. In this case, we are looking at Jasno-99, a Boeing 747-800, at 300 knots, level at thirteen thousand feet."

He rolled his pointer to the second read-out, bearing no luminescent numbers. "This is a raw-data radar-return. The controller knows there is an aircraft at this point, but she has no data on call-sign, aircraft type, airspeed, or altitude."

Ryan rolled his pointer to the third scope read-out, another altitude-transponder squawk, converging with the two other read-outs. "We are looking at Bison-28, a C-130 cruising at 290 knots, level at fifteen thousand feet. The three aircraft are clearly converging. The controller notes the first altitude-squawk read-out, Jasno-99, at thirteen thousand feet; and the second altitude-squawk read-out, Bison-28, at fifteen thousand feet. Despite the appearance of a potential collision, the controller knows the two aircraft have 2,000-feet of vertical separation."

Ryan shifted his pointer to the raw-data radar-return. "On the other hand, as the two altitude-transponder read-outs converge with this raw-data radar-return, the controller has no clue as to separation in the vertical plane. Her traffic-advisory call to the Boeing 747-800 and the C-130 will be along the lines of 'Traffic converging, six miles, four o-clock, altitude unknown.' The pilots of the Boeing 747 and the C-130 will not know where to look for the converging traffic: High, low, or level."

"What are the minimum aircraft separation requirements?" For aircraft at the same altitude, under radar control, the minimum horizontal separation is three miles. For aircraft at different altitudes, under radar control, the minimum vertical separation is 1000-feet; with odd-thousands (31, 33, 35,000-feet) for eastbound aircraft, and even-thousands (28, 30, 32,000-feet) for westbound aircraft. For those aircraft flying VFR, the rule of thumb has eastbound aircraft at odd altitudes, plus 500 feet (5,500 and 7,500 feet); while westbound aircraft lay claim to even altitudes, plus 500 feet (4,500 and 6,500 feet).

There are exceptions to the three-mile separation rule. Separation requirements are generally increased behind "heavy" aircraft, due to the threat posed by "wake turbulence." Conversely, at a number of busier airports, separation requirements are reduced to allow for more closely-spaced departures and arrivals. London-Heathrow, advertised as the "busiest two-runway airport in the world," is one such airport.

As we made our way between the radar scopes and controllers, I was reminded of my first radar lecture. As with so much of aviation, the science is simple. Think of radar scanning the skies, just as you would think of a flashlight scanning the perimeter of a darkened room, from a position at the center of the same darkened room. When the flash-light's beam of light strikes a mirror, located in a far corner of the darkened room, the light is reflected back to the flashlight.

Likewise, when a radar's beam of energy strikes an aircraft located in the far corner of the sky, the radar's energy is reflected back to the radar; hence, the term "radar-return." Just as our flashlight reflection can tell us in which corner of the room a mirror is located, so too the radar energy reflected off an aircraft can tell a controller in which corner of the sky, or along which line (azimuth) an aircraft is located.

Furthermore, if the radar knows the speed at which the radar energy traveled, and the time interval between radar energy transmission and reflected radar energy reception, the radar can solve for distance. Simple *speed-time-distance* arithmetic (A car traveling at a *speed* of sixty miles per hour, for one hour of *time*, will cover sixty miles of *distance*.) Armed with both pieces of information; the azimuth along which an aircraft is located, and the distance along that line; the radar can pinpoint aircraft location.

On our earlier re-route overhead Syracuse, our weather-radar "painted" the weather off our right wing. The paint was a mix of greens, yellows and reds. The colors reflected the intensity of the precipitation. Light precipitation (rain shower) reflected relatively little radar energy, and was depicted as a green radar-return. Heavy precipitation (intense thunderstorm) reflected far more energy, and was depicted as a red radar-return. Yellow radar-returns depicted the Goldilocks intensity, not too heavy, not too light (heavy rain, standard thunderstorm). As a general rule, we *try* to avoid the yellow, and we make *every effort* to avoid the red.

Ryan's tour wrapped up with the Flow-Control display. With a few keystrokes, the screen came alive with dozens of aircraft read-outs super-imposed upon the outline of North America and the surrounding coastal waters. Each of the read-outs appeared to be pointing toward the New York metropolitan area. "This screen captures every aircraft currently airborne, enroute to Newark, at its approximate location." He continued: "From an air traffic control perspective, every airport's flight-operations and air traffic controller staffing, is designed to safely accommodate a finite number of arrivals per hour, under clear-sky conditions. Exceed that designed arrival rate, or complicate the weather picture, and delays become inevitable. For example, Newark, our departure airport, is generally configured and staffed to accommodate forty aircraft arrivals per hour. Under less-than-standard conditions, that aircraft arrival rate will often be reduced to substantially fewer aircraft arrivals per hour.

"At any time, with a few taps on the keyboard, the FAA Central Flow Control Facility can compare the designed arrival rate with the forecasted/actual arrival rate. This comparison, hand-in-hand with weather observations and forecasts, will dictate the Window Seat Pilot experience: On-time with no delays, or holding patterns, delaying vectors, or ground-stops."

Back to our flight …

One of the more pleasant upsides to the airline life, is the opportunity it presents to meet some interesting people. As noted earlier, I am most often flying with eight others, with whom I have never before flown. Working the mathematics across an average of five flights per week, over the course of thirty airline years, that makes for a good number of opportunities to meet some very interesting people, making for an equal number of very pleasant memories.

Less than an hour into our journey, I already know what I will most recall about Fran: His hands do as much talking as his words, as they are forever in motion, no matter what story he may be telling, and he clearly loves to tell a good story. On the subject of baseball, it is game over. On that subject, he cannot stop the talking or the hand-waving. For very good reason: As noted earlier, after playing Division One baseball as a college student, Fran has coached three high school baseball teams to state championships.

"Traffic-Traffic-Traffic." Our Traffic Collision Avoidance System (TCAS) interrupts the seltzer and the lime, the apple and the raisins. Fran's latest baseball story will have to wait.

Two sets of eyes turn to our Navigation-Displays. We have an "amber" target at our twelve o'clock, six miles out, fourteen hundred feet below, climbing at 1200 feet per minute. I hit all exterior lights. Fran kills all interior lights. We lean forward and scan the night sky, low at our twelve o'clock. We are searching for the red/white beacon on the left wingtip, the green/white beacon on the right wingtip, and the red-rotating beacon on the upper fuselage. We are prepared to disengage the auto-flight systems, for manual evasive action.

Fourteen hundred feet below us, with an identical "Traffic-Traffic-Traffic" warning echoing in their ears, and our "amber" target on their Navigation-Display; unseen hands have likewise hit all exterior lights, and killed all interior lights; while two sets of eyes are likewise scanning the night sky (searching for us), high at their twelve o'clock; with hands poised to disengage auto-flight systems.

Within moments, the amber target on our Navigation-Displays indicates a decreasing rate of climb, morphs from amber to white, and levels off a thousand feet below us at FL 320. On the flight-deck a thousand feet below us, our aircraft has likewise morphed from an amber target to a white target. No threat. Crisis averted. Our TCAS system annunciates "Clear of traffic."

Our altitude-transponder was "talking" to their altitude-transponder, calculating closure rates. In the event the other aircraft had continued its climb through the "Collision Buffer," our display would have morphed from amber to red, and our TCAS would have directed us, via both audio-command and visual-display, to take specific collision-avoidance actions. In this instance, we would likely have been commanded to "Climb, Climb, Climb" at a target rate-of-climb. We would have disengaged the auto-flight systems, advanced the throttles and manually followed those climb commands until hearing the reassuring "Clear of Traffic" call.

In a similar manner, the aircraft converging from below would likely have heard the TCAS command "Monitor Rate of Climb," with specific climb restrictions displayed on their Primary Flight Display (PFD). That flight-crew would have likewise disengaged their auto-flight systems, throttled back and manually followed the TCAS guidance, relaxing at the comforting words "Clear of Traffic."

The amber TCAS alerts are encountered, per pilot, on average, a few times each month. The red TCAS warnings, and their associated avoidance commands, are encountered, per pilot, on average, a few times each year. Compliance with TCAS avoidance commands is mandatory. So long as both aircraft are equipped with altitude-transponders, and so long as both flight-crews properly respond to TCAS alerts, the system generally works well. In those instances in which either aircraft lacks altitude-transponder equipment, as was the case with the raw-data radar-return on Ryan's tour, the avoidance strategy remains "see and avoid."

The TCAS system is a prime example of how enhanced safety equipment can both raise the bar on safety expectations ("safer"), and at the same time erode prior margins of safety ("less safe"), for what might arguably be considered "a wash." For the first twenty-five years of my aviation career, there was no TCAS. Lacking TCAS, pilots relied upon air traffic control traffic-advisories and the "see and avoid" concept. Today, many pilots feel naked without their TCAS. Indeed, many pilots will refuse to fly an aircraft with an inoperative TCAS system. These pilots likely view TCAS as an example of "We are safer with TCAS."

On the flip-side, safety margins once called for two thousand feet of vertical separation. Today's standard calls for one thousand feet of vertical separation. The North Atlantic Tracks, lacking radar coverage, were once spaced sixty-miles apart. Today, they are spaced fifteen miles apart. Vertical separation has been cut in half. Lateral separation is a quarter of previous separation requirements. Some pilots might view the reduced vertical and lateral separation as "We are less safe."

The net result? Operationally, we can pack more aircraft into a given block of airspace. Are we safer due of TCAS? Are we less safe due to reduced separation? A net gain, a net loss, a net wash?

That "safer" or "less safe" question pervades the entire system. As yet another example, most modern aircraft are now equipped with anti-skid protection; hence, the "We are safer" conclusion. On the other hand, those anti-skid systems now allow flight-crews to operate on shorter runways, under more slippery conditions; hence the "Are we less safe?" question.

Reflection

My favorite aviation quote is from Chuck Yeager, the first man to break the speed-of-sound. "I would rather be lucky than good."

On 11 May 1996, at 2:04 PM, ValuJet Flight 592, a DC-9 with 110 souls on board, departed Miami enroute to Atlanta. A mere six minutes after takeoff, at 2:10, the flight-attendant team informed the flight-deck of an on-board fire. After declaring an emergency, the Captain requested, was granted, and executed an immediate one-hundred and eighty degree turn, for an emergency return to Miami. Time was not on her side. Less than three minutes later, the aircraft, with all aboard, was lost in the Everglades. A mere nine minutes from takeoff to perish. A mere three minutes from being informed of an emergency, to impact. The two pilots, simply ran out of time; as a fire within the forward cargo compartment burned through flight control cables, electrical systems and the flight-deck floor, rendering controlled flight impossible. In the midst of a rapidly unfolding disaster, they never stopped flying the airplane.

On 15 January 2009, at 3:25 PM, USAirways Flight 1549, an Airbus A-320 with 155 souls on board, departed New York's LaGuardia Airport for Charlotte, North Carolina. Two minutes after takeoff, the aircraft was struck by a flock of Canadian Geese. As a result of the bird strike, the aircraft lost power on both engines, attaining a maximum altitude of just over 3000-feet. After declaring an emergency, the pilots requested, and were granted, carte blanche. Rapidly running out of altitude and options, the two pilots opted to put the jet into the Hudson River. All aboard survived.

In both instances, the flight crews faced dire scenarios. In both instances, the flight crews reacted in a timely and professional manner, exercising proper judgment and aircraft control. In the case of ValuJet 592, the crew simply ran out of time. In the case of USAirways 1549, the crew was blessed with the Hudson, as they rapidly ran out of altitude and options amid the concrete jungle of the New York / New Jersey metropolitan area.

Both crews were "good." One crew was "lucky." Had those two crews traded scenarios, the one crew might be here today, while the other crew likely would not be here today. The lesson inherent in the two scenarios gives cause for humility. "I would rather be lucky than good."

In life, as in flight: No matter how good you may be, a bit of luck is always welcome; indeed, luck may be the deciding factor.

106

Position: Approaching St. John's, Newfoundland

Oceanic Clearance

We have burned fuel, lightened our load and climbed to Flight Level 350. We will enjoy a bump in fuel efficiency and a boost in the tailwind component.

The Canadian province of Nova Scotia is at our six o'clock, as we approach the western shores of Newfoundland. Our journey has taken us through airspace controlled by New York Center, Boston Center and Moncton Center. With over two dozen radio hand-offs since the Newark "Rotate" call, we are now speaking with Gander Center.

We will shortly go "feet wet" over the North Atlantic. With that in mind, we begin our preparations for the overwater portion of our journey. Unlike the radar-environment which has prevailed during the overland portion of our journey, the upcoming over-water portion will be in a non-radar environment. It is time for the Extended Twin Operations (ETOPS) Checklist.

However, before we get to the checklist, a few comments regarding ETOPS. Our flight over the North Atlantic, requires we remain within 180-minutes of an ETOPS alternate at all times. Our two ETOPS alternates are Goose Bay, Canada and Manchester, England. Between the two ETOPS alternates, we have one critical-point, often referred to as an "equal time point."

Our critical-point will determine to which ETOPS alternate we will divert, in the event we experience one of two specific ETOPS scenarios: Either the dual-emergency of an engine-failure coupled with a loss of cabin pressure, requiring a descent to 10,000-feet; or, the single-emergency of a loss of cabin pressure with two operating engines, and a descent to 10,000-feet. While in ETOPS airspace (more than one-hour from an adequate alternate), if we experience either of those two scenarios prior to the critical-point, we will reverse course, and proceed west, to Goose Bay (behind us). If we experience either of those two scenarios following the critical-point, we will continue east, to Manchester (ahead of us).

An emergency other than the two ETOPS scenarios (a major system failure, a medical emergency, or a cargo fire), may require a divert plan of greater or lesser urgency. It will be our job to keep those additional divert scenarios in mind, as we "cross the pond."

First item on the ETOPS Checklist, we tune our two HF (High Frequency) radios to this evening's designated frequency (5616), and check-in with Gander Oceanic, the first of two controlling authorities for the overwater portion of our journey.

"Good evening, Gander Oceanic, Flight 28 is level at FL350, approaching St John's, SELCAL is Juliet Charlie Bravo Sierra."

Gander Oceanic replies, moments later, with "Flight 28, you are cleared on Track Whiskey, FL350, Mach .80, cross Novep at time 0506 Zulu. At 30-West, contact Shanwick Oceanic on HF frequency 8864. Standby for SELCAL check."

We note our clearance, we provide our read-back, we wish our Gander controller a pleasant evening, and we standby for the SELCAL check.

As was the case with the overland portion of our journey, two-way radio contact with Air Traffic Control is mandatory while in oceanic airspace. Flight-crews have two options: Monitor the HF (High Frequency) radio for the duration of the oceanic crossing (constant static, mind-numbing chatter, endless noise); or, enjoy the sweet sounds of silence, punctuated with an occasional SELCAL (Selective Call) chime. The SELCAL option is the universal preference.

The SELCAL feature allows Gander Oceanic to contact us via an address unique to our aircraft: J-C-B-S (Juliet, Charlie, Bravo, Sierra). To initiate the SELCAL check, Gander Oceanic types J-C-B-S and hits the SEND prompt. Moments later our SELCAL chime sounds, our SELCAL light illuminates and a SELCAL message displays on our forward instrument panel. We reply via voice: "Gander Oceanic, Flight 28, SELCAL checks good."

Why Juliet, Charlie, Bravo, Sierra? When transmitted over a radio, with its lack of clarity, and its frequent static, the human ear may note little difference between A, J and K; or between B, C, D, E, G, P, T, V and Z; or between I and Y; or between M and N. Fifteen of twenty-six letters.

The chance for miscommunication is high. The consequences of miscommunication can be unpleasant. Hence, the phonetic alphabet: Alpha, Bravo, Charlie, Delta, Echo, Foxtrot, Golf, Hotel, India, Juliet, Kilo, Lima, Mike, November, Oscar, Papa, Quebec, Romeo, Sierra, Tango, Uniform, Victor, Whiskey, X-Ray, Yankee and Zulu.

Speaking of Zulu, why Zulu-Time?

The globe-spanning nature of aviation, requires a global standard for time-reference. With aircraft routinely taking off in one time zone, reporting to air traffic control in a second and third time zone, with time-estimates for waypoints in a fourth and fifth time zone, the potential complications are many. What time did we cross this mandatory reporting point? What time will we cross the next mandatory reporting point? What time does the curfew start? (Yes, airports, to include London-Heathrow, have noise-abatement curfews).

For example, our Gander Oceanic clearance required us to cross Novep at the time of 0506. Would that be 0506 Newark time, 0506 London-Heathrow time, or 0506 local/Gander time? We, and all others, require a standard time-reference. That standard time reference is Zulu-Time. Zulu-Time is Zero-Time. Zero-Time is the local time at zero-degrees longitude. Zero degrees longitude passes through the town of Greenwich, England. Hence, Greenwich Mean Time or GMT. The global standard time is the local time in Greenwich, England.

Why do we utilize HF (High Frequency) radios? The VHF (Very High Frequency) radio we have been using, since our Newark push-back, has limited range, and is therefore unsuited for overwater operations. By contrast, the HF radio utilizes the reflective properties of the Ionosphere, an outer layer of our atmosphere, roughly thirty-five miles above the surface. HF transmissions bounce off the Ionosphere, extending well beyond the horizon. This "over the horizon" capability allows HF signal reception virtually around the world. Aircraft can routinely communicate with New York while airborne between Los Angeles and Tokyo, and with Honolulu while airborne between London and New York.

We have nailed the overwater communication requirement with our SELCAL-check. On the navigation side of the ledger, we run through three quick steps. First, we confirm agreement between our wet-compass heading of 082-degrees and our three independent Inertial Navigation Systems (Left, Right and Center are all reading 084-degrees). The allowable tolerance is five degrees. We are within limits.

Second, we tune the St John's (Newfoundland) ground-based navigation aid (CYYT, frequency 113.50). We note our azimuth and distance (095-degrees and 63 miles) from that navigation aid. We compare this raw data with our Flight Management Computer (FMC) azimuth and distance (093-

degrees and 65 miles). The allowable tolerance is four nautical miles and six degrees. We are within limits. Third, we confirm active GPS updates to our FMC. All systems are in agreement. Our communication and navigation checks are complete.

Next up, our altimetry. We confirm our three independent altimeter readings (Captain, First Officer, Standby) are in agreement, well within the plus/minus 200-foot limitation.

As we cross the pond, we will (1) be in voice contact with air traffic control via an Ionosphere bounce, on HF radio and SELCAL; (2) our navigation systems will keep us on the assigned track; (3) our altimeters will keep us on the assigned altitude; and (4) adherence to our airspeed requirement will ensure in-trail separation along the track. We will do so without the assistance of ground-based radar, an air traffic controller, or a ground-based navigation aid.

While we received our oceanic clearance via HF radio, a number of flight crews will employ the satellite-based CPDLC (Controller Pilot Data Link Communication) for clearance request and issuance. Like ourselves, they will request a particular NAT Track, mach number and altitude. They will do so via keypad rather than voice. Like ourselves, they will include an ETA for their oceanic entry-point.

Gander Oceanic will reply, via CPDLC, with their oceanic clearance details (NAT Track, mach number, altitude, entry-point time). After reviewing their clearance, flight-crews will exercise the digital version of the radio read-back, by replying with the CPDLC "Accept" prompt, confirming they have received and understood their oceanic clearance. To put a bow on the package, Gander Oceanic will close the loop with a final "Clearance Accepted" message.

The datalink option in the request, issuance and acceptance of oceanic clearances, has a companion in the "flight-following" realm. While the overwater portion of our flight takes us well beyond the range of ground-based radar, we are never beyond the range of space-based satellites. An increasing number of aircraft are equipped with satellite-compatible transponders, feeding real-time data to a constellation of satellites. Their satellite-compatible transponders provide latitude, longitude, altitude, heading and speed data; enabling oceanic controllers to construct a picture very similar to the picture utilized by the radar controllers of the New York, Boston and Moncton air traffic control centers.

This technology, ADS-B (Automatic Dependent Surveillance-Broadcast), is on a trajectory to one day replace radar as the primary surveillance method for controlling aircraft, both overland and overwater. It is one component of a rapidly evolving "Air Traffic Management" industry, in which technology is advancing at a blistering pace, rendering obsolete the lessons this aviator learned as recently as five years ago, much less forty years ago. It promises to ease the safety concerns of congested airspace (allowing more aircraft into departure and arrival corridors), bolster fuel efficiency (allowing more direct routing), minimize carbon footprint (less fuel burn over a more direct route), ease ground and airborne delays (aircraft separation, more efficient routing), and enhance weather-turbulence avoidance (more flex built into the system, enabling inflight weather deviations).

Regarding the blistering pace of technological advance, in the minds of many, aviation is increasingly a matter of information management, perhaps more so than flying; which begs the question: As we load up on systems and automation, have we lost touch with "flying the airplane?" What will the pilot of the future do when the systems and the automation fail? Will he/she still know how to fly an airplane? It is a challenge confronting flight-training departments and regulatory authorities around the world.

A recent International Civil Aeronautical Organization (ICAO) study examined seventy-seven "flight-path related" accidents and more than three hundred "flight-path related" incidents. "Automation dependency" was a factor in 36-percent of those accidents and incidents. The rate between 1990 and 2009 was 22-percent. The rate between 2010 and 2021 was 49-percent, more than doubling in rate. Not an optimal trend-line.

For the moment, in the midst of the technological revolution, I am grateful to have both Fran and Erica along with me this evening. They are both of a generation (not yet gray or wrinkled) which is fully up-to-speed with the digital tsunami engulfing aviation.

Reflection

Pilots are taught, from Day One, to be ahead of the aircraft, to anticipate, to plan, and to prepare for the what-if scenarios.

Pilots are required to have Destination Alternates if unable to land at the planned destination; along with Enroute Alternates in the event of an engine-failure, a loss of pressurization, or any number of other critical failures.

Pilots are required to carry "Reserve" fuel, in the event of any unknowns. Pilots are required to carry "Alternate" fuel, in the event a diversion becomes necessary.

Pilots, almost universally, prefer the pad of a longer runway for both departures and arrivals: More acceleration distance for the take-off, more deceleration distance for the landing or for the aborted, rejected takeoff.

Pilots, almost universally, prefer the dual pads of more airspeed and more altitude: Altitude keeps us clear of terrain. Airspeed, as noted earlier, is life. High-and-fast offers options that are unavailable when low-and-slow.

Pilots, almost universally, prefer more fuel: More fuel allows for more time, more time allows for more options, more options allow for more life opportunities.

In life, as in flight: Anticipate. Be ahead of the aircraft. Have a pad. Have a back-up plan.

North Atlantic Track Entry

The Automation Tour

The North Atlantic Track System (NATS), to include our NAT Track Whiskey, changes every twelve hours, reflecting the prevailing flow of traffic: Westbound tracks early in the day, eastbound tracks later in the day. The NAT Tracks are constructed to optimize ever-shifting, high-altitude winds; with an eye toward maximum tailwinds for eastbound flights, and minimal headwinds for westbound flights.

Thirty years ago, there were four Tracks. This evening, there are eight Tracks. Thirty years ago, they were vertically separated by two thousand feet. This evening, they are vertically separated by one thousand feet. Taken together (twice the number of Tracks, twice the number of altitudes available on those Tracks), the changes highlight the significant increase in traffic over the North Atlantic.

Back to our flight: First up, we comply with the Strategic Lateral Offset Program (SLOP). With a few key strokes, we program our Flight Management Computer (FMC) for an offset, two-miles to the right of our assigned oceanic track Whiskey.

Why offset, and parallel our track, by two miles? In an ironic twist, with the widespread use of GPS navigation, aircraft now run the risk of being "too accurate" and potentially "too close" to one another.

Lacking a radar controller with the "big picture" display; with the earlier-discussed, satellite-based ADS-B program still in its infancy; and with vertical separation along the North Atlantic

Tracks now halved to one thousand feet; the most common inflight error (altitude deviation) now constitutes a notable threat. With that in mind, the random SLOP offset (one or two miles to the right of course) is designed to mitigate the "too accurate" and potentially "too close" dilemma. More to the point: It is now a mandatory offset.

We have randomly selected two miles. If we, or any other aircraft, commit an altitude deviation, the lateral SLOP offset will help to minimize the likelihood of any unpleasant consequences. Yes, "safer" now requires that we deliberately go off-course!

Having set our SLOP offset, we expand our Navigation Display range, and note three aircraft ahead of us, and two aircraft behind us, offset to the right of Track Whiskey, by one or two miles. We are not alone.

We tune our left VHF (Very High Frequency) radio to the optional Airliner-Common frequency of 123.45, and our right VHF radio to the mandatory Emergency-Guard frequency of 121.50. Airliner-Common is often animated and crowded, as it is utilized by flight-crews to trade turbulence reports, wind read-outs and sports scores (Air Force football beating Navy and Army). Emergency-Guard is generally silent, must be monitored by all flight-crews, at all times, and is utilized for May-Day calls, air-defense-intercept procedures and any number of emergency matters.

Much of aviation is about pacing. We have completed the required procedures. It is time to recline the seat just a bit, and absorb the here and now. We start with our engine instruments. Our "EPR" (Engine Pressure Ratio) gauges read 1.59 for the left engine and 1.58 for the right engine. Fuel flows are even, at 4100 pounds per hour, per engine. Oil pressure, temperature and quantity look good. The engines look good. We shift attention to our flight instruments.

The Navigation-Display provides a bird's-eye view of our path. We are inbound to our next waypoint (Fifty degrees west longitude), with a two-mile offset to the right, holding a four-degree wind correction to the right. The TCAS (Traffic Collision Avoidance System) displays a handful of aircraft, ahead and in-trail, above and below. Gander and St. John's, two possible alternate airports, are displayed at our six and seven o'clock positions.

The Primary Flight Display (PFD) is the home for the all-important "hub" instrument, the artificial-horizon (blue sky above, brown earth below, white horizon, fluorescent airplane super-imposed). We are wings-level, with a pitch of roughly 3-degrees nose up. The PFD displays a speed of Mach 80, a Ground-Speed of 571 knots, a True Airspeed of 480 knots, an Indicated Airspeed of 290 knots and a wind vector of ninety-one knots out of the southwest. Our weather radar shows clear skies ahead, with a one-degree nose-down tilt.

The "Flight Mode Annunciator" (FMA), located just above the PFD, indicates the flight modes currently in play: SPD, V-NAV, L-NAV, CMD.

The first FMA annunciation, refers to our auto-throttle system. There are three possible auto-throttle modes: SPD, EPR, or blank. At the moment, while displaying SPD, the auto-throttle system is controlling thrust to hold a selected speed (Mach .80). While on our takeoff roll, the FMA displayed EPR, as the auto-throttle system controlled thrust to meet a selected takeoff thrust setting (1.62 Engine Pressure Ratio). On our arrival into London's Heathrow, roughly ten minutes prior to touchdown, I will disconnect the auto-throttle system, the annunciator will go blank (indicating no active auto-throttle mode), and I will hand-fly the jet.

The second FMA annunciation, refers to our vertical mode. There are five possible vertical modes: V-NAV, V-S, FL-CH, G-S, or blank.

Our current V-NAV (Vertical Navigation) display indicates our auto-flight system is slaved to the Flight Management Computer (FMC), currently calling for level flight at Flight Level 350. As we approach London-Heathrow, we will construct a vertical path within the FMC, from cruise altitude to touch-down, to include all altitude and airspeed restrictions. While in V-NAV, our auto-flight systems will ensure we meet each of those altitude and airspeed restrictions. *In VNAV, the FMC program prevails.*

In the V-S (Vertical Speed) mode, our auto-flight systems will maintain a selected vertical speed. On climbs and descents of a few thousand feet, pilots may opt to select a shallow vertical speed of 500 feet per minute, in an effort to provide our Window Seat Pilots with a nice, smooth, barely perceptible, climb/descent experience. On the flip-side, in an effort to avoid areas of weather, pilots may opt to select a maximum rate of climb or descent, to climb above, or pass below, the weather. Earlier this evening, as we broke through the cloud layer on departure, we de-selected V-NAV (climbing at 6000 feet per minute), and selected V-S (climbing at 100 feet per minute) to allow for a few moments of cloud-surfing. *In V/S, the selected vertical speed prevails.*

In the FL-CH (Flight Level Change) mode, our auto-flight systems select a pitch angle and a thrust setting to maintain a selected airspeed while in the climb or descent. Depending upon the geometry, the auto-flight systems may command a steep angle or a shallow angle, with a commensurate thrust setting. *In FL-CH, the selected airspeed prevails.*

In the G-S (Glide-Slope) mode, our auto-flight systems will track the three-degree glide-slope associated with an Instrument Landing System (ILS). More on the ILS as we approach London-

Heathrow. *In G-S, the three-degree glide-slope prevails.* In the "blank" mode, there is no vertical guidance.

The third FMA annunciation, depicts our lateral mode. There are five possible lateral modes: L-NAV, HDG-SEL, HDG-HLD, LOC or blank.

Similar to the V-NAV (Vertical Navigation) mode, the L-NAV (Lateral Navigation) mode slaves our auto-flight systems to the lateral path we have programmed into the Flight Management Computer (FMC), and as displayed on the FMC Legs-Page, taking us from one waypoint to the next, in sequence. *In L-NAV, the FMC program prevails.*

The HDG-SEL (Heading Select) mode, and its close cousin the HDG-HLD (Heading Hold) mode, direct the aircraft to fly the "selected" heading, or to "hold" the present heading. *In either mode, heading prevails.*

The LOC (Localizer) mode directs the auto-flight systems to track the course centerline associated with an Instrument Landing System (ILS). More on the ILS as we approach London-Heathrow. *In LOC, the localizer signal prevails.* In the "blank" mode, there is no lateral guidance.

The final FMA annunciation, refers to our auto-pilot mode. There are three possible auto-pilot modes: CMD, F-D and blank. Our current CMD (Command) mode confirms our auto-pilot is flying the jet: Climb, descend, turn, or hold steady.

The F-D (Flight-Director) mode indicates two things. First, the auto-pilot is no longer flying the jet. However, flight-guidance commands (climb, descend, turn right, turn left) are being sent to the vertical and lateral steering-bars overlaying the artificial horizon. In this mode, a pilot simply follows the steering bars: Up, down, left, right.

In the "blank" mode, the auto-pilot is no longer flying the jet, and flight-guidance commands are not being sent to the steering bars (which disappear). In this mode, the pilot is "cycling without the training wheels."

In the days prior to auto-flight systems, auto-pilots, auto-throttles and steering-bars; a pilot generally knew what the aircraft was doing, for he or she (and nothing else) was in command. There was little room for doubt. He or she was making it happen.

With the advent of auto-flight systems, auto-pilots, auto-throttles and steering-bars, there is often uncertainty: Where are we going? Why is it doing that? As an example, in our earlier-discussed Cali incident, in the moments prior to impact, the cockpit voice recorder captured the two pilots asking: "Where are we? Where are we headed? Where are we? What happened here? I do not know."

In such instances, the remedy is simple: Kick off the automation, and hand-fly the jet. That simple remedy poses a challenge: What if the pilot has not hand-flown a jet in quite some time?

Reflection

Unlike many other professions, when things begin to fall apart, the clock never stops ticking, the engines continue to burn our finite amount of fuel (limiting our options), we continue to cover the ground at ten miles a minute, and we (often) continue to descend toward unforgiving terrain.

There is no side-bar at the bench, there is no time-out to confer with a mentor. There is no "do over" or "recess" or "take five" or "sleep on it" or "try again tomorrow." There is only here. There is only now.

There is a premium placed on sound judgment, timely decision-making, and crisp execution; while operating under pressure. Right here. Right now.

In the aviation business, an error in judgment, decision-making, or execution, often does not offer an opportunity for post-event reflection or regret, over a glass of wine, or a cup of tea.

It can be a very pleasant business, until it is not. Aviators are paid for those "until it is not" moments of judgment, decision-making and execution: Right here. Right now.

Feet Wet

A pproaching our first oceanic reporting point, we refer, once again, to our ETOPS Checklist. With each successive reporting point, we will run the same drill.

We construct a "Howgozit" (how goes it) post-position point, at 0521-Zulu, ten minutes beyond the 0511-Zulu estimate for our upcoming waypoint. We place the Howgozit point on our Navigation-Displays. We confirm L-NAV and V-NAV are engaged. Our altimeters are within limits. The upcoming segment's magnetic course (093 degrees), magnetic heading (094 degrees), time (44 minutes), and distance (412 nautical miles) are in agreement (FMC Legs-Page and flight plan).

As a personal technique (not a requirement), I note our pitch angle (approximately three degrees nose-up) and our engine power setting (approximately 1.59 EPR). If we were to lose power to our flight instruments, or if our automation were to fail, we will know that a three-degree nose-up pitch angle, and a 1.59 power setting, will ensure stable/level flight.

As an added technique (again, not a requirement), I note our ground-speed (571 knots) and our winds (235 degrees at 95 knots). If we were to suffer a complete failure of our navigation systems, all of which are entirely dependent upon electrical power, we could utilize the recorded ground-speed and wind data, along with our "wet compass," to reach safe shores, much as the seafarers did, crossing these same waters, centuries ago.

Lastly, as we pass overhead our reporting point, we tune our HF, and we make the required position report.

"Good evening, Gander Oceanic, Flight 28, checks 48-North and 50-West, at 0511-Zulu, FL350, Mach .80, estimating 52-North and 40-West at 0555-Zulu, next is 51-North and 30-West, fuel 40.9."

With each North Atlantic crossing, to keep the mind sharp, and to keep the reactions well-scripted, we take a few moments to review the procedures for an emergency divert. This first over-water reporting point provides a convenient prompt for doing so.

Should an emergency diversion be required, Fran will hit all our exterior lights and broadcast a "Mayday" call on both the Emergency-Guard frequency of 121.50 and the Airliner-Common frequency of 123.45. He will state the nature of our emergency, our position, our altitude, and our intentions. By doing so, he will alert all aircraft in our vicinity to be "heads-up" for our ETOPS divert. His call will likewise clear the radio frequencies of idle chatter, allowing for uninterrupted emergency communications.

If we have lost pressurization, we will both execute the "Immediate Action Item" reviewed hours earlier, on the chair-fly drive to work.

"Oxygen, On, One Hundred Percent. Crew Communications, Establish."

We will don our quick-don oxygen masks and select 100-percent oxygen ("Oxygen On, One Hundred Percent") and we will "Establish Crew Communications" (not an easy task in the event of a rapid decompression, with the roaring wind, the bitter cold, amid papers and objects flying about the flight deck). Once we are both safely on oxygen (the time of useful consciousness at our current altitude is 15 seconds), I will fly the jet, and Fran will run the emergency checklist.

Utilizing the "Heading Select" function, I will enter a thirty-degree bank turn to the right, establishing a five-mile parallel offset from Track Whiskey. The five-mile offset will place us three miles beyond any aircraft flying a two-mile SLOP offset, helping to ensure traffic separation while we descend. While in the turn, I will monitor my Navigation-Display for TCAS readouts of nearby aircraft.

Once established on the five-mile offset, and with Fran's confirmation, I will set ten thousand feet (a safe, oxygen-rich altitude) in our Altitude Select Window, select idle thrust, command a maximum rate of descent, select maximum permissible airspeed and deploy full speed-brakes (thereby killing Lift and accelerating our descent). While doing so, I will continue to monitor my Navigation-Display for TCAS readouts, to avoid any aircraft that may be below us.

Descending through the floor of the NAT Tracks, at FL290, and while continuing the descent to 10,000-feet, I will pivot to the FMC Alternate-Page and select a route taking us direct to the closest ETOPS alternate (currently, Goose Bay, Labrador, at our seven o'clock). After *verifying* Goose Bay at the top of the FMC Legs-Page, and a dashed white line to Goose Bay displayed on the Navigation-Display, after *verbalizing* the modification and after asking Fran to *verify* the same; I will Execute the divert command, *monitor* a morph from a dashed-white line to a solid-magenta line, and engage the L-NAV function. *Verbalize, verify, monitor.*

Once level at 10,000 feet, Fran and I will remove our oxygen masks, and cover the bases. Together, we will complete the Depressurization checklist. We will hold a conference call with Cherie and her Flight Attendant team, inform and reassure our passengers with a public address announcement, and place a sat-comm call to our dispatcher: Inside, outside, backside.

If we have lost an engine, I will maintain aircraft control while Fran runs the Engine Failure checklist. To compensate for our asymmetric thrust (one engine at cruise-thrust setting, one engine at zero-thrust), I will add rudder. Once again, operating in the "Heading Select" function, I will begin a right turn for our five-mile offset, utilizing fifteen-degrees of bank. I will disconnect the auto-throttle system, and select maximum continuous thrust on the operating engine.

I will turn to the FMC Engine-Out page, and note our engine-out altitude of FL250 and our engine-out speed of 242 knots. With Fran's confirmation, I will set, *verbalize,* and *verify* FL250 in our Altitude Select Window and execute the FMC engine-out function. I will *monitor* as the auto-flight systems command a V-NAV descent to FL250 at our engine-out speed of 242 knots.

As was the case with the loss of pressurization scenario, once below the floor of the NAT Tracks, at FL290, I will select the FMC Alternate-Page and, with Fran's concurrence, I will execute a route taking us direct to the closest ETOPS alternate. Having executed the divert command, I will engage our L-NAV function. Following our level-off at our engine-out altitude of FL250, working with Fran, we will then cover the bases.

Throughout either scenario, while Fran's primary focus is the applicable emergency procedure, and while my primary focus is "flying the jet," we will both monitor the other's performance. He will monitor my aircraft control. I will monitor his checklist execution. Regarding his checklist execution, under *no* circumstances will either of us shut-down *any* engine without the other pilot's confirmation that we are shutting down the correct engine. Likewise, throughout either scenario, we will request inputs from our flight attendants. Of particular note, in a loss of pressurization scenario, we will seek a structural integrity report (have we lost a door, a window, or any portion of the cabin surface). In an engine-failure scenario, given that our engines are not in our field of vision, we will seek an "eyes on target" report of engine condition (flames, visible damage, evidence of oil or hydraulic leaks).

Their "eyes on target" vantage point can often offer critical, life-saving information. In one instance, when a flight-crew erroneously shut-down an operating *right engine*, and while that flight-crew announced the *right engine* shut-down on the public address system, *the passengers and flight-attendants were aware of flames on the malfunctioning left engine.*

Yet, that critical information was never solicited by the flight-crew, and never relayed by the flight-attendant crew. By the time the flight-crew recognized their error (they had shut down the *operating* right engine, rather than the *failing* left engine, leaving them with *no* operating engines), they had run out of time and altitude. With tragic consequence.

Recall our crew-brief: "While security concerns mandate the door will remain locked throughout the flight, it need not be a barrier to communication. If you see, hear, or sense something, please give us a call." Communication: There is no substitute.

Lastly, in any inflight emergency, we will ask Erica, and any other qualified pilots, to join us on the flight-deck to assist with the emergency.

Regarding inflight emergencies, the generation of now-retired pilots, with whom I once had the great pleasure of flying, would insist, with good reason, on an initial, critical step: Light a cigarette. Take no action until you have lit a cigarette, and until you have enjoyed a few relaxing puffs. Their advice was on target. Today, flight students are taught to hack the stopwatch, take a deep breath and relax, before taking any corrective actions.

In the midst of a sudden emergency, in the grip of the "startle effect," hasty action can make for deadly action. The industry literature has a number of instances in which flight-crews, while in the midst of a panicked rush, have inadvertently, incorrectly, and tragically, shut-down the sole operating engine: Leaving all aboard with no operating engines.

In addition to the "wrong engine" scenario outlined moments ago, on 4 February 2015, an ATR-72 departed Taiwan's Taipei airport. As the flight passed through 1200-feet on their departure, their right engine lost thrust. In response, the Captain stated "I will pull back on the number one [left] engine." Despite the First Officer's objections, the Captain shut down the sole operating [left] engine. A tragic outcome ensued. The final accident report stated: "If the flight-crew had done nothing more than confirm the loss of thrust on the right engine and returned to land using the remaining engine, the accident and loss of life would not have occurred."

From a similar accident report: "*The speed with which the pilots acted was contrary* to both their training and the instructions of the Operations Manual. *If they had taken more time* to study the engine instruments it should have been apparent..."

Light a figurative cigarette. Take a deep breath. Pop a stick of gum. Punch the clock. Save time (and lives) by taking your time. Harkening back to the pre-departure brief: We will not rush for anyone, at any time, for any reason.

As we wrap up our review of an emergency divert, we are approaching our Howgozit point, ten minutes down-range from our most recent position report at Fifty-West. We re-confirm L-NAV and V-NAV are engaged. We re-confirm we are on course. All is well.

Why conduct a ten-minute, post-position Howgozit check? Why re-confirm L-NAV and VNAV engagement? Why re-confirm on course?

On 1 September 1983, a Boeing 747, with 259 souls on board, departed Anchorage, Alaska, enroute to Seoul, South Korea. Shortly after takeoff, air traffic control directed the crew to fly on a heading of 220-degrees until intercepting a course inbound to a ground-based navigation aid. The crew properly selected "Heading Select" for their lateral guidance. While on the assigned heading of 220-degrees, the crew did indeed intercept the inbound course to the navigation aid. However, having intercepted the inbound course, the crew never de-selected the "Heading Select" mode. Hours later, while still in "Heading Select" mode, over 500 nautical miles north of course, the aircraft passed through then-Soviet-controlled, restricted airspace, and was shot down, leading to the loss of the aircraft and all 259 on-board.

Shortly thereafter, then-President Ronald Reagan declassified the (previously classified) GPS (Global Positioning Satellite) systems, making GPS navigation available to all. Reagan did his part. We will do our part. We will conduct our Howgozit check with each waypoint passage.

On a recent North Atlantic crossing, the ten-minute, post-position Howgozit check caught me, and my First Officer, inexplicably in the "Heading Select" mode, with our Navigation-Display showing us four miles off course. Following a quick correction to course, and a re-selection of the L-NAV mode, we racked our brains with the question: "How did that happen?". We had verbalized. We had verified. Clearly, we had failed to monitor.

That episode, along with a handful of others over the course of a forty-year career, highlights the intrinsic nature of the human factor and the ubiquity of human error. Armed with a strong predisposition to "do the right thing," fully committed to checklist-discipline, a faithful adherent to the *"verbalize, verify, monitor"* mantra, we had nonetheless found ourselves four miles off-course.

Upon arrival at our destination, my First Officer and I both submitted a Flight Safety Action Program (FSAP) report. The FSAP program is an industry-wide initiative encouraging the voluntary submission of flight-safety threats, errors and incidents. Each report is reviewed by a team of relevant stakeholders (The FAA, the airline, and a pilot flight-safety representative). The details of each report add to an ever-growing body of data identifying threats, recommending pre-emptive actions, and facilitating data-sharing within the industry. With the exception of willful disregard of procedures or regulations, the submission of an FSAP report, protects pilots from any subsequent FAA "certificate action." The program is credited for significant improvements in industry safety.

We resume our "tour" of the flight-deck, turning our attention to the overhead panel. First up, I flip through our three independent and redundant Inertial Navigation Systems. The "Present Position" function is in full agreement across the three systems.

Next up, hydraulics. We have three independent hydraulic systems. Together, the three systems power our flight controls (ailerons and rudders for "left or right" and elevators for "up or down"), our "high lift devices" (trailing-edge flaps and leading-edge slats), our landing gear extension and retraction, our nose-wheel steering and brakes, and a hydraulically-driven electrical generator. Each of those functions is powered by at least two of the three hydraulic systems, thereby ensuring double- or triple-redundancy in the event any one, or two, hydraulic systems were to fail. While not ideal, we could suffer the loss of a single hydraulic system, with minor consequence. Likewise, we could suffer the loss of two hydraulic systems, with minor consequence. Our simulator check-rides, every nine months, frequently include either, or both, scenarios.

While there is no emergency checklist for the hypothetical loss of all three hydraulic systems, one crew has successfully handled such a nightmare scenario. On 19 July 1989, a McDonnell Douglas DC-10 enroute from Denver to Chicago, suffered a catastrophic, uncontained engine failure in the tail-mounted engine (one of three engines), due to an undiagnosed stress fracture in an engine fan blade. The debris from the uncontained failure, penetrated hydraulic lines within the aircraft's tail, leading to a virtually impossible total loss of all three hydraulic systems, a scenario for which there was no emergency procedure. In short: The flight crew had zero control over any flight control; left or right, up or down. The aircraft was little more than a gliding, winged-rock with two operating engines.

Employing textbook crew resource management skills, and through the use of differential power on the two operating, wing-mounted engines, the flight crew managed to guide "the rock" to a Sioux City runway. One hundred and eighty-four of the two hundred and ninety-six aboard the flight survived. Amid an unimaginable scenario, for which there was no procedure, the flight-crew never stopped flying the airplane.

We have discussed redundancy *across* our three hydraulic systems. Safety is further enhanced by redundancy *within* each of the three systems. Our left hydraulic system is powered by an engine-driven pump, as well as an independent electric hydraulic pump. The right hydraulic system is similarly powered by an engine-driven pump, and an independent electric hydraulic pump. Our center hydraulic system is powered by two independent electric pumps, along with a "ram air turbine" (RAT). The RAT consists of a spinning propellor-like assembly. Airflow over the RAT will generate sufficient hydraulic pressure to power the primary flight controls (our ailerons and rudders for left/right, and our elevators for up/down).

In summary, our hydraulics include three independent systems and seven independent pressure sources. System pressures, from left to right, currently read 3110, 3030, and 3030 psi. All hydraulic quantities are "in the green." All is well with the hydraulics.

Regarding the Sioux City incident, as is the case following any serious safety incident, corrective action was taken. Hydraulic systems are now engineered to retain sufficient "stand-by" hydraulic fluid, in the event a breach occurs within a hydraulic system, thereby ensuring operation of critical aircraft systems, to include the flight controls that were absent in Sioux City.

Redundancy is likewise engineered into our electrical system. Each of our two engines drives an independent generator. Each generator is capable of carrying a full electric load. The loss of a single generator would be of minor consequence, as the remaining generator would "pick up the load" for the failed generator. In the event we were to lose both engine-driven generators, our auxiliary power unit (APU) generator would likewise pick up the load and provide sufficient electric power for all major systems.

In the very unlikely scenario in which we were to lose both engine-driven generators and the APU generator, a "hydraulic motor generator" (HMG) powered by the left hydraulic system (a hydraulic motor powering an electric generator) would supply electric power to all key/critical systems.

In the "over-the-top" unlikely event that we would we lose both engine-driven generators, *and* the APU generator, *and* the HMG, our battery-powered, stand-by electric system would provide essential power for between thirty and ninety minutes.

If we were to lose both engine-driven generators, *and* the APU generator, *and* the HMG, *and* our battery-powered stand-by system, our engines would continue to hum, our stand-by (raw data) instruments would continue to provide good information, and our FAA-required flashlights would prove their value.

As unlikely as it might seem, the above-described "total electrical loss" *has* happened. Having been dispatched with an inoperative APU (auxiliary power unit), on a night flight between Anchorage and Seattle, an aircraft (identical to our aircraft this evening) lost both generators. Complicating the scenario, the HMG (Hydraulic Motor Generator) failed to come on line. Down to a mere thirty minutes of battery-supplied stand-by power, the flight-crew successfully pointed the aircraft in the direction of an emergency divert airfield. Shortly thereafter, while established on the divert heading, the aircraft lost stand-by power. Nonetheless, the flight-crew completed the approach, and the landing, with no/zero electrics. It has been my good fortune to share a flight-deck with the Captain of that flight. His signature? Humility.

The redundancy list continues. Two independent pressurization systems, with a manual back-up. Six electric fuel pumps, arrayed across three fuel tanks, each pump powered by an independent electric power source, each pump capable of supplying both engines, with a gravity-feed backup in the unlikely event all six pumps fail. Three braking systems (Normal, Alternate, Reserve), further backed-up with "Stand-By" accumulator-braking.

Two independent fire/overheat detection loops encircling our engines. Two independent smoke detector units in our cargo compartments. Two independent fire extinguishing bottles per engine. Two independent fire extinguishing bottles per cargo compartment. Along with the earlier-discussed two HF radios, we have two VHF radios, two VOR navigation receivers, two ILS (Instrument Landing System) receivers, two Global Positioning (GPS) systems and three Inertial Navigation System (INS) systems. Not to be forgotten, we have two engines: The aircraft can fly just fine on one engine. Indeed, single-engine flight is a central feature of our every-nine-month simulator check-rides.

While not a recommended technique, the aircraft can fly just fine without any engines. On 23 July 1983, due to a fuel calculation error (ubiquity of human error), a Boeing 767 lost both engines, due to fuel starvation, at forty-one thousand feet (roughly eight miles above the surface). Despite the two-engine flame-out, the two pilots managed to "glide" the aircraft to a safe landing, while utilizing the RAT (ram air turbine) to power their flight controls.

Roughly eighteen years later, an Airbus 330 experienced a fuel leak over the North Atlantic. That fuel leak led to the eventual loss of both engines, due to fuel starvation, at thirty-five thousand feet (roughly seven miles above the frigid North Atlantic), while sixty-five miles from Lajes airfield in the Portuguese Azores Islands. Once again, the two pilots managed to "glide" their aircraft to a safe landing while utilizing the RAT to power their flight controls.

No loss of life. System redundancy. Two stories to last a lifetime.

Reflection

While "I would rather be lucky than good" ranks as a most instructive aviation quote; Tenerife, Canary Islands, ranks as a most instructive aviation episode.

On 27 March 1977, two Boeing 747 aircraft (One Pan Am and one KLM) collided on Tenerife's active runway, while in the midst of heavy fog. Five hundred and eighty-three lives were lost, making the incident the single deadliest accident in aviation history. While several factors were at play; to include heavy ground fog, non-standard taxiway and runway marking, non-standard radio terminology, and radio call interference; one factor stands out as most instructive.

Just prior to the start of their takeoff roll, and again, in the first moments of their takeoff roll; the KLM First Officer, and the KLM Second Officer, both verbally questioned whether or not they had been cleared for take-off, and whether or not the Pan Am 747 was still on their takeoff runway. In both instances, the Captain, occupying the prestigious position as KLM's Chief of Pilot Training, confidently assured the two more junior pilots that all was well.

All was not well. The KLM, on its takeoff roll, for which the First Officer (correctly) feared they had not received clearance; collided with the taxiing Pan Am, which was, as the Second Officer (correctly) feared, still on the runway.

The instructive element of the episode? Listen to your crew. Age, education, experience, position, qualifications, seniority, or title, should never be equated with "I am right" and "You are wrong."

In life, as in flight: Check the ego. Leave it in the parking lot.

Front Seat, Over The North Atlantic

Gustave And The Chip Log

The clouds, sentinels of our route, pass silently beneath our wings, at a speed of over 900 feet per second. We make our passage, guests of the moment, respectful passersby. We race with the winds, we mingle with the clouds, we dance with the stars. Silent, graceful, touched.

I never tire of it. Time and again, I long, I ache, I yearn. Please let me disconnect the auto-flight systems. Please let me play, as I once did, back in the day. Please let me once again enjoy the moments when I must crane my neck, to look back over my shoulder, to find the horizon appearing from below, at my six o'clock.

The Aileron Roll. The Barrel Roll. The Clover Leaf. The Immelmann. The Loop. The Split S. And my all-time favorite: The Cuban Eight. Or, let me simply throttle up, pull back, point the nose to the heavens, and climb until I run out of "smash." Then, let me roll inverted, let me pull the nose down, through the horizon, let me once again feel the g's. Having done it all, let me do it all over again.

Let me twist and turn, let me dance and flirt with the towering columns of cloud; tease the edges of this one, twist and punch through the billows of the next; unbounded vision one moment, cloud-blind the next moment; to possess in both moments, a timeless and unmatched sense of freedom; to witness, in seeming isolation, the silent power and beauty of nature.

I would crawl on my hands and knees, over crushed glass, for one more aerobatic flight among the puffy whites of my playground of yesteryear. I have been blessed.

Back to reality. Fran and I are enjoying the silence. Alone with our respective thoughts. His hands are no longer flying about the flight-deck. For the moment, my face, arms and my torso are safe.

The flight-deck has taken on a serenity. The lights have been dimmed. The conversation has ebbed. We are alone with the sounds of flight: The soothing symphony of the rushing airflow, the hum of the computers, the whir of instrument cooling fans, the distant and steady thunder of the engines. An occasional radio call punctuates the peace, leaving in its wake an even deeper peace. We slice silently, cleanly, smoothly, through the night sky.

While the Window Seat Passenger has a bit of a view through the cabin windows, nothing beats the view from the front seat: The hedge-rows and stone-walled fields of Europe's rural farmlands and the terraced rice paddies of Asia's hillsides; the snow-capped peaks of the Andes, the Himalayas, the Rocky Mountains and the Swiss Alps; the glaciers of Greenland and the vast expanse of the Arctic Ice Cap; the countless ice-bergs of the northern seas; the "no-two-alike" cloud formations, the setting or rising of the sun, or this evening's rising moon.

Our horizon consists of a roughly horizontal cloud bank, with a bit of a 20-degree tilt, extending from the upper left, leaning slightly downward to the lower right. At our one o-clock position, the leading edge of a rising full moon makes its initial appearance. Given our altitude, the effect is similar to time-lapse photography. In the space of mere few minutes, from the initial glimpse, with the cloud tops bathed in a pale, surrealistic light; the white disc begins its silent, steady ascent; quarter, half, three-quarters and full. It seems to pause for a moment, upon the tops of the now fully illuminated cloud deck, to survey its vast domain; before continuing its ascent to perch among the stars; whereupon it is bathed in the pink glow of the setting western sun well to our rear. The beauty of nature at its finest.

The flight-deck offers an astronomer's paradise: The unfettered view of the brightest planets, the Big Dipper and the Little Dipper, and the three stars of Orion's belt, first pointed out to me by my father, so many years ago. The same father who, years ago, took me to the observation decks of many an airport, to watch in wonder as the jets of the day did their magic.

To our left, the beauty of the Aurora Borealis, the Northern Lights. An ever-shifting, fading, strengthening, weakening, dancing array of blues, violets, yellows, greens and reds.

The Northern Lights trace their origins to solar storms. Those storms on the surface of the sun (93-milion miles away), emit high-speed, charged particles which scatter throughout the solar system. Just as metal filings are attracted to magnets, so too these charged solar particles are drawn to the Earth's magnetic poles, both north and south, producing the Northern Lights or Aurora Borealis (northern hemisphere) and the Southern Lights, or Aurora Australis (southern hemisphere).

After their 93-million mile journey from the surface of the sun, as they enter the highest reaches of our atmosphere (ninety-five percent of the particles fall to within 55-80 miles above the Earth), these charged particles collide with, and fracture, atmospheric nitrogen and oxygen atoms, leaving in their wake highly-charged nitrogen and oxygen ions. These charged ions emit radiation of various wavelengths in the electro-magnetic spectrum, each wavelength accounting for a particular color in the magnificent display we are witnessing this evening.

The flight deck likewise offers a geologist's paradise. The front seat, seven miles above the surface of the earth, offers an unparalleled vantage point to note the geologic features marking the passage of time: The sea-beds of now-vanished inland seas;

the valleys, both narrow and broad, carved by the advance and retreat of Ice Age glaciers; the evidence of the inexorable power of rivers and windblown-sands to carve the land; weaving patterns and shapes to beckon, rival and challenge the most-gifted artist; the marriage of river valley and farmland; the contrasts of forested green with the stark white of the snowline.

The artistry is not merely of nature's making. Humanity has likewise put pencil to paper, paint-brush to canvas: The tailored and terraced fields along mountain slopes; the stone-wall and hedge-row bordered farmlands of the valleys. At night, densely-packed lights mark the collections of humanity inhabiting our urban centers, those lights gradually fading through the dimmer lights of suburb, to the vast darkness below.

The symmetries of the parallel avenues and the perpendicular boulevards of our urban centers, are matched by their country cousins, the parallel and perpendicular "section lines" marking fields of corn, wheat, and rye, punctuated here and there with the stately grain silo. Linking the urban centers, the vast river systems which have always linked humanity. And, everywhere, the endless ribbons of asphalt, railroad track, powerlines, or dirt road. And always, upon those roads, the round-the-clock parade of headlights and tail-lights, linking friend and family, commerce and trade.

Roughly 2300 years ago, a gentleman by the name of Eratosthenes, of Cyrene (modern-day Libya), estimated the circumference of the Earth. He did so by measuring the distance between the cities of Alexandria and Syene (both in modern-day Egypt) and by measuring the difference in the shadows cast by the sun, in each city, at noon, on the Summer Solstice. Armed with the above calculations, he arrived at an answer that was within a one-percent error of the Earth's 24,901-mile circumference.

At first blush, those nearly twenty-five thousand miles appear significant. However, from the vantage point of the flight-deck, we are (to borrow a tune) a small world after all. Ribbons of asphalt link one coast with another. The red-light / green-light wingtips of aircraft at our twelve o'clock link one continent with another. The collection of the world's airlines at the largest airports, constitute a virtual "assembly of nations." Yes, we are a small world. Every flight is a marvel, every view is a lesson, every moment is an opportunity for reflection and gratitude.

Thirty-five thousand feet below, though breaks in the living wonder of the clouds, rests the moonlit and wind-tossed seascape of the frigid North Atlantic, the Nordic sea-faring path between Europe and the New World, a path we will cross in mere hours, at 75-degrees Fahrenheit, with the inflight entertainment rolling, with the Chilean Sea Bass, or the Thai Tilapia, served on a hot plate.

Seascape and landscape below, the Northern Lights to the left, the moonlit clouds a mere arm's reach away. Beauty unsurpassed. Fran turns to me: "Thoughts?" I pause, contemplate and reply: "Spectacular." Moments later, I turn to him: "You?" He likewise pauses and replies with his hands at peace on his arm-rests: "Ditto. Spectacular."

Not wanting to waste the view, I reach down for the interphone, and place a call to our First Class galley. As hoped, Cherie answers. I ask her if she would like to catch a view of the Northern Lights. She most definitely would. I remind her to bring her camera or cell-phone. She asks if she can get us anything. Fran and I would both love an Earl Grey tea. No cream. No sugar.

She replies with a cheerful "I will make it hap'n, Cap'n."

Our flight attendants are allowed access to the flight-deck, but not the pilot seats, anytime other than the "Sterile" flight segments below ten thousand feet. With two flight-deck jump-seats, there is always a place for them to catch a few minutes of quiet time. Cherie, and her flight attendant team, are always welcome.

As it turns out, while we have never before flown together, Cherie and I ran into each other, decades ago. Literally. She remembers the moment. I do not. Having said that, the head of thick, black curls tumbling over her shoulders, is sparking some distant memories, as she recounts our first meet.

Roughly twenty-five years ago, Cherie, from Rochester, New York, accustomed to the cold, went out for a snowfall run while on a winter layover in Cleveland, Ohio. She did so, just as I, having been raised in Munich, Germany, likewise accustomed to my snowfall runs, came in from my own run. Entering and exiting from the same door, at the same moment; we literally ran into each other. Twenty-five years later, we are sharing a flight-deck and enjoying the Northern Lights, while we each enjoy a cup of Earl Grey. Yes, it is a small world.

Cherie shares her life story, while sipping at her Earl Grey, and while enjoying the air-show surrounding us. After having earned a degree in nursing, she opted to "spend one year as a flight-attendant." Thirty years later, she is still living that "one year" as a flight attendant. The freedom, the travel and the passenger interactions have sustained her passion for the job. She is a people-watcher. She is looking forward to spending the afternoon and evening in London's Trafalgar Square, watching the world walk past, followed up with a bit of Thai or Indian, "The best part of a London layover" as she puts it. She opines: "Were it not for their colonies, the English would have no cuisine."

As we approach the halfway point between our fifty-degrees west longitude position and our forty-degrees west longitude position, we note we are running three minutes ahead of our scheduled ETA of 0555-Zulu. Our groundspeed has crept up on us. The winds have shifted, our tailwind is up by about 40 knots.

As noted earlier, aircraft separation over the North Atlantic is based on proper altimetry (for above/below separation), course discipline (for left/right separation), and speed control (for "in-trail" ahead/behind separation). With each position report, we provide our speed, our position crossing time, and our estimate for the next reporting point. At fifty-degrees west longitude, we reported Mach .80, time 0511-Zulu, and a forty-degrees west longitude estimate of 0555-Zulu. We must maintain that position estimate within plus or minus two minutes. Failure to do so may impact (no pun intended) aircraft separation, and may lead to a "come see me" phone call. While we have held a steady Mach .80, we have not maintained our allowable tolerance of plus or minus two minutes (we are three minutes ahead of our scheduled ETA).

The corrective action? If running ahead of schedule, we do not slow down. If running late, we do not speed up. Rather, it is time for another radio call with Gander Oceanic. Fran makes it happen with an updated estimate for forty-degrees west longitude: 0552-Zulu.

Regarding our speed, one of the more frequent Window Seat Pilot questions is "How fast are we going?" That question, and its answer, brings me back to the Summer of 1980, and an Oklahoma afternoon, with a jet trainer strapped to my back, my head encased in a form-fitting helmet, sucking on oxygen at twenty-eight thousand feet. With seat-belt and shoulder-harness secure, a parachute on my back, ejection seat handles at both knees, my right hand on the throttles, my left hand on the stick, and both feet on the rudder pedals, while steady on a westerly heading of 270-degrees, it was time for the "slow flight" demonstration.

As I eased back on the airspeed, I likewise eased back on the nose to maintain my Lift vector (increase angle-of-attack, increase coefficient of lift), thereby remaining level at twenty-eight thousand feet. As the airspeed bled down to 120 knots, I rolled the jet up on its left wing, and glanced at the Oklahoma section lines six miles below. I rolled the wings level.

My brain, registered the following message: "Something does not look right." I rolled the jet up on its right wing, and scanned the Oklahoma section lines once again. I rolled the wings level. Something was indeed "not right." The section lines were appearing from behind me, they were not disappearing ahead of me. I was flying backwards.

Aviators work with three separate airspeeds: True-airspeed, indicated-airspeed and ground-speed. We start with true-airspeed. Imagine any block of air. True-airspeed is how fast an aircraft travels through that particular block of air. True-airspeed remains a constant, unaffected by altitude or temperature. Due to its constant nature, true-airspeed is the speed entered on flight-plans. It is the speed air traffic control references for traffic separation. In view of its importance, any true-airspeed deviation greater than 10-knots, or 5-percent, must be reported to air traffic control. My true airspeed, through that block of air, on that Oklahoma afternoon, was 156 knots. Our true-airspeed this evening is approximately 480 knots.

An aircraft's ground-speed is how fast it moves over the ground. It is the sum of true-airspeed (the speed of an aircraft through a block of air), plus or minus the speed with which headwinds or tailwinds are pushing that block of air.

The Oklahoma winds were out of the west at approximately 170 knots. While flying into the headwind, with a true-airspeed of 156 knots, the 170-knot headwind had me flying backwards at a ground-speed of minus 14 knots.

Like those Oklahoma winds, our winds this evening are out of the west at 91 knots. Unlike that Oklahoma afternoon, we are not on a westerly heading; rather, we are on an easterly heading; hence, those 91 knots constitute a tailwind. We are traveling through a block of airspace at a true-airspeed of 480 knots. Adding our 91-knot tailwind to our 480 true-airspeed, gives us a ground-speed of 571 knots.

The last, and conceptually the most challenging, of our three airspeeds is indicated-airspeed. In the earliest days of aviation, indicated-airspeed was the only airspeed "indicated" on the flight-deck; hence, the label "indicated-airspeed." While flight-decks now display all three types (Indicated, True, and Ground) the label "indicated-airspeed" has endured.

Air density varies with temperature and altitude. High-altitude and high-temperature air is "thin" air. Low-altitude and low-temperature air is "thick" air. Thin air has fewer air molecules. Thick air has more air molecules.

As noted earlier, air molecules passing over the surface of our wing provide the Lift enabling us to fly. Airspeed is one of a handful of pilot-controlled factors (wing curvature, wing surface area, angle-of-attack, co-efficient of lift, and airspeed) influencing the Lift Equation.

Knowing how many air molecules are passing over our wing, at any given moment (speed), is *key* to deciding how to employ the other elements of Lift: When to increase or decrease angle-of-attack and coefficient of lift, when to increase or decrease wing curvature and wing surface area (extend or retract wing flaps and wing slats). Given that speed is the only Lift factor that is squared, carrying with it an outsized impact on Lift, it plays a *critical role* in flight-deck decision-making. We *must know* how many air molecules are passing over our wing, at any given moment in time (speed).

Around the time our friend Daniel Bernoulli was strolling along the Venetian canals, a French engineer by the name of Henri Pitot was studying the flow patterns of rivers and canals. He was particularly interested in exploring ways to measure "fluid flow velocity."

During the course of my ramp-dance, hours ago, I paid particular attention to four forward-facing probes, located along the left forward and right forward fuselage, two on each side, ensuring they were clean and free of debris. Those tubes are referred to as "pitot tubes," in honor of our friend, Henri Pitot.

While in flight, air molecules are constantly flying into our four pitot tubes, just as bugs constantly impact the glass of our automobile's windshield as we drive along any highway. Like those bugs impacting our windshield (fewer bugs at low speed, more bugs at high speed), the frequency with which those air molecules enter our pitot tubes, is a function of our true airspeed through a block of air (our speed along the highway) and the thickness of the air through which we fly (determined by temperature and altitude).

Independent pitot systems (redundancy) count the number of air molecules entering our four pitot tubes, and display the summation as indicated-airspeed. The pitot systems "count" the air molecules by measuring their cumulative "ram air pressure" as they enter the pitot tubes.

As discussed earlier, we extend our flaps and slats (dirty wing) at low speeds, and we retract our flaps and slats (clean wing) at high speeds. While on our departure, our indicated-airspeed (168 knots, 188 knots, 208 knots) dictated when we *retracted* our flaps and slats. Our indicated-airspeed will likewise dictate when we *extend* our flaps and slats on arrival. Likewise, indicated-airspeed (148 knots) was Fran's cue for his "Rotate" call (increase angle of attack, increase coefficient of lift) while on the take-off roll. Indicated-airspeed provides Lift. Indicated-airspeed is life.

Ground-speed gets us there. Indicated-airspeed provides the Lift to keep us airborne. True-airspeed plays a critical role. For the aspiring aerodynamic engineer, there are two additional speeds: Equivalent-airspeed and calibrated-airspeed; neither of which is displayed on the flight-deck; neither of which has ever been a part of this pilot's "real world" calculations.

No discussion of airspeed would be complete without addressing the question of why it takes so much longer to fly west, from London to Newark; than it does to fly east, from Newark to London. With the exception of minor route variations, the distance between the two locations does not change. Similarly, with minor exceptions, the true-airspeed does not change. Why then, does the westbound trip take so much longer than the eastbound trip?

The difference rests with the Headwind and Tailwind components. The enroute winds are predominantly out of the West. Hence, tailwinds and faster ground-speeds for eastbound flights, Newark to London; and headwinds and slower ground-speeds for westbound flights, London to Newark. While some Window Seat Pilots may be content with the above answer, others may ask: Why are the winds predominantly from the West?

The air residing over the Equator is closest to the sun, and is therefore the Earth's consistently warmest air. The laws of nature dictate warm air rises; therefore, air over the Equator rises. The air over the North and South Pole is farthest from the sun, and is therefore the Earth's consistently coldest air. The laws of nature dictate cold air falls; therefore, air over the Poles falls.

Falling polar air must go somewhere. Likewise, rising equatorial air must go somewhere. Nature provides the answer in the form of a simple air-cycle. Falling cold air flows south, from the Poles to the Equator, replacing rising Equatorial air; while rising Equatorial air flows north, from the Equator to the Poles, replacing falling Polar air.

How would a north-south, equator-pole-equator air-cycle treat easterly and westerly journeys differently? Once again, we turn to yet another engineer-mathematician, Gustave-Gaspard Coriolis.

In 1835, Gustave demonstrated the Earth's rotation serves as the link between the north-south, polar-equatorial air-cycle, on the one hand; and eastbound tailwinds and westbound headwinds, on the other hand.

Long before digital-downloads and live-streaming, the turntable (aka the record player) reigned supreme. Imagine a record spinning on a turn-table. Imagine we hold a ruler over the record (while it is spinning) oriented from the center to the circumference, as in a radius. With the ruler in one hand, with the record spinning below, and with a piece of chalk in the other hand; imagine we draw a straight chalk line, along the ruler's straight-edge, on the surface of the spinning record.

Imagine we switch the turn-table off, we lift the record, and we examine the straight-edge chalk line we have drawn on the record surface. That straight line will appear as a curved line on the record surface, due to the record's spinning as we drew our straight line.

Likewise, the north-south air-cycle and the Earth's rotation. As the north-south air-cycle winds travel in a straight line, between the Equator to the two Poles, they are curved ninety degrees (the Coriolis Effect) by the spinning of the Earth. In the Northern hemisphere, the winds are curved to the right, flowing West to East. In the Southern hemisphere, the winds are curved to the left, likewise flowing West to East.

The north-south air-cycle, the Earth's rotation, and the subsequent curving of the winds, more fully answers our question. We now know why winds are consistently out of the West, why tailwinds are the norm from Newark to London, why headwinds are the norm from London to Newark, and why it takes so much longer to fly from London to Newark, than it does to fly from Newark to London.

The difference can be substantial. With our average 61-knot tailwind, and our 480 knot true-airspeed, our 541 knot ground-speed will cover the 3089 miles between Newark and London in five hours and forty-two minutes. Our companion flight, from London to Newark, dealing with the same average wind, now a 61-knot headwind, flying the same 480 knot true-airspeed, will require seven hours and twenty-four minutes to cover the same 3089 miles, at a 419-knot ground-speed; a difference of one hour and forty-two minutes.

Four factors influence our airspeed. First factor: Aircraft structural limitations. Just as a paper-thin kite may do well in a light breeze, just as a backyard oak can withstand some strong winds; so, too, an aircraft is designed and constructed to withstand the stresses of a particular airspeed. Eventually the backyard wind may reach a speed at which our paper-thin kite, and our backyard oak, may experience unpleasant scenarios. In a similar manner, an aircraft can only take so much airspeed. Our structural limitation? We are limited to .86 Mach, eighty-six percent the speed of sound.

Second factor: Rules. Just as there are automobile speed limits on interstate highways and within residential areas; so, too, there are speed limits in holding patterns, while enroute, below ten thousand feet, and along this evening's North Atlantic Track. Holding airspeeds are limited to 200 knots through 6000-feet, 235 knots through 14,000-feet, and 265 knots above 14,000-feet. Enroute speeds are limited to a 5-percent or 10-knot variation from assigned true-airspeed. We are limited to 250 knots below 10,000-feet. And, as we cross the North Atlantic this evening, we are limited to a 0.01 deviation from our assigned Mach speed.

Third factor: Every engine has its limits. Our engines can operate for twenty seconds at an Exhaust Gas Temperature (EGT) of 897-degrees, for five minutes at an EGT of 877-degrees, or for an unlimited duration at an EGT of 795-degrees. Those engine limits, in turn, limit our airspeeds.

Fourth factor: Fuel efficiency. Just as an automobile has a particular relationship between speed and fuel efficiency; so, too, an aircraft has a fuel efficiency sweet-spot. In an industry in which fuel often constitutes the number one expense, fuel efficiency constitutes a major influence on airspeed selection.

Before we wrap up our discussion of airspeed, one final detour into terminology. Where did the term "knot" come from? In the days of yore, upon the seas thirty-five thousand feet below us, the speed of a sea-going vessel was measured with a piece of wood called a "chip-log." The chip-log was attached to a length of rope, and tossed overboard from the stern of a vessel. A series of knots were tied into the rope, at intervals of forty-seven feet and three inches. As the length of rope attached to the chip-log passed through the hands of one sailor, tasked with counting the knots as they passed through his hands; a second sailor kept time on a thirty-second hour-glass. At the expiration of the thirty-second period, the knot-count was translated into "knots" of speed, with each "knot" equating to roughly 20.25 inches per second, or "one nautical mile per hour." One knot.

The navigators of the early sea-going vessels, seeking remote islands for fresh water and food, in the vastness of the ocean; faced with nourishment or starvation, success or mutiny, life or death; relied on a rudimentary chip-log, and a knotted length of rope.

How fast are we going? 480 Knots True, 290 Knots Indicated, 571 Knots Ground Speed. So much for fond Oklahoma memories. Back to our flight. We are approaching forty-degrees west longitude, amid the stars, the moon, the clouds and the silence.

Reflection

Roughly eight billion of us share this pebble, labeled Earth. There are no solo positions out there. Every position has an interface with someone.

"Plays well with others" is critical to success in any endeavor.

It has been my privilege to spend a good bit of time with my airline's pilot-interview team. Without exception, every one of our interview questions includes an element designed to gauge the "plays well with others" component.

"Setting the tone" is key. When it comes to tone, there are no vacuums. Every situation has a tone. That tone will be set by someone. Be that someone. Set the right tone. With the first handshake, with the first eye-contact, with the first spoken word.

In life, as in flight: Play well with others. Set the right tone. From the first moment.

Be it the airline business, or any other business, every action we take, every decision we make, must be customer-focused. The customer is our only reason for being. The customer is Job One.

Mahatma Gandhi did not earn his enduring fame as a customer service agent. However, his words offer timeless advice on the matter:

"A customer is a most important visitor on our premises. He is not dependent on us. We are dependent on him. He is not an interruption on our work. He is the purpose of it. He is not an

outsider on our business. He is a part of it. We are not doing him a favor by serving him. He is doing us a favor by giving us an opportunity to do so."

How do I define my mission in the airline business? I do not think of myself as a pilot. Rather, I think of myself as a customer service agent, who happens to fly. Customer service is my Job One. Take care of the customer.

In life, as in flight: The customer is Job One.

"Break Time"

Cherie, seated on the flight-deck jump-seat, has drifted off to sleep. We do not wish to disturb her. We have dimmed the lights, killed the speakers and donned our headsets. With hushed voices, we make our report.

"Good evening, Gander, Flight 28, checks 52-North and 40-West at 0552-Zulu, FL350, Mach .80, estimating 52-North and 30-West at 0635-Zulu, next is 52-North and 20-West, fuel 35.5. Over."

"Roger, Flight 28, Gander Oceanic copies your position. At 30-West, contact Shanwick Oceanic on 8864."

Once again, we confirm L-NAV and V-NAV engaged. With the flight plan in hand, I pencil in our time at 40-West as 0552Z, with 35,500 pounds of fuel. I likewise pencil in our three-degree nose-up pitch and our 1.59 EPR engine thrust setting. We are three minutes ahead, and up 400 pounds on the fuel. As a reminder for our required SELCAL Check with Shanwick Oceanic, at our 30-West waypoint, I pencil-in our assigned HF frequency of 8864. Lastly, we once again pull up the weather for London-Heathrow, Goose Bay and Manchester. All remains well.

It is time for my break. A brief tap to Cherie's shoulder brings her back to consciousness. A quick call to our cabin team brings Erica to the flight-deck. While Fran takes a trip to the cabin for his physiological need, I brief Erica on the flight progress to date.

We are V-NAV and L-NAV. We are cleared on Route Whiskey, FL350, Mach .80. We are three minutes ahead, and up 400 on the fuel. We are on a two-mile offset. Goose Bay remains our ETOPS alternate, as we have not yet passed our ETOPS critical (equal-time) point. The weather looks good for London-Heathrow, Manchester and Goose Bay. All systems are good, with our center fuel tank at 3500 pounds. In roughly twenty-five minutes, we will switch over to our main fuel tanks, located within our wings. With Fran's return, and with instructions to wake me for any emergency checklist, any Insufficient-Fuel message, or any possible diversion scenario, I head to the cabin for my break.

My physiological need calls for a 185-foot stroll to the aft galley. Passing through the First Class galley, Cherie thanks me for the tour of the Northern Lights and for not disturbing her nap. I remind her: "You have the tough job, we have the easy job. Visit and nap anytime you wish." I resist the temptation to sample the pastries arranged on the cart for our Window Seat Pilots. Along with the receding hairline, I am fighting the middle-aged spread.

Making my way down the aisle, to the aft galley, I note our nervous flyer, Hannah of Anchorage, remains in what appears to be a deep sleep. Upon my arrival in the aft galley, I find two of our flight attendants, Evette and Claire, sitting on their jump-seats, left and right, updating their manuals with their latest revisions, while discussing their favorite layovers.

Evette has led a self-described "gypsy life." She was born and raised in Alaska (yes, two Alaskans on the jet). Mother of three gymnasts, she has spent a good bit of time in Florida, Texas, and Oregon, and is in the midst of a middle-aged return to Alaska. With a light laugh, as she brushes her auburn bangs from her eyes, she tells me her Alaskan life was all about hiking, her Florida life was all about windsurfing, her Texan life was all about triathlons, and her Oregon life was all about giving birth. And what will her new Alaskan life will be all about? Her reply: Heaven.

I comprehend. My first assignment, following flight training, was in Alaska. To this day, decades later, that Alaskan assignment offered the most memorable flight experiences, amid the most spectacular beauty. With the exception of a few urban areas, the entire state, from sea level to eighteen thousand feet, was "uncontrolled airspace." Pick an altitude, pick an airspeed, pick a heading, point the bird, and fly. No permission required. Aviator heaven.

Evette's favorite layover experience is people-watching in Rome's Piazza Navona. She takes great delight in trying to spot the Americans in the crowd. Baseball caps are no longer the give-away, nor is the New York Yankees apparel, for both have gone global. With a smile, she claims she can still count on the almost uniquely-American preference for sneakers, amid the prevailing sandals and the anything-other-than-sneakers favored by the vast majority of the global population; a distinction she claims is evident among the thousands of global passengers occupying her aircraft cabins.

Claire, of Baton Rouge, Louisiana, sporting a soft-southern accent, occupying the right jump-seat, is nursing a tall glass of Coke, garnished with a handful of lemon slices. Her inflight bag, resting at her feet, has a few additional cans of Coke tucked inside, along with a zip-lock bag of lemon slices. As a connoisseur of soft drinks, she claims a distinct distaste for the sugar found in internationally-bottled soft drinks, as she much prefers the high fructose corn syrup of domestically-bottled soft drinks (hence, the layover cans of Coke tucked into her inflight bag). With an appealing grin and twinkle in her eyes, she claims the corn syrup and lemon slices, check the squares for her daily servings of fruits and vegetables.

Claire's favorite layover? The beer gardens of Munich. Recalling my childhood days in Munich, and my many Munich lay-overs, I can appreciate her choice. People-watching opportunities in the Munich beer gardens are world-class caliber, a very nice complement to the beers, pretzels, schnitzels and views.

Hoping to get some sleep, I dispense with my standard cup of tea, and take a moment to enquire about our Window Seat Pilots. Evette and Claire tell me they are, for the most part, in good spirits, despite the delay out of Newark. The passenger entertainment systems are working like a charm. The cabin temperatures have been perfect. All good.

As I make the return journey to my nap-nest, I am asked a question, by a still-wide-awake Window Seat Pilot: "How do you find your way from Newark to London, at night, while over the North Atlantic?" It is a great question. Do I opt for the short answer or the long answer? Do I opt for brief humor, or do I take the time for a comprehensive answer? My love for the science, coupled with respect for my Window Seat Pilot, points me toward the latter option: The comprehensive answer. My nap can wait.

The Window Seat Pilot of the moment is Anne, of Albuquerque, New Mexico, originally of West Virginia. She is an Air Force veteran, having served a number of years in the command post business. She is unable to sleep. An upside to our upcoming discussion? My answer to her question will likely put her to sleep.

Our Flight Management Computer (FMC) computes a navigation solution based upon a handful of inputs: Two independent streams of Global Positioning Satellite (GPS) data, three independent Inertial Navigation Systems (INS) data streams, as well as any available ground-based navigation signals.

We start with twenty-four GPS satellites orbiting 11,500 miles above the Earth. Those satellites allow for global coverage, providing three-dimensional position accuracy (latitude, longitude, altitude) to within 10 meters. Each of the twenty-four satellites transmits a two-part, satellite-unique signal. A GPS receiver, upon "hearing" those two-part signals, will conduct a modified triangulation exercise to determine its three-dimensional position.

The first part of every satellite-unique signal provides the GPS receiver with the GPS satellite's identification and position, answering the twin questions: "Which satellite am I hearing?" and "Where is that satellite located?" The second part of the signal allows the GPS receiver to calculate distance from the satellite (speed-time-distance calculations), thereby defining a "sphere of potential position," with the satellite at the sphere's center. This first satellite signal will place the GPS receiver (our aircraft) at any point on that "sphere of potential position."

Reception of a second signal will define a second "sphere of potential position." The intersection of any two spheres will define a circle. With that in mind, the GPS receiver (our aircraft) will be located at any point on that "circle of potential position."

Reception of a third signal will define a third "sphere of potential position." The intersection of three spheres can only be defined as two points, with the GPS receiver (our aircraft) now narrowed down to one of two points in space.

Reception of a fourth signal will create a fourth "sphere of potential position." Four spheres can only intercept at a single point in space. The GPS receiver (our aircraft) will be located at that single point: Defined in three dimensions of latitude, longitude and altitude.

Our INS systems likewise calculate our position in three dimensions. However, unlike GPS or radar, our INS systems do so in an entirely autonomous manner, independent of any ground-based or space-based inputs.

Having said that, the INS system does require an initial, pre-departure, present-position entry. Prior to our Newark push-back; three of us independently confirmed our INS present-position. That pre-flight confirmation was key to all subsequent INS operations.

With the first movement of our aircraft, the INS systems kicked into gear, as on-board accelerometers measured our acceleration in three planes of motion: Forward-backward, left-right, and up-down. In an on-going, real-time manner, from Newark departure to London-Heathrow arrival, every INS acceleration measurement (in all three planes of motion) is "broken down" into measurements of aircraft velocity (in all three planes of motion). The three velocity measurements are further "broken down" into measurements of distance change (in all three planes of motion).

Each measure of distance change is applied to each former present-position. Therefore, the INS present-position displayed at any point during the course of our journey, is the sum of all previous accelerations, speed and distance changes, applied to the initial, pre-departure, present-position.

The initial, pre-departure, present-position is therefore key; requiring both an accurate initial input and a stable accelerometer platform. Regarding the initial input, an error of a single degree of latitude (a simple typo) will produce a sixty-mile error prior to any aircraft movement, with all subsequent calculations applied to that original sixty-mile error.

Regarding the accelerometers, an accelerometer error of 1/1000 the force of gravity, an error of approximately three one-hundredths of a foot over one second of time, would cause a present-position error of approximately forty miles over the course of a single hour, to say nothing of the accumulated error over the course of a seven-hour flight from Newark to London-Heathrow.

A child's game offers a nice illustration of the INS operation. Imagine a blindfolded child starting from the center of a room, and subsequently led around the room by a friend's hand; left and right, forward and backward, slowly and quickly; coming to rest after several turns, and asked "What is your present position in the room?"

If the blindfolded child was aware of her initial present-position within the room, and if she was able to track the number of steps in this direction, a turn in that direction, the number of steps in this second direction, and so on through each subsequent series of steps and turns, she would have a rather accurate sense of her position when asked "What is your present-position?"

Just as the child tracks steps and turns, applying them to each prior present-position; so too, the INS tracks all accelerations, speeds and distance changes, and applies them to each prior present-position; in all three dimensions: Up-down, left-right, forward-rear.

While knowing present-position is helpful, the INS can further assist by working the calculations going forward. Knowing present-position (latitude-longitude and altitude), and knowing the next waypoint (latitude-longitude and altitude), the INS can direct the auto-pilot to travel in a particular direction, at a particular speed, for a particular interval of time, from one waypoint to the next, Newark to London-Heathrow.

Returning to our analogy: If the blindfolded child knows her initial present-position; if she knows the positions of windows, doorways, furniture and appliances within the room; she will have all the data required to navigate to any position within the room; simply by turning in this direction or that direction, for this or that number of paces, from window to doorway to sofa to refrigerator.

Radio-updating provides a final input. Scattered around the globe, navigation aids (navaids) were once the back-bone of air navigation. Each navaid has its own phonetic identifier, Morse Code identifier and transmission frequency.

One of the last navaids prior to our going feet wet was the VOR-DME located in Gander, Newfoundland: Transmitting on

117.3, with a YQX phonetic identifier and a matching Morse Code identifier.

The Gander VOR-DME transmitter spins at a rate of 1800 revolutions per minute, transmitting 361 signals in each revolution around the 360-degree compass rose. The extra (361st) signal, is the reference-signal.

As the transmitter passes through each of the 360 degrees of the compass rose, it transmits a signal identical to the reference signal (amplitude and frequency) with one variation. Each of those 360 signals will have a unique, identifying phase-shift from the reference-signal baseline: A 30-unit phase-shift for the 030-degree radial, a 90-unit phase-shift for the 090-degree radial, a 330-unit phase-shift for the 330-degree radial, and so on, around the compass rose.

The FMC radio-updating function auto-tunes the two closest VOR-DME transmitters, identifies the two transmitters (based on their reference signals), and calculates our radial from each of the two transmitters (based on the phase-shifts from the reference-signals, for example the 030-degree radial and the 090-degree radial). High school geometry tells us two lines (our two radials) can intersect at only one point. That one point of radial-intersection, is our present-position.

The FMC may choose to utilize the DME (Distance Measuring Equipment) portion of the VOR-DME transmitter. The DME option requires a brief conversation between the ground-based DME transmitter, and our on-board DME receiver.

The on-board DME receiver opens the conversation with an outbound radio signal traveling at 880 feet per second. Upon receipt of the aircraft's signal, the DME transmitter replies with a signal of its own, likewise traveling at 880 feet per second. With receipt of the DME transmitter reply, the system logic applies the now-familiar, speed-time-distance calculation, to fix our DME distance along the previously-identified VOR radial.

Armed with the radial (VOR phase-shift from the reference signal), and our distance along the radial (DME), we will know our present-position.

Our VOR-DME update function will remain in the "search" mode as we make our way across the North Atlantic, searching for any ground-based navaid transmissions. As we approach the coast of Ireland, and as ground-based navaid signals become available, the VOR-DME update function will resume, providing an input to our Flight Management Computer (FMC) navigation solution.

I am reminded of two earlier-life VOR-DME stories. During the pre-INS, pre-GPS days of the now-ancient Cold War, "meaconing" was a tactic deployed with occasional, deadly effect. Meaconing involved establishing a "false" navaid, transmitting a proper VOR-DME signal, on the proper frequency, with the proper Morse Code identifier. An unknowing flight-crew, having received the false signal, having verified the false Morse Code identifier, was often lured into tracking a false VOR-DME radial across hostile international borders, into mountains, or into range of surface-to-air weaponry. These stories often did not have happy endings. One such story is thought to have taken the lives of a college classmate, and his six-person crew.

A happy-ending story, occurred on an earlier-life flight from Honolulu, Hawaii to Anchorage, Alaska. The standard crew complement included a navigator. The pilots flew, the flight engineers monitored the aircraft systems, the loadmasters supervised the air-drops and the aerial refuelings, and the navigators got us from Point A to Point B.

At some point in that pre-INS and pre-GPS flight, roughly midway between Honolulu and Anchorage, the navigator announced we had lost our OMEGA navigation system (a now-outdated, long-range navigation system). We took comfort in the knowledge we still had a LORAN navigation system (yet another, now-outdated, long-range navigation system). Shortly following the loss of the OMEGA, the navigator announced we had also lost the LORAN. We took comfort in the knowledge that our navigator was trained in the art and science of "celestial navigation." Armed with his sextant, our navigator could calculate our present position via angular measurements between the visible horizon and any number of celestial bodies (the moon, the sun, the planets, or any one of fifty-seven navigation stars).

Having set up his sextant, the navigator announced the sextant was broken. At that point, we put the sandwiches down, we lay the crosswords to the side, and we set a wind-corrected, wet-compass course for the Alaskan mainland. Lacking the auto-tune function we take for granted this evening, we methodically rotated through a dozen or more VOR-DME navaids as we approached the coast of Alaska. We eventually scored a hit on a navaid, we rode that navaid radial inbound, and we spent a wonderful night in Dutch Harbor, Alaska. With a story to last a lifetime.

That experience (everything that could fail, did fail) is one of the reasons I take a moment to note the actual winds and ground-speed as we pass each oceanic waypoint, neither of which is procedurally required.

Back to Anne of Albuquerque's question: "How do you find your way from Newark to London, at night, while over the North Atlantic?" Throughout the course of our flight this evening, the Flight Management Computer (FMC) utilizes the two independent GPS inputs, the three independent INS inputs, and any available VOR-DME inputs, to calculate a composite FMC-Position.

One additional answer can be found in the swim leg of a triathlon. How do you know you are swimming in the right direction, in open water, without the convenience of stripes painted upon the floor of a pool, or floating lane dividers on the water's surface? The answer is both simple and a bit painful: So long as someone is kicking you in the forehead, and so long as you are kicking someone else in the forehead, you are likely swimming in the right direction.

So too, with the NAT-tracks over the North Atlantic. So long as we have blinking red, green and white strobe lights at our twelve o'clock, so long as we have multiple contrails aligned with our flight path, and so long as our TCAS displays aircraft at our six o'clock and at our twelve o'clock, we are likely flying in the right direction.

The industry has come a long way. As young aviators; pre-INS, pre-GPS, pre-FMC; my colleagues and I manually tuned hundreds of VOR-DME frequencies, identified an equal number of Morse-Code identifiers, and conducted countless cross-country flights, by hopping from one navaid to the next, along highways in the sky. Those highways in the sky had names: Victor Routes below 18,000-feet (V-214) and Jet Routes above 18,000-feet (J-177).

Those highways remain in place. They are constructed by stitching together a series of VOR-DME legs, from departure airport to arrival airport. Each leg is defined by an outbound radial from one VOR-DME, a leg midpoint defined by DME (Distance Measuring Equipment), and a subsequent inbound radial to the next VOR-DME. We have come a long way.

And where is Anne of Albuquerque headed? She will be hiking Exmoor and Dartmoor National Parks, in the southwest of England. Been there. Done that. Bring a raincoat.

Reflection

What words of wisdom would I offer an aspiring young aviator?
Do the right thing. Every time.

It has been my privilege to have served as a member of my airline's "Event Review Committee" (ERC). The ERC reviews roughly thirteen thousand flight safety reports, submitted annually, by our fellow pilots.

An overwhelming majority of the reports I have reviewed, would never have been submitted, if the flight-crew had simply followed procedure, if they had simply done the right thing.

Virtually every accident that has occurred, over the course of my forty-plus years as a professional aviator, has occurred because someone failed to do the right thing.

In life, as in flight: Do the right thing. Every time.

Reflections

I have reclined the seat, placed the pillow, spread the blanket and kicked the shoes. Ear plugs and eye shades are in place. Sleep may or may not be in the cards this evening. But, at o-dark-thirty, I am slowly entering another zone, a cross between melting and collapsing.

As a child, I was a frequent Window Seat Pilot, having crossed the North Atlantic several times. The airlines of the day were Pan American World Airways and Trans World Airlines, better known as Pan Am and TWA. The jets were single-aisle, four-engine Boeing 707s and McDonnell Douglas DC-8s. The inflight entertainment featured a single movie, displayed on a screen hanging from the cabin's ceiling, via a movie projector mounted above the aisle.

As an eighteen-year-old, I was upside down over the Nevada desert, in the back-seat of a McDonnell Douglas F-4 Phantom II, rocketing along at 300 knots, at 300-feet, in what was referred to as an "incentive ride".

A few short years later, while enrolled in a program labeled "flight-screening," I was at the controls of a single-engine Cessna, flying a race-track pattern overhead the Colorado Rockies. Stalls, steep turns and basic aircraft control were my main focus. With a grade-book sign-off and my "initial solo" behind me, I was on my way to eighteen months of flight-training.

Flight training was not an easy road, with a wash-out rate approaching fifty percent. To put that wash-out rate in perspective, every student entering flight training was a college graduate, who had already passed the "flight-screening" program, who had

163

already logged over a dozen hours of flight time, and who had already flown solo.

Why the high wash-out rate? Learning-curves and the syllabus timeline. Where other flight training programs allowed for more time to catch up, the taxpayer-funded flight training had but one rule: Keep up with the syllabus-timeline, or find another line of work. Hack it, or pack it.

The training was not an easy road in another respect, as two classmates lost their lives while attempting to earn their wings, just as several others would lose their lives as fully qualified pilots in the years to follow. Military aviation can be an unforgiving business.

At the age of twenty-two, I was solo and super-sonic, flying the T-38 Talon, affectionately referred to as "The White Rocket." Flight training spanned the full spectrum: The classic aerobatics (Aileron Roll and Barrel Roll; Cloverleaf and Cuban Eight; Immelmann, Loop and Split-S); day and night formation (two-ship and four-ship, fingertip, close-trail and extended-trail); low-level tactical navigation and high-altitude cross-country navigation. We learned what it took to be a good flight-leader, and what it took to be a good wing-man.

And we rode the "the tickle."

There were no glass-cockpits. There were no inertial navigation systems. There were no global positioning systems. There were no flight management computers. There were two ejection handles and a parachute.

Following flight training, with wings on my chest, life morphed from T-38 Talons overhead Oklahoma to the C-130 Hercules on a global scale. Life was day and night low-level, single-ship and formation, air-drop and air-assault, covert infiltration and covert exfiltration, lights-out and comm-out, low-level air-refueling and night vision googles, radar warning receivers and flak jackets, chaff and flares, break-left and break-right.

While my military path to the airline business may have been the norm thirty years ago, such is not the case today. Military aviation today is less than one-third its Cold War size. Consequently, a mere handful of my First Officers are former military aviators. The vast majority of new entrants have received their flight training and initial flight experience in the private sector, earning their required ratings and certifications at the local airfield or at any number of universities offering an aviation track. They have gained their early flight experience as flight instructors, and gained their initial industry foothold in the regional airline or the corporate aviation environment.

Fran, for example, earned his college degree, and his aviation qualifications, while attending school in North Dakota. Armed with his college degree, he enlisted in the Air Force and spent four years as a "boom operator" on a KC-135, a converted Boeing 707 designed to provide air-refueling. As the boom operator, Fran guided the KC-135's refueling probe (the "boom") into the receiving aircraft's equivalent of a fuel cap. A most delicate task. He went on to earn a Master's Degree in Aviation Science, and embarked upon a pilot career that passed from flight instructor, to regional jet pilot, to a position as a First Officer at a major airline. His story is one of passion paired with perseverance.

Erica attended a small liberal arts college in New England, spent a number of years flight-instructing, and earned her foothold in the airline business while flying single-engine, commuter aircraft, solo, to and from New England's coastal islands, amid the often-harsh New England weather. As with Fran, Erica's story is one of passion paired with perseverance. It is my good fortune to be sharing a flight-deck with the two of them.

What do I most enjoy about the airline business? Show up, fly the jet, go home. There are no mid-night Zoom meetings with marketing teams, conducting a meeting twelve times zones apart. There are no evening conference calls with the sales team, while coaching third base, or while sharing dinner with my wife and my two boys.

Most appealing: No politics. The date-of-hire, seniority-based system, sets in concrete an environment in which no pilot is gunning for another pilot's job; where one pilot's willingness to work through the weekend, or over the holiday, does not put another pilot out of the running for a promotion; where summer vacation opportunities, weekend duty assignments and the heft of pay-checks, are not contingent upon one's golf game; where putting one's marriage and family first, does not cost one their job, or impact their career advancement.

Is there a downside to the seniority-based system? Absolutely. No matter how well I may do my job, no matter how well Fran or Erica may do their jobs, our progression up the ladder will not reflect our level of competence. Our seniority numbers and our dates-of-hire, will forever dictate our position within the overall scheme.

What do I least enjoy about the airline business? Time away from family. I have often told my boys; if I could do it all over again, knowing what I know today; if I had to choose between flying and family, I would have chosen family. Too much time away.

Having said that, my time with family is all about family. When I am with family, there are no phone calls. Coaching third base is about the bunt or the steal, not answering a sales call. Dinner with family is about relaxation, conversation and choice of dessert; not a business call interruption.

How would I compare military flying with airline flying? Mara, a very sharp-minded twelve-year-old, my seat-mate on a flight to Buffalo, New York, painted a very clear contrast for me. Having asked me the question, and having patiently endured my long-winded answer, she replied: "Airline flying is like ice-skating, while military flying is like hockey." Mara had hit the nail on the head.

In the airline business, the job is all about flying the jet. End of story. However, in military flying, the job is *not* about flying the jet. Rather, the job is about the air-drop, the air-assault, the air refueling, the time-over-target, the formation, the break-right and the break-left, the radar-warning-receiver, the chaff and the flares, all while monitoring and participating in three or four different radio conversations. The flying must come naturally.

Similarly, in ice-skating, the job is about the skating. End of story. However, in the midst of a hockey game, the job is *not* about the skating. Rather, the job is about the puck, the goal, the passing game, the attack, the offense, the defense. The ice-skating must come naturally.

When am I most alive in the course of a flight? I am most alive on three occasions. First, and most passionately, whenever I have an opportunity to interact with the Window Seat Pilots. I take advantage of every opportunity to do so. Every delay is my opportunity to walk the aisles, pass out snacks and drinks, answer the questions and allay the fears. Every delay is my opportunity to offer flight-deck tours, featuring Window Seat Pilots seated at the controls, one hand on the yoke, one hand on the throttles, digitally capturing a smile and a memory.

On those occasions when time allows, prior to heading down the jet-way, I often linger at the departure gate, and ask a handful of younger Window Seat Pilots to assist me with the flight-plan, walking them through the many considerations that enter into each flight.

My interaction with the Window Seat Pilots continues throughout the flight, as I ask air traffic control for a detour over

Niagara Falls, the Grand Canyon, Monument Valley, Lake Tahoe, Bryce Canyon and Zion National Parks, or Yosemite's Half Dome. On each such tour, I take great delight in rolling the jet into a series of left and right S-turns, offering the Window Seat Pilots, on both sides of the aircraft, spectacular views of nature's beauty. As was the case with our moments of cloud-surfing, the detours burn a bit of fuel and time. However, the added fuel burn is insignificant, the impact on arrival time is insignificant, while the Window Seat Pilot views are without equal.

At the conclusion of each flight, as I stand at the door, thanking our Window Seat Pilots for their business, I take great delight in offering the company flight-plan to one of them, as a souvenir of his or her flight experience.

Does any particular Window Seat Pilot experience stand-out? Absolutely. On those occasions wherein we have ferried military units into war-zones, I have made it a point to shake the hand of every deplaning soldier, sailor, airman and Marine, while thanking them for their service. Any one of them could be my son, a United States Marine, now on his fourth deployment.

At the other end of the spectrum, I will never forget the child who took it upon himself to eat my ham and cheese sandwich and sip my Earl Grey tea, while sitting in the Captain's seat, as I gave him a flight-deck tour. Nor, will I ever forget his mother, who sat impassively on the jump-seat, and watched, without comment, as her son did so.

I will always chuckle as I recall the question hurled at me, wrapped in warm humor, as the passengers deplaned, following a particularly firm landing: "Captain, did you land this airplane, or were we shot down?"

Lastly, there is the passenger who, after having exchanged harsh words with a flight attendant, made it a point to inform me: "Captain, I likely fly more often than you do." My reply, while sipping my Earl Grey tea? "Sir, thank you for your business; however, just to be clear, you sit, I fly."

Second, I can think of few joys greater than actually flying the jet. In an earlier life, it was the "yank, bank and crank". No auto-pilot. No auto-throttle. No flight-director. Upside-down and pulling the g's while looking back, over my shoulder, for the horizon. The 300-foot low-levels in mountainous terrain, well below the ridgelines, with the tree-tops rushing beneath at over 400 feet per second, focused on a "time over target." Bone-jarring assault-landings on dirt strips carved out of South American and Asian jungles. The "break right" and the "break left" to counter simulated threats. The black-of-night landings on night vision goggles. The finger-tip and the fluid-tactical formation. The night aerial refuelings, flown three to five knots above stall speed. Not to be forgotten: The sweet-slam. Igniting the White Rocket's afterburners on the take-off roll, and the forceful slam into the seat-back as they kicked in. Together, they count as among my most-treasured lifetime memories, in a life blessedly filled with treasured memories. If I could turn back the clock, and live that earlier-life all over again, I would do so in a heart-beat, with a cold box-lunch, at a small fraction of my current pay-check. It has never been about the Benjamins.

In the context of airline flying, there are few joys greater than to hand-fly a super-smooth take-off rotation, followed by an equally smooth departure and climb-out, with a few moments of moonlit cloud-surfing. Disconnecting the auto-flight systems, and deviating just a few degrees from course, for just a few moments, to softly tease and caress the brilliant edges of the clouds with our silver wingtips, always brings a warm smile. Battling moderate turbulence and crosswinds, to nail a super-smooth touchdown, on-speed, and on centerline, is a particular joy.

On the cerebral side of the ledger, there is a quiet satisfaction and contentment in the energy-management challenge of bringing a 240,000 pound jet from 39,000-feet (potential energy), flying at 500-knots (kinetic energy), to a smooth touchdown (zero energy) over the course of a finite 120-mile ground track, meeting any number of mandatory airspeed and altitude restrictions along the way, with a handful of air traffic control amendments thrown into the mix. Doing all of the above, without spilling the coffee.

Unseen by The Window Seat Pilot, the energy-management challenge (descent points, airspeed selection, throttle control, speed-brake usage, flap and slat extension, landing gear extension) constitutes the bulk of inflight instruction and evaluation for both new, and experienced, pilots. When done smoothly, it is impressive; often prompting the height of professional aviator praise: "Nice job."

Third, I am most alive when the well-ordered symphony begins to fall apart, as in maintenance issues, weather issues, air traffic control issues, emergencies and divert issues. I enjoy the challenge of keeping an eye on the ball in the midst of the turbulence engulfing the symphony; maintaining poise, projecting calm, keeping a healthy team-dynamic intact, keeping the focus on the customer experience, rising to the occasion, and "making the mission happen."

What was my last most-alive experience? My last flight into London-Heathrow. A night approach, with a cloud ceiling roughly 2500-feet above the surface. The forecast had called for rain, and a *right* crosswind, steady at 20-knots, with gusts up to 30 knots. No problem. We could handle a 20-30 knot crosswind. Challenging, but do-able.

As per my norm, given my still undiminished joy in hand-flying the jet, I had disengaged the auto-flight systems roughly ten minutes prior to landing. Shortly after rolling out on final approach to the runway, I had reason to wonder if I had bitten off more than I could chew.

The rain was torrential. Throughout the approach, from roughly 3500-feet all the way down to touchdown, the aircraft was rocked with moderate turbulence, defined as "standing or walking will be a challenge," as we wrestled a 36 knot *left* crosswind. Strapped into our seats, with shoulder harness and seatbelts secure, simply reading our constantly bouncing flight instruments proved to be a challenge. Complicating matters, as we passed through 2000-feet, our 36 knot *left* crosswind switched to the forecast 20-30 knot *right* crosswind, a 66-knot reversal.

Our airspeed was bouncing plus-or-minus 10-knots from the target airspeed, making for 20-knot airspeed swings. The moderate turbulence and the gusting crosswind, had me in the constant-correction mode. My right hand was working the throttles to maintain target airspeed; throttle-up, throttle-back; constant correction, all the way down. My left hand was working the yoke; aileron into the wind to counter the crosswind, sometimes more aileron, sometimes less aileron; constant correction, all the way down. My feet were working the rudder pedals, in tandem with the aileron inputs: More aileron required more opposite rudder, less aileron required less opposite rudder; constant correction, all the way down.

While working the ailerons and the rudders, left and right; I was working the yoke forward and aft, directing the elevators up and down, to maintain glide-path; constant correction, all the way down.

While flying the approach, there was no conscious or deliberate processing of information. Rather, my mind, my hands and my feet; became one with the jet, one with the winds and one with the turbulence; constant corrections all the way down. Eyes inside, eyes outside; confirming on-speed, confirming on centerline, confirming on glide-path.

I nailed the landing. On-speed, on centerline, at the thousand-foot marker. Textbook. The roll-out, the taxi-in, and the ride to the hotel, was not a time of self-congratulatory comment. Rather, it was a time of humble reflection. I am paid to fly those approaches. I delivered. Just as any other professional pilot would have delivered.

Was that my most memorable landing? No. My most memorable landing occurred while in the midst of my initial C-130 flight training. Up to that point in my flight training, the optimal landing was super-smooth, on-speed, on-centerline, within the touch-down zone. On this New Mexico afternoon, I was one of a handful of students seated in the cargo hold of a C-130, awaiting my turn in the Co-Pilot seat. While on headset, with no access to a window, I monitored the flight-crew as they extended the trailing-edge flaps, as they extended the landing gear and as they ran the Before Landing Checklist. I noted the thrust reduction and the slight change in nose-up pitch angle, anticipating a super-smooth landing from the two very experienced instructor pilots at the controls. Much to my surprise, rather than the expected super-smooth touchdown, I experienced a bone-crushing, spine-compressing impact, accompanied by unending expletive-laced congratulatory praise for an outstanding landing.

That landing was my introduction to the "assault landing," in which the kinetic energy vector is dissipated in the downward direction (via the "controlled crash"), thereby allowing for a much shorter landing roll-out: Less kinetic energy to dissipate in the forward direction, as required for a dirt-strip, carved out of the jungle.

Regarding landings: What is considered a "good" landing? The light-hearted answer is captured in the expression "If you can walk away from the landing; then, it is a good landing." The text-book answer is on-speed, on centerline, in the touch-down-zone. My comment following a rough landing? It was not my fault. It was not her fault. It was the asphalt.

What are the biggest changes I have witnessed in the airline business? One change leaps to the top of the list: The degree to which automation has become the norm. When properly programmed, our auto-flight systems will set our takeoff thrust. Following takeoff, those same systems will maintain our airspeed, our lateral path, and our vertical path through six hours of climb, cruise and descent; wrapping up with an auto-landing, to include flaring for touchdown and retarding our throttles to idle thrust. Closely related to the automation, are the ubiquitous computer-generated flight-deck displays, entirely reliant upon flight data computers and symbol generators.

My fear? What happens when the automation and/or symbol generators fail? What happens when the automation is misunderstood? Recent industry literature is replete with examples in which automation failed, automation was misunderstood, or symbol generators (display issues) led to unpleasant scenarios. The fear is not mine alone. The industry, as a whole, recognizes, and is addressing, this issue.

Have I had inflight emergencies? Yes. Have I been frightened while in the midst of those emergencies? No. One is generally not frightened while in the midst of an emergency. One simply reverts to training. That training follows three tracks. First, to remain calm, to maintain aircraft control, and to correctly analyze the situation. Second, to employ the basic tenets of human factors and "Crew Resource Management" training. Third, to utilize the appropriate checklists, and to properly execute the appropriate emergency procedures. We do so, every nine months, while in the simulator: One simulated emergency after another. It is a testament to the quality of our training, and to the quality of our simulators, that after each real-world emergency, the shared comment has generally been "That was just like the simulator."

Regarding our earlier discussion of the DC-10 total hydraulic failure, wherein the flight-crew controlled an aircraft that was little more than a rock with two operating engines, after having lost all flight controls; the Captain stated: *"We were too busy [to be scared]. You must maintain your composure in the airplane, or you will die. You learn that from your first day of flight training."* That "maintain your composure" mindset is one of the key character traits expected of all flight-crew members; most particularly, the Captain; most particularly, in the midst of an emergency.

Have I ever been lucky? I am lucky every time I fly. Three instances of luck stand out. The first occurred while in flight training, decades ago. Had I not been lucky on this particular day, I would not have lived to see my twenty-third birthday.

I was on my initial-solo in a twin-jet trainer. I entered the airport traffic pattern, 1500-feet above the surface, at 300 knots, lined up with the centerline of the landing runway. At a position midway down the length of the runway, I visually cleared the (parallel) downwind leg to my left, rolled into sixty-degrees of left bank ("left break"), added thrust, and began to pull the nose across the horizon; working my way through a level, 180-degree, 2-G turn, planning to roll out on the (parallel) downwind leg of the traffic pattern.

Unbeknownst to me, another student, following a touch-and-go landing, had rolled out on the same (parallel) downwind leg of the traffic pattern, at the same altitude, 1500-feet above the surface. However, this student had failed to make the required, standard radio call, "Closed-Downwind." This required, standard radio call had but one purpose: To alert any aircraft preparing for a "left break" (me) that a potential traffic conflict may be in the offing. Alerted to the potential traffic conflict on the (parallel) downwind leg of the traffic pattern, an aircraft (me), would delay the "left break" until clear of the potential traffic conflict.

On this particular day, I was the aircraft in the "left break." On this particular day, I did not know a potential traffic conflict was in the offing. While in a sixty-degree left bank, I was belly-up, and blind to any other converging aircraft on the downwind leg.

Midway through my turn, while concentrating on maintaining my airspeed and my altitude, while pulling the nose across the horizon, I heard a non-standard radio call, repeated several times, each time with a greater note of urgency: "In the break, roll out." New to the flying business, accustomed to standard radio calls, it took a few extra moments for me to process the non-standard call.

It dawned on me. I was "In the break." Perhaps I should "roll out" of the turn. I did so. I rolled wings level, just in time to see the underside of another jet pass directly over my position, close enough to see the streaks of oil on the underside of the fuselage. Had I not rolled out, it is possible (perhaps likely) my raised right wing (while in a left turn) may have struck the underside of the other jet, bringing two young lives to an end. On that day, I was lucky.

Four lessons. First, "standard operating procedures" are written in the blood of those who have preceded us. Second, there are consequences in failing to do the right-thing, in failing to adhere to "standard operating procedures." In this case, the right-thing was to make the "Closed Downwind" radio call. The consequence of failing to do so, could have been the tragic, and wholly unnecessary, loss of two young lives. That is one phone call my mother did not have to receive. Third, error is a timeless and ubiquitous part of the human condition: To be human, is to err. It was far too early in my aviation career for me to be good. On that day, I was lucky. Fourth, despite my being directly in front of him, the other pilot never saw me: Trust, do not depend.

Second instance of luck: While still enrolled in flight training, while on a solo ride in the White Rocket, I experienced an episode of g-induced loss-of-consciousness (G-LOC), in which the g-forces imposed on my body, pulled the blood from my upper body (brain and eyes) to my lower body, leading to loss of sight and loss of consciousness. I woke to the sound of rushing air, my feet on the two rudder pedals, my right hand on the stick, my left hand on the throttles. I had blacked-out. I was blind. I was floating in a zero-g condition, with no sense of weight.

While blind, my mind was processing at a rapid clip. I suspected I had lost consciousness due to excessive g-forces drawing the blood from my brain. The key question was whether I had lost consciousness while pulling down, while inverted, at the top of a loop, with the nose of my jet now pointed down; or whether I had lost consciousness while pulling up, through the bottom of a loop, with the nose of my jet now pointed up.

If I was pointing down, not knowing how long I had been unconscious, I may have had little time left to make a decision, little time to eject, little time until impact, little time left to live. If I was pointing up, I had time. One characteristic of G-LOC is that the victim may experience a brief amnesic period coincident with the onset of the G-LOC episode. Hence, I was missing that key element of information: Pointing up? Pointing down?

What to do? Eject, or ride it out? Which was the greater negative? Embarrassment following ejection from a perfectly good jet? Or, death while riding a perfectly good jet into the fields of Oklahoma? I would have to explain my embarrassment. I would not have to explain my death. In a testament to peer pressure, I opted to avoid the embarrassment. I opted to cross my fingers, and ride it out.

My vision returned. My nose was pointed up, my wings were level, nothing but blue sky at my twelve o'clock. I rolled the jet over on its right wing, allowed the nose to drop back down to the horizon, rolled left, leveled-off, called it a day, and never spoke a word of the incident. For decades. On that day, I was lucky.

Third instance of luck: Twenty years later, while leading a low-level, three-ship formation through the Adirondacks; after wrapping a tight left turn around the corner of a ridgeline, roughly 300-feet above the ground, at 250-knots; I rolled out wings-level, only to see another C-130 at our twelve o'clock, far too close for comfort, belly-up (and blind) to us, at roughly the same altitude. Had I not rolled out of my turn when I did, or if either of us had opted to widen our turn just a bit, twelve crewmembers would not be here today. On that day, I was lucky.

Which brings us to a uniquely military expression: Air discipline. The C-130 belly-up at our twelve o'clock, was the number-three aircraft in our three-ship formation. The pilot had deviated from the flight-planned route, to scout his lakeside fishing cabin, without informing the formation; with the intent to rejoin the formation, following the check of his fishing cabin. He had violated air-discipline with potentially tragic consequences.

A noteworthy aviation experience: Joe-Spit-The-Ragman. I met Joe decades ago, in the midst of a maintenance delay, while I was serving as a Second Officer (in the now-obsolete Flight Engineer position) on the Airbus A-300. I do not recall the nature of the maintenance delay, nor do I recall the location. However, I do recall the delay seemed, at the time, to be without end.

At one point, over the course of the trouble-shooting; after seemingly endless back-and-forth consultation with maintenance; Joe had offered his two cents on the matter, wrapping up with "But what do I know, I am just Joe-Spit-The-Ragman." As it turned out, Joe's comments held the key. His aircraft systems knowledge, humbly delivered, saved the day. We closed up. We launched. We completed the mission.

In the far-flung airline business, Joe and I never again crossed paths. However, I have never forgotten that encounter, and the lesson inherent in his on-target words, delivered with humility. The lesson: Age, education, experience, qualification, rank, and title; may, and often do, offer value-added. However, the absence of those markers, does not imply a lack of value-added. Time and again, as evidenced in the industry literature; age, education, experience, qualification, rank and title; have often failed to save the day. On the other hand, the quiet, humble comment, often delivered by the least among us, has often saved the day. There is a Joe-Spit-The-Ragman out there, in every line of work, in every scenario. Listen to Joe-Spit.

An impactful quote? *"When anyone asks me how I can best describe my experience in nearly forty years at sea, I merely say 'uneventful'. Of course, there have been winter gales, and storms, and fog and the like. But, in all my experience, I have never been in any accident, of any sort, worth speaking about. I have seen but one vessel in distress in all my years at sea. I never saw a wreck, and I have never been wrecked, nor was I ever in any predicament that threatened to end in disaster of any sort."*

The words were spoken by Edward J. Smith, the Captain of the Titanic, nine days before the Titanic struck an iceberg, while under his command, taking the lives of 1,513 crew and passengers. It can happen. To anyone. At any time.

What do I say to young children who tell me they want to be a pilot when they grow up? I tell them they must choose. They can be a pilot, or they can grow up, but they cannot do both, as pilots never grow up. Pilots are simply kids, playing with bigger toys, in a bigger sandbox. Our sandbox is not the twenty-by-twenty foot, ten-inch pile of sand at the neighborhood park. Our sandbox extends from the surface of the earth, to the heavens; from left to right, and fore to aft; for as far as the eye can see.

What do I say to young children, and their parents, when they tell me I have a great job? I tell them, the best job in the world is being a Mom or a Dad. Hearing my sons call me "Dad" always elicits a deep heart-felt response. Hearing the word "Captain" simply does not come close. Having said that, when Henri, the Santo Domingo station manager addresses me as "El Commandante" he never fails to elicit my smile in return.

As I feel the weight of my eyelids, my mind is not with Henri, or with the children. Rather, it is with the men and women with whom I have flown. Harlan, my Flight Commander during flight training; a veteran of multiple combat tours in the revered McDonnell Douglas F-4 Phantom II, affectionately known as "The Double Ugly" and the world's largest distributor of MIG parts. When I sought his advice on how to strengthen my neck muscles, strained while wearing my flight-helmet in the midst of six or seven g-forces; he suggested a neck-strengthening exercise that would first require me finding a girlfriend. It was Harlan's "In the break, roll out" radio call, over forty years ago; that allowed me to raise my two boys, and type these words today.

John, the C-130 flight-engineer; decades older than I, having flown the C-130 longer than I had been alive; who, while sound asleep in cruise flight, would calmly call out, with eyes closed: "What's happening with the number three engine?". His call would prompt a glance at the number three engine instruments: Sure enough, we had a problem with number three.

Greg, who enjoyed dropping down to the lowest of low-level flights; in the furthest reaches of the Alaskan wilderness, to cavort with the caribou herds; and in the remotest portions of the Arctic Ice Cap, to play with the polar bears; always saving enough time and fuel for a low-level circle of the spectacular majesty that is

Mount McKinley; a mountain that took the life of a flight training classmate, a superb baseball player, a quintessential "good guy."

Eric, my first squadron commander, who, while on a low-level flight along the hauntingly beautiful and barren Aleutian Island chain, offered me the advice: "The most important job you will ever have, is the one you have right now."

Bob, with whom I shared a 300-foot low-level flight from North Carolina, all the way to Nevada. Ten years later, the ubiquitous hand of human error reached out and tapped Bob on the shoulder, as he "flew west" while on a night air-refueling mission off the Oregon Coast.

Kurt, who could always be counted upon to find, and enjoy, the finest of cigars, in the remotest of jungles, while wearing nothing but his flip-flops and his ever-present, signature smile.

In the airline business, Doc, my first Captain, the poster-boy for the hard-charging, chain-smoking, beer-guzzling, skirt-chasing, roaring-with-laughter, profanity-spewing stereotype airline pilot of his generation; a Captain, who treated every member of the team with unparalleled respect.

Bob, my first airline instructor, who had flown in the Korean War; who, at the age of sixty-eight years, had fathered two children with his twenty-six-year-old mail-order bride; who retired to Florida's Marathon Key, with his wife and two young children; while doing one hundred push-ups a day.

Marx, who, in the worst days of the war, had smuggled an orphan out of Vietnam in his luggage, thereby saving one young child's life, while sacrificing his own promising military career.

Kit, who had flown in both extremes; in a single-engine, propellor-driven, forward-air-control aircraft, skimming tree-tops and dodging bullets, while wearing a sweat-soaked t-shirt; and in the high-flying SR-71 Blackbird, still holding world speed-records, beyond the reach of any bullet or missile, while wearing a pressurized space suit.

Paul, who had demonstrated valor, above and beyond the call of duty; a valor about which only a handful of others knew, a valor about which he never spoke; until one survivor, owing his life to Paul's actions, wrote a memoir; thereby allowing Paul to be awarded our nation's second-highest award.

Ron, with his often-used pick-up line: "You can trust me, I played the Christ child in the Christmas play."

Diamond Jim, Dakota-raised, wearing leather flight-gloves, on every flight, from engine-start to destination arrival; who had every VOR-DME frequency memorized, from East Coast to West Coast; who offered me a sterling example of gentlemanly behavior, behavior I sought to emulate, behavior which garnered me some remarkably pleasant encounters.

Frank, friend, simulator partner, Chief Pilot, and my only come-see-me phone call.

Sam, who flew one of the finest approaches I have ever witnessed, under some of the most demanding conditions I have ever experienced; who "flew West" long before his time.

Honorable mentions to Brad, Herb, Mike, Jim, and Bill; five of the finest men with whom I have ever flown; five men who have likewise "flown West" long before their time.

Not to be forgotten, the many men and women I have had the pleasure of interviewing, as part of my airline's pilot-hire interview-team. The wealth of experience they bring to the job, and the maturity they have gained through those experiences, has been humbling in the extreme.

Lastly, the many men and women I have observed in the simulator, and in-flight; while I have held the roles of Second Officer, First Officer, Captain, Line Check Airman, Simulator Evaluator, and FAA Aircrew Program Designee: Their near-flawless execution of flying skills (often under great stress), their unwavering adherence to the life-saving tenets of threat-and-error management, their consistent displays of the quintessential good-pilot traits, their ever-present good cheer, and the laughter we have shared.

Each of them, and countless others, are what have made, and what continue to make, this life a supreme joy. And, with that grateful thought, I drift off to sleep.

Awake Amid The Bumps

Nap-time is done. As I take the 180-foot stroll through the sleeping cabin to the aft galley, for my cup of tea, we hit our first substantial "bumps" of the journey, a shot of moderate turbulence. An unseen hand on the flight-deck hits the "Seat Belt" sign. I drop myself into the closest available seat. Having secured my seat belt, I prepare to ride out the turbulence.

To my left, my Window Seat Pilot turns to me with evident concern in her eyes. Her first question: "May I hold your hand?" Not waiting for an answer, she takes my hand; and, while I am keenly aware of her tight grip, she asks her second question: "Where does turbulence come from?"

With the "Seat Belt" sign illuminated, with her grip tight upon my hand, conscious of her incredible blue eyes, deep enough to go for a dive, warm enough to never come back up for air, I surrender to her question, and I offer her my best reply.

Two fond memories of Thermodynamics 210, come to mind. First, the PV=nRT equation relating pressure, volume and temperature. Second, the one take-away lesson that remains with me to this day: Think of air, and the behavior of air, just as you would think of water, and the behavior of water.

Recall the title of Daniel Bernoulli's book (_Hydro_-dynamica) in which he lays out his theory of Lift, discovered as he strolled the Venetian _Canal_. Recall the nature of Henri Pitot's research: _Rivers, canals_ and _fluid flow_ velocity. Recall the Gustave-Gaspard Coriolis effect: Equally applicable to the _ocean currents_ of our _hydro_-sphere, and the _fluids_ within our inner ear. Think of air, and the behavior of air, just as you would think of water, and the behavior of water.

There are fast water currents, just as there are fast air currents (as in the jet-*stream*). There are calm waters, and there are pockets of calm air. There is smooth sailing, and there are smooth flights. There are choppy waters, and there is choppy air. Indeed, pilots and air traffic controllers routinely utilize all three words (calm, smooth, choppy) when reporting inflight conditions.

We can swim with the current, just as we can fly with the wind. We can lose ground while swimming against the current, just as we can fly backward against a strong Oklahoma headwind. Ailerons and rudders will turn an aircraft through the air, just as rudders will turn a boat through the water. Differential thrust will swing an aircraft's nose, just as the differential application of oars will swing a boat's bow. A submarine's elevator will raise or lower a submarine's depth, just as an aircraft's elevator will raise or lower an aircraft's altitude. Harbor signs caution "Leave No *Wake*," while flight crews strive to avoid *wake*-turbulence. Amid the wind-tunnels of an aerodynamic laboratory, engineers refer to the portion of an aircraft in contact with the airflow as a *wet* surface.

Bodies of water; be they rivers, lakes, or oceans; often experience turbulence wherever they merge. In a similar manner, air turbulence is frequently encountered wherever two or more bodies of air meet along a "front." The phenomena has a name: Frontal turbulence.

Streams of water frequently encounter turbulence, in the form of rapids, whenever they encounter rocks along the bed of a river. In a similar manner, air turbulence (mountain *wave*) is frequently encountered whenever air (jet *stream*) encounters mountains. As was the case with "calm, smooth, choppy," pilots and air traffic controllers routinely utilize the words "jet *stream*" and "mountain *wave*" when reporting inflight conditions.

A third form of turbulence is often encountered with rising warm air, or with falling cold air, with updrafts and downdrafts often exceeding rates of 6000 feet-per-minute. Think "*water fall*." Decades ago, while conducting a low-level search along the upper slopes of Alaska's Mount McKinley, while heading downhill, just below the summit, with our power near idle, scanning the slopes for a missing aircraft; we were suddenly caught in the midst of a powerful "waterfall" of air, that had "crested" the summit to our rear, "poured" over the lip, and "plunged" downward. We were a "boat tossed upon the stormy seas."

We were along for the ride. We were not flying. We had no flight-control authority. Our elevators, ailerons and rudders were unresponsive. We were simply caught in the "wave." At some point, we were "tossed out," much as an ocean *wave* tosses debris upon a shoreline. We regained control authority, and we returned to base.

Recalling an earlier question regarding fear, the McKinley episode is likely the only episode during which I may have flirted with fear. There was no training upon which to fall back. There was no procedure to execute. We were at the mercy of nature. No amount of flying proficiency, no number of simulator experiences would alter the outcome. Back to Chuck Yeager's quote. On that day, we were lucky.

Having said that, I do not recall being afraid while in the moment. We never stopped trying to fly the airplane. We kept trying to exert some element of control authority; some rudder, some aileron, some elevator; hoping for a bite of the airflow, hoping for a bit of control effectiveness.

My Window Seat Pilot, still gripping my hand, having introduced herself as Marlena, now biting her lower lip, asks her third question: "Is turbulence, whatever its source, dangerous?"

It can be. Her grip tightens. However, it rarely is. Her grip relaxes. Turbulence may fall into any of four levels of intensity.

The most common form of turbulence is Light turbulence. Light turbulence is a daily occurrence. Drinks *may* splash, you *may* have a dry-cleaning bill, but walking through the cabin is *not* a challenge. The next level of intensity is Moderate turbulence. Drinks *will* consistently splash, you *will* have a dry-cleaning bill, and standing or walking *will* be a challenge. Moderate turbulence is an every now-and-then occurrence. The next two levels, Severe and Extreme, are very rarely encountered. In my forty years of aviation, I have never encountered, nor do I know of anyone else who has ever encountered, Severe turbulence (standing or walking is impossible) or Extreme turbulence (aircraft control is practically impossible). In either case, if you were to encounter Severe or Extreme, your drinks and your dry-cleaning bill is *not* likely to be your focus.

As her grip on my hand relaxes further, she asks her fourth question: "Can we avoid turbulence?" Yes, we can. Sometimes. Thunderstorms and "towering cumulonimbus" cloud formations are frequently associated with turbulence. We visually avoid them. While flying in limited-visibility situations, turbulence can often be identified via our onboard weather radar. Most weather radars display three colors (green, amber and red), corresponding to three levels of precipitation intensity (light, medium, heavy). Many weather radars (such as ours) have an additional color option: Magenta for turbulence. Visual avoidance (thunderstorms and towering cumulonimbus) and weather radar (red and magenta) will often suffice as a turbulence-avoidance strategy.

However, the avoidance of "clear air turbulence" (CAT) poses a trickier challenge. As the term implies, CAT occurs in "clear air" with few markers. An entire industry has developed to provide flight-crews with CAT forecasts. Those CAT forecasts are a key part of our pre-flight weather briefings; often detailing the locations, altitudes and directions of CAT movement. Utilizing those CAT forecasts, flight-dispatchers attempt to construct flight plans to avoid areas of known CAT turbulence, and often add an extra dose of "deviation fuel" to allow for possible detours around CAT turbulence, in the event it is encountered while enroute.

Once airborne, flight-crews have a number of options for CAT avoidance. For decades, we have relied upon pilot-reports (PIREPs) submitted by our fellow pilots. Dispatchers and air traffic controllers have then verbally forwarded those PIREPs to other flights.

In those areas where an air traffic control relay is not an option (over the North Atlantic), flight-crews will often utilize the Airliner-Common frequency of 123.45 to inform other flights of CAT turbulence encounters.

The datalink revolution impacting aviation has found a role in turbulence avoidance. Our datalink systems allow us to transmit a turbulence report (location, altitude, intensity) which will (with no human relay) automatically trigger an alert in any other data-link equipped-aircraft approaching the reported turbulence.

Many flight-crews are armed with an even more advanced turbulence avoidance tool. Their personal-electronic-device, having replaced their forty pounds of paper, is equipped with an integrated accelerometer which will "feel" every "shake" the aircraft experiences. Furthermore, it will categorize every "shake" as light, moderate, severe, or extreme turbulence. Lastly, it will then automatically transmit that "shake report" to every other similarly equipped flight-crew; thereby taking the flight-crew, the dispatcher and the air traffic controller out of the relay-chain.

The Seat-Belt sign has been turned off, and Marlena's grip has relaxed sufficiently, to allow me to gently disengage, as I reach to unfasten my seat-belt.

Her last question: What are our options, should we receive a turbulence report while airborne? We can (fuel-permitting) deviate laterally around the turbulent area, or we can (if possible) deviate vertically above or below the turbulent area.

Having done my best to answer her question, I bid Marlena a fond farewell, and I resume my journey to the aft galley, in search of my tea. I do not get far. Ryan and Tessa, the two children I spotted hours ago, as they observed the Newark air-show through the terminal's rain-streaked windows, are now straining their necks to look out their window overlooking the right wing. I spot their mother and father, sound asleep across the aisle.

With my own two boys in mind, I drop into the aisle seat, and say "Hello." I learn they are on their way to Estonia, via London-Heathrow. I tell them I have always wanted to tour Estonia, along with the neighboring countries of Latvia and Lithuania. Young Ryan tells me "It is not too late." I smile at the notion that I am taking "How To Live Your Life" advice from a six-year old. Tessa suggests, "You can stay with us, when you visit." Again, I smile. How do I turn down an invitation from a pair of six-year olds?

Tessa points out that their right wing has a green strobe light at the wingtip, while their parent's left wing has a red light on its wingtip. She asks, "Did they run out of green lights? Or, did they run out of red lights?" Again, I smile. Living beneath Newark Airport's traffic pattern, my own son Jason, prior to his kindergarten years, had noticed the same wingtip-lighting configuration.

I compliment Tessa for being as observant as she is. I explain: Every aircraft has a red light on the left wingtip and a green light on the right wingtip. This allows other aircraft to determine in which direction an aircraft is flying, when that aircraft is spotted at night. I draw a simple diagram on a chocolate-stained napkin.

Ryan has a tougher question: "What are the things on the back of the wing, that curve up and down; and the things on the top-middle of the wing, that pop up and down?" I flip the napkin and begin to draw, as I continue speaking. Speaking and drawing, at the same time. No caffeine. I am self-actualizing.

Along the trailing edge of each wing, we have an aileron, one per wing. When a pilot rolls into a turn, the ailerons on one wing curve downwards (increasing wing curvature), increasing Lift, while ailerons on the opposite wing curve upwards, decreasing Lift. The first (increased Lift) wing climbs, while the second (decreased Lift) wing falls. The aircraft turns. Some aircraft have two ailerons on each wing, an inboard aileron (closer to the cabin) and an outboard aileron (closer to the wingtip). On these aircraft, the outboard aileron is often "locked out" at high speeds.

As for the wing panels located on the upper surface, in the middle of the wing: When a pilot rolls into a turn, beyond a pre-set bank angle, those wing-mounted "spoilers" will deploy (pop-up) on the falling wing, interrupting the airflow over the surface of that wing, "spoiling" the Lift over that wing, thereby increasing the turning moment.

Immediately following our touchdown in London-Heathrow, the spoilers will deploy (pop-up) on both wings, spoiling the Lift over both wings, thereby allowing the full weight of the aircraft to settle upon the landing gear, greatly enhancing braking effectiveness. A failure of the spoilers to deploy on landing (or on an aborted takeoff), could reduce our braking effectiveness by up to sixty-percent. With that in mind, we will check for, and confirm, spoiler deployment, immediately following touchdown. If the spoilers have failed to deploy, we will take immediate corrective action to manually deploy them. The spoilers, also known as "speed-brakes," are often utilized in flight, as we deploy them on both wings to kill Lift and expedite a descent, or to assist in aircraft deceleration.

Much as I would love to continue the conversation, I must return to the flight-deck, and allow Fran to get started on his crew-rest. I bid Tessa and Ryan a fond farewell.

Reflection

Threats to aviation safety? The potential over-reliance on automation, the potential erosion of basic flying skills, and the potential loss of situational-awareness. Two recent incidents highlight all three trends.

First, an experienced, senior flight-crew, comprised of four pilots, with over one hundred years of combined professional flight experience, flying a highly-automated wide-body aircraft. When forced to hand-fly an approach and landing, the flight-crew failed to comprehend the logic of their auto-throttle system, failed to note a thirty-four knot loss of airspeed, and consequently landed short of the runway. An unpleasant scenario ensued, with loss of life. A perfectly good airplane, on a perfectly clear, blue-sky-sunshine day.

Second, a highly-automated wide-body aircraft, experienced a partial / temporary loss of airspeed data. The crew failed to set a proper engine-thrust setting (the engine instruments were unaffected by the partial / temporary data loss); they failed to set a proper pitch angle (pitch displays were unaffected by the partial / temporary data loss); they failed to respond to repeated aerodynamic stall warnings. Result? An unpleasant scenario in which all aboard perished.

What did the two episodes have in common? They were both "highly-automated" aircraft.

All industry stake-holders have drawn attention to the perils of an over-reliance on automation, an erosion of basic flying skills, and a loss of situational-awareness.

In life, as in flight: Never lose touch with the basics.

Ears Popping

Cherie has my number: A fresh cup of Earl Grey as I return to the flight-deck. Thank you, Cherie. Fran briefs me, as Erica steps into the cabin for a physiological need. We are LNAV and VNAV. We remain on a two-mile right offset. We are on schedule with fuel. We are on schedule with time. We are still Mach .80. We have climbed to Flight Level 370. We have passed our ETOPS critical point (equal-time point). Weather is unchanged at both London-Heathrow and Manchester. The pilot-reports are calling for a smooth ride ahead. With Erica's return, Fran heads back for his crew-rest. He will return in just under an hour and fifty minutes.

I have returned to the flight-deck while Erica and I are in the middle of our "window of circadian low." The primary window of circadian low occurs between 0300 and 0500. Within this window, sleepiness is at its greatest, and performance capabilities are at their lowest. Unfortunately, this is the time period in which trans-Atlantic flight-crews are most often conducting their descent, approach and landing at the conclusion of an all-night flight. This less-than-ideal situation is compounded by the fact that the overwhelming majority of flight-crew *errors* (by a wide margin) occur during the descent, approach and landing phase of flight, independent of time of day. Indeed, roughly sixty-five percent of *accidents*, industry-wide, occur in the approach and landing phase of flight.

Why are we entering the most error-prone, most accident-prone, phase of flight, while in the midst of our science-confirmed window of circadian low? As was the case in our earlier discussion of flight delays, passenger preference drives the schedule. The standard North-Atlantic schedule allows leisure and business travelers to put in a full day of activity at their North American locations, head out to the airport at the conclusion of their day, take an all-night flight across the North Atlantic, and arrive in Europe at the start of the next day: To conduct their business, or to embark on their morning tour.

The economics of the airline business works hand-in-hand with passenger preference on the return leg to North America. Aircraft generate no revenue while sitting on the ground; hence, they are often departing on their return journey to North America a mere two hours after touching-down in Europe. Leisure and business travelers can plan for a reasonable wake-time in Europe, enjoy a full breakfast, head out to the airport, catch a mid-morning flight to North America and arrive mid-afternoon or early-evening, just in time for a hotel check-in, an evening meal, or a connecting flight to points further west.

While Erica and I are both in the midst of our window of circadian low, our challenge differs. Having just returned from my brief nap, for the next fifteen to thirty minutes, I will be in the midst of "sleep inertia" also known as "sleep-drunkenness." Either label refers to the period immediately following a nap or regular sleep episode, where performance is impaired and vigilance is reduced. Sleep-inertia may be severe, may last from minutes to hours, and may be accompanied by micro-sleep episodes. Not an optimal scenario. We do not want to lose an engine and execute a divert while in the midst of sleep-inertia or sleep-drunkenness.

Sleep-inertia is the reason I select the second break: I do not want to wake from the third break, and conduct a descent, approach and landing, while in the midst of my sleep-inertia.

Fatigue has been a significant contributing factor in a number of aviation, railroad, trucking and maritime accidents. As a consequence of those accidents, a number of studies have examined the nature of fatigue. Those studies have suggested a handful of mitigating strategies, and led to several changes in the regulations governing duty-time and flight-time. Those regulations govern the number of hours we may fly (daily, weekly, monthly, annually), the length of off-duty and in-flight rest periods, and the requirements for augmented (three-pilot, four-pilot) crews.

The changes to those regulations have had an impact. By way of example, the earlier-discussed, Newark blizzard episode, in which we were still legal to fly a seven-hour flight to Glasgow, Scotland, after an all-night, no-rest, eleven-hour duty-period, would no longer be permitted under the updated regulations.

I have my cup of tea in hand. No cream. No sugar. Erica has returned with her coffee. No cream. No sugar. The studies tell us caffeine can be an effective fatigue counter-measure. Caffeine takes roughly 15-30 minutes to enter the bloodstream. Its effects may last up to five hours after ingestion. Our caffeine-challenge this evening: Take just enough to maintain alertness for the remainder of the flight, but not too much to interfere with much-needed rest, upon our arrival in London-Heathrow, after our all-night flight.

Regarding naps while on duty, and in the seat: Although a number of very reputable foreign airlines allow such naps, our FAA does not allow them. That said, every pilot crossing the North Atlantic this evening, is well aware of the many studies demonstrating that "power naps," often as short as twenty minutes, are the most effective strategy for restoring alertness and performance.

Those same studies suggest short activity-breaks can likewise increase alertness. Hence, my hourly flight-deck stretching routines, and my 180-foot strolls to the aft galley for my cup of tea: Always at least once per flight, often more than once per flight. Stretch the legs, clear the mind, get the blood flowing, fight fatigue.

In our effort to stay ahead of the fatigue challenge, Erica and I have set the flight-deck lighting to full illumination, we have the speakers set to maximum volume, and we have chilled the flight-deck just a bit.

As she sips her coffee, raven-haired Erica turns to me, smiles, and asks "Do you still send postcards to your two boys?" I am a bit stunned. "You do not remember me, do you?" I am disappointed. Have I failed to recall two of my crew-members; first Cherie, and now Erica? Still smiling, Erica rescues me: "I was a blonde, back then." Thank you, Erica.

She recounts meeting me while on a Birmingham, England layover. I was part of the inbound flight-crew, and I was heading to bed. She was part of the outbound flight-crew, and she was heading out to fly. I had become lost amid the confusing hallways of the layover hotel.

After a brief hallway chat regarding my layover plans, Erica had set me on the correct path to my room. While engaged in that brief hallway chat, I had been holding two postcards, which I had purchased at the airport. Erica had commented, with a smile, at the time, "No one does postcards anymore." In reply, I had advised her of my habit of sending each of my boys a postcard, while on every layover, from the day each of them had been born. They each now have four shoe-boxes filled with "Dad" postcards.

Having rekindled my memory of our brief hallway conversation; I now recall her informing me, at the time, of her habit of indulging in a massage on every layover. Her mantra: "No one treats me better than I treat myself." My love for my children had made an impression upon Erica. Her healthy focus on self-care had made an impression upon me. So much so, that her words of self-care had prompted my own monthly massage habit. Thank you, Erica.

The repeating chime of the Master-Caution aural alert, and its companion, the flashing Master-Caution light at our twelve o'clock position, interrupts the comfort of our peaceful flight-deck. Our feet drop from our improvised foot rests, our seats return to the upright position, we put the tea and the coffee to the side. In the midst of our window of circadian low, we must clear our minds, and address the non-normal. I reach out and silence the mind-numbing aural alert.

Aviate, navigate, communicate. The first step is Aviate. I turn to Erica: "You have the jet. I have the checklist". *Maintain aircraft control.* Ensure the airplane is still flying. A quick scan confirms we are on speed, on altitude, on course, with all auto-flight systems fully engaged. Erica confirms.

Analyze the situation. We examine our instrument displays. Our Engine Indicating and Crew Alert System (EICAS) is displaying a Cabin-Auto alert. Turning our eyes to the overhead panel, we examine our cabin altitude, climbing through 9700-feet, well above our earlier 7200-feet. Not good. We examine our differential pressure, dropping through 5.2 psi, well below our earlier 9.1 psi. Not good. We examine our cabin rate-of-climb indicator, climbing at 1700 feet per minute. Not good. The outflow position indicator displays a full-open position. Not good. Flight-crew, cabin-crew and Window Seat Passenger ears are popping. We are depressurizing.

Take proper corrective action. With aircraft systems knowledge in mind, and after seeking Erica's confirmation, I reach up and flip our pressure-control from Primary to Alternate. After a brief pause, we note our pressurization indications begin to stabilize, and then begin to reverse. The cabin altitude is descending towards normal, the differential pressure is climbing towards normal, the cabin rate-of-climb has stabilized, the outflow valve indicator shows a slowly closing outflow valve. *Maintain aircraft control, analyze the situation, take proper corrective action.* We have done so.

We have two automatic pressure-control systems. These systems have but one job: Control the position of the cabin outflow valve, to maintain proper cabin pressure. For reasons unknown, the Primary pressure-control system has failed. We have selected the Alternate system. The Alternate system has re-established control over the cabin outflow valve. Had both automatic control systems (Primary and Alternate) failed, we would have reverted to manual control. Another example of system redundancy.

In the unlikely event the manual control had failed (a triple system failure), we would have been busy. First up, the Immediate-Action items, reviewed on the chair-fly drive to the airport, earlier this evening, with the stained and rubber-banded index cards laying in my lap.

Oxygen Mask and Regulators	*"On, 100 Percent"*
Crew Communications	*"Establish"*
Seat Belt Sign	*"On"*

With our cabin altitude passing through 10,000-feet, on its way to our current flight altitude of 37,000-feet, we would have donned our oxygen masks (supplying 100-percent oxygen), we would have established crew communications (not an easy task with the possible roar of inflight winds and the blowing of unsecured items about the frigid-cold flight-deck), and we would have hit the seat-belt sign (one does not want to be unsecured in a rapid-decompression).

If we had been unable to arrest the climb in cabin altitude, oxygen masks located in the ceiling panels overhead our Window

Seat Pilots, would have automatically deployed as we passed through 14,000-feet in cabin altitude.

With the Immediate-Action items complete, we would have executed the earlier-reviewed ETOPS critical-scenario diversion: An expedited emergency descent to the oxygen-rich altitude of ten-thousand feet, with a divert to the applicable ETOPS alternate. At this point in our flight, having passed our ETOPS critical point, that ETOPS alternate would be Manchester, England.

Back to the here-and-now. We have selected the Alternate pressure-controller. The cabin has stabilized. To cover the bases, we pull out the Quick Reference Handbook, flip to the Abnormal Section, scroll through to Air-Systems, and review the applicable checklist. Utilizing the Challenge/Response method described earlier, Erica and I run through a handful of clean-up items. All is well. Checklist complete.

I am heads-down, completing an Electronic Log-Book entry. Federal Air Regulations require flight-crews to make a log-book entry for any/all maintenance issues. Where that once entailed a pen applied to paper, sufficiently firm to be legible through three sheets of carbon copy, we now simply type away at a keypad, and hit the Send prompt. Armed with an early, satellite-relayed, heads-up, our London-Heathrow maintenance technicians can review the applicable log-book-history, obtain any required spare parts, and meet us upon arrival, thereby minimizing the likelihood of a maintenance delay for the return journey to Newark.

Why do we pressurize the aircraft? Imagine a tall stack of bricks. If you placed the fingers of your hand beneath the bottom brick, you would feel far more pressure upon your fingers, than if you placed your fingers beneath the top brick. More bricks above, more pressure upon your fingers. Fewer bricks above, less pressure upon your fingers.

So, too, with air pressure. With more air above, there is more pressure on each air molecule. With less air above, there is less pressure on each air molecule. Therefore, there is far more air pressure at sea level (the bottom brick), than at our current cruise altitude of thirty-seven thousand feet.

While our good friend Daniel Bernoulli was keeping pace with discarded wine bottles in Venice's Grand Canal, and while Henri Pitot was studying fluid flow, two equally inquisitive gentlemen, John Dalton and William Henry, were exploring the relationships between the pressure, temperature and volume of gas. The two were close friends, both residents of Manchester, England, both publishing their respective discoveries within one year of each other.

John Dalton, like others we have discussed, was a remarkable person. Born into an English Quaker family, he was prohibited from attending university in England, as attendance was strictly limited to members of the Church of England. As such, John's formal education extended only so far as elementary school.

Despite a hurdle that would shut down many others, both then and today, John became a renowned physicist, meteorologist and chemist; eventually earning membership in the Royal Society of London, and an honorary degree from Oxford University. He is known as the "father of chemistry," being the first to formulate the notion of the atom, leading him to develop the first table of relative weights of atoms.

For our purposes, his research taught us two lessons. First, the pressure upon the oxygen we breathe, will decrease as we climb in altitude (similar to our stack of bricks); with the pressure at thirty-seven thousand feet, roughly one-fourth the pressure at sea level (bottom brick). Second, at a time when most of his peers believed the atmosphere was a compound of its own right; he rightly claimed that our atmosphere was seventy-nine percent nitrogen and twenty-one percent oxygen.

More importantly, he rightly concluded that at both sea level, and at thirty-seven thousand feet, the percentage of oxygen within the air we breathe, remains the same: Twenty-one percent at sea level, and twenty-one percent at thirty-seven thousand feet. Put the two lessons together: There is the same percentage of oxygen at thirty-seven thousand feet, as there is at sea level; there is simply less pressure upon that oxygen, at thirty-seven thousand feet. John Dalton's Law.

William Henry, having earned his medical degree, and having engaged in research and publishing in both physics and chemistry; discovered "Henry's Law," which states that the solubility of a gas into a liquid is directly proportional to the pressure of the gas above that liquid. In other words, if we want to "push" a gas into a liquid, we must have enough pressure upon that gas to make the "push" happen.

Every time a Window Seat Pilot opens a can or bottle of a carbonated beverage, they see Henry's Law come into play: The carbonation (gas) within the beverage (liquid) is released as soon as the pressure upon that gas is reduced. Pop the top of the bottle or the can (release the pressure), pour the carbonated beverage into a clear glass, and watch the gas (bubbles) escape from the liquid (beverage). More spectacularly, loosen the cork on a bottle of Champagne, and watch as the explosive pressure within the bottle launches the cork across the dining room. William Henry's Law.

Let us bring the two lessons together. John Dalton taught us the pressure upon oxygen (gas) is less at thirty-seven thousand feet, than it is at sea level. William Henry taught us we need sufficient pressure to get that oxygen (gas) into a liquid (our vital, life-sustaining blood).

Pair the two findings, and we have the potential for an unpleasant scenario: Not enough pressure at thirty-seven thousand feet (John Dalton) to push the oxygen gas into our liquid blood (William Henry). If oxygen cannot get into the blood, then the oxygen will not get to the eyes or to the brain. No oxygen, no vision. No oxygen, no brain. If the pilot cannot see, if the pilot's brain is out of action, we have the makings of an unpleasant scenario. Recall the Boeing 737 decompression scenario enroute from Cyprus to Athens, in which all aboard perished due to oxygen-starvation.

By pressurizing the aircraft cabin (our cabin altitude currently reads 7,200-feet while we are flying at 37,000-feet), we provide sufficient pressure within the cabin, to force the oxygen (gas) into our blood (liquid); allowing us to see, think, fly and live. We pressurize to live. We pressurize to avoid unpleasant scenarios.

Knowing "Why" we pressurize, often leads to "How do we pressurize?" We do so by tapping into compressed (high-pressure) air from our two engines, routing that compressed air through two air-conditioning packs, and releasing that air-conditioned, compressed air into the cabin.

The incoming high-pressure air is only half the story. If we were to blow continuously into a balloon, the balloon would eventually pop. So, too, with an airplane. If we were to direct high-pressure air into our aircraft, with no outflow, we would run the risk of eventually "popping." An unpleasant scenario. As the saying goes, something has to give.

How do we keep from "popping?" The answer: While our engines provide a continuous, fresh flow of compressed, high-pressure air into the cabin; our pressure-controllers (Primary, Alternate, Manual) regulate airflow leaving the cabin, by controlling the position of the cabin outflow valve. Air in. Air out. Balance. A constant stream of incoming air, and an equally constant stream of outgoing air.

200

What happened this evening? The Primary pressure-controller failed. The cabin outflow valve defaulted to the full-open position. With the escape of pressurized cabin air, through the fully-opened outflow-valve, our cabin altitude began to climb. Had we not corrected the matter, our cabin altitude would have eventually equalized with the ambient air pressure at 37,000-feet. Time of useful consciousness at 37,000-feet? Fifteen seconds.

What of the opposite scenario? What if the cabin outflow valve had failed to the fully-closed position (rather than the fully-open position)? Would our aircraft have "popped?" No, it would not have "popped." Our aircraft is equipped with an over-pressure relief valve, which will open to release excessive cabin pressure. Moreover, with the flip of two switches, Erica and I can opt to cut off the compressed, high-pressure air entering the cabin: No incoming air, no "popping."

Our ears, however, do "pop." Why do they do so? Newark Airport rests roughly at sea level: Low-altitude, high-pressure air. While on the ground, the tissues within our bodies, much like sponges in water, soaked themselves in Newark's low-altitude, high-pressure air.

Following takeoff, as we gained altitude (lower pressure), a pressure differential developed between the higher-pressure air within our bodies, and the lower-pressure outside our bodies. Given the laws of nature, the high-pressure air within our bodies sought to "escape" to the lower-pressure regions outside our bodies. Our eardrums blocked one of the escape routes, and "popped" with the rush of air attempting to escape. Our sinuses may have likewise blocked one of the escape routes, often leading to sinus pain.

During our descent into London-Heathrow, the reverse will hold true. Our body tissues will be soaked with the high-altitude, low-pressure air of our 7,200-foot cabin altitude. As we descend for our 195-foot arrival into London-Heathrow, the high-pressure air *outside* our bodies, will seek to "escape" *into* the low-pressure regions within our bodies. Our ears will pop, as our eardrums will be blocking the *inward* rush of the higher-pressure air we encounter on our descent. Our sinuses may likewise experience discomfort and pain.

To cope with ear and sinus discomfort, experienced Window Seat Pilots suggest chewing gum, yawning, or rotating the jaw. The reasoning is rather simple: The ear-tube is linked to the sinus-tube, which is linked to the nose-tube, which is linked to the mouth/throat-tube (think Ear-Nose-Throat physician). By chewing gum, yawning, or rotating the jaw, the Window Seat Pilot hopes those tubes will allow high-pressure air to escape, thereby easing the ear and sinus discomfort.

As a wrap, not all aircraft are pressurized. Military fighter, attack and reconnaissance aircraft are rarely pressurized. Flight-crews operating these aircraft utilize oxygen masks providing 100-percent oxygen, often under positive pressure, thereby compensating for both John Dalton's Law (100-percent oxygen, rather than 21-percent oxygen) and William Henry's Law (positive pressure, rather than ambient pressure).

I am often struck by the many, now long-forgotten, minds that had the curiosity, the courage, and the conviction of their beliefs, to conduct their research and allow the miracle of flight that, today, we so take for granted. Daniel Bernoulli and Lift. Gustav Pitot and Indicated Airspeed. John Dalton, William Henry and Pressurization. Orville and Wilbur Wright, a cast-iron engine, a bicycle chain, and the miracle at Kitty Hawk. We are forever in their debt, even as we may wonder which of the young Window Sea Pilots aboard any of the flights crossing the North Atlantic this evening, will one day be known to the world, for their own discoveries.

Reflection

There is a time to (respectfully) say "No Sir, No Ma'am".

The Summer of 1988. A heavy-weight aircraft, on a hot and high-altitude day (92-degrees at 5,400-feet), surrounded by mountains. The high-altitude, high-temperature, thin air; coupled with a heavy aircraft and mountainous terrain; made for a challenging scenario.

While taxiing for takeoff, the number-three engine blew oil, coating the entire right side of the aft fuselage. We returned to parking. Maintenance re-serviced the oil, conducted a brief engine-run, and signed the logbook: "Cannot Duplicate."

I refused to take the aircraft. A senior officer (non-aviator), holding a rank several grades higher than mine, ordered me to take the aircraft. I replied with a very respectful "No Sir." After much back-and-forth, maintenance conducted a second engine-run. In the midst of the second engine-run, the number-three engine once again blew oil, coating the entire right side of the aft fuselage.

Subsequent trouble-shooting revealed an engine oil filter clogged with contaminants. An oil pressure relief valve had blown. The first engine-run had been terminated prior to reaching an over-pressure sufficient to trigger the pressure relief valve.

Had we accepted the "Cannot-Duplicate" after the first maintenance engine-run, we may have lost the engine shortly after takeoff; on a high-temperature, high-altitude day (thinner air, fewer air molecules, less Lift); while heavy-weight, surrounded by high terrain. A potentially unpleasant scenario.

In life, as in flight: There is a time to (respectfully) say "No Sir, No Ma'am."

Sunrise, Clouds, Contrails

Sunrise over the North Atlantic. This morning, Erica and I are privileged to witness an ever-changing, ever-deepening menagerie of cloud formations and hues: Shadows upon sunlight, and sunlight upon shadows, billowing cumulus towers among trailing stratus wisps. Whites virgin pure, brilliantly edged, softly warmed, and shaded gray; set upon blues of deep dark, amid blues of soft warm. Autumnal oranges, rich golds, shy pinks and brilliant reds. Shifting, shading, beckoning, welcoming. A garden of colors, lights and shapes. Nature's artistic brush, forever in flight across the canvas of our sight.

It has been said, by many a parent, to many a child, "No two snowflakes are alike." So too, with clouds. No two clouds are alike. While I have enjoyed the thrill of aerobatics, formation flying, low-level routes and supersonic flight; while I will always treasure the ramp-dance; it has been my time spent among the clouds that has brought me my karma. The clouds have been my home. The clouds have been my playground.

Ever-silent in their majesty, ever-glorious in their beauty; these clouds are forever giving birth, growing, aging and dying; experiencing a cycle of life not unlike that of our own lives. Indeed, meteorologists assign thunderstorms to three life stages: Cumulus (marked by updrafts), Mature (marked by the start of rain on the surface) and Dissipating (marked by downdrafts). At 37,000-feet we are witness to the full span of their lives, up close and personal.

The first lesson in the study of weather, the preeminent truth, is that temperature shapes and drives all weather. Recall our discussion of the equatorial and polar air cycles: Rising warm air, falling cold air. Consider, too, the sea-breeze and shore-breeze phenomena. As the day's sunlight falls equally upon both sea and shore, the waters absorb heat, while the land surface reflects heat. As the land surface reflects the heat, air over the land surface warms and rises, thereby creating a low-pressure region (vacuum), which, in turn, draws in the air from over the sea, creating a sea-breeze. As night falls, the sea releases the heat which it has absorbed. As the sea releases its heat, the air over the sea warms and rises, thereby creating a low-pressure region (vacuum), which, in turn, draws in air from over the shore's surface, creating a shore-breeze.

Temperature drives weather. This truism applies to any discussion of cloud formation. Each of the clouds rushing by at over 900 feet per second, shares a humble and simple birth. Each traces their origin to a moist body of air, somewhat warmer than neighboring bodies of air. They stand out. They are different. They billow to a different drum.

As is the case with any hot-air balloon, warm air must rise. With that in mind, our somewhat warmer moist body of air begins its ascent. As our body of air ascends, it cools at a standard rate of 2-degrees per 1000-feet of altitude. As our body of air cools, it approaches saturation. Eventually, with sufficient cooling, it becomes saturated.

Beyond the saturation point, any further increase in altitude, any further decrease in temperature, will lead to condensation. A cloud will be born. Our somewhat warmer moist body of air (now a cloud) will continue its ascent until temperature-equalization is achieved with the surrounding air. No longer "somewhat warmer" than the surrounding air, the growing will stop. For some bodies of air, that temperature-equalization will lead to a relatively flat stratus cloud. For other bodies of air, the temperatures within may feed an energy dynamo that propels an ever-climbing cloud. This cloud billows, puffs and towers. Hence, the term "*towering* cumulonimbus."

Just as each of us requires a helping-hand in our early days, so too with clouds. The entire process; the ascent, the cooling, the saturation, the condensation, the cloud formation; requires a further helping-hand ingredient. That helping-hand comes in the form of microscopic particles suspended in the atmosphere; salt, dust and by-products of combustion. These particles are collectively referred to as "condensation nuclei."

To illustrate the role of condensation nuclei, imagine a warm, humid, south Florida Summer day (our moist body of air). Following a game of tennis, we remove a chilled glass of iced-tea from the fridge, step outside, and place it on the glass-topped patio table, as we reach up to adjust the umbrella for shade.

Moments later, having adjusted the umbrella to our liking, we reach for the iced-tea glass and find the surface is now coated with a film of condensation, running down the surface of the glass, leaving a puddle on the surface of the table.

Question: Where did the water on the surface of the iced-tea glass come from? Why did water spontaneously form on the surface of the glass of iced-tea, while not previously forming on the glass-topped patio table, as we played tennis?

The answer: The glass of chilled iced-tea provided both cooling and condensation nuclei amid the moist body of air. Hence, water condensed (cloud formation) upon the surface of the iced-tea glass. By contrast, while the glass-topped patio table (potential condensation nuclei) had been present amid the moist body of air, throughout our entire tennis game, it had been unable to provide the added cooling required to prompt condensation (cloud formation).

Condensation requires all three elements: Moisture, cooling, and condensation nuclei. In the context of an already moist body of air (south Florida Summer), the glass-topped table offered only one of the remaining requirements (condensation nuclei), while the *chilled* surface of the iced-tea glass offered both the remaining requirements (condensation nuclei and cooling).

To close out the discussion, that same chilled glass of iced-tea, placed on a patio table, after a game of tennis, in the dry air of Albuquerque, New Mexico, would not be coated with moisture after the umbrella adjustment. There would be no condensation. There would be no cloud formation. Would there be cooling? Yes. Would there be condensation nuclei? Yes. Moist body of air? No. Not in Albuquerque, New Mexico. All three elements are required.

So, the clouds greeting us this morning, amid our spectacular sunrise, have formed due to a temperature differential and a heat-fueled ascent. They have formed due to cooling while ascending, vapor-saturation (prompted by the cooling), and an assist provided by condensation nuclei. Once formed, they have topped-out at the point of temperature-equalization with the surrounding air; or, a point where their inner, upward energies have exhausted themselves.

Back to our flight. Erica and I are in need of a caffeine boost. I call back to the First Class galley, and ask Cherie for an additional shot of caffeine: Earl Grey for me, no cream, no sugar. Coffee for Erica, no cream, no sugar.

Would we like some leftover ice-cream sundaes, still chilled, on dry ice, with our choice of toppings? Tempting, but "No Thank You." Erica, decades younger than I, will take one for herself. No one treats her better than she treats herself. Her preference? Raspberry-chunk, caramel topping, crushed nuts, whipped cream, with a cherry on top.

As we approach our next position, at 52-North Latitude and 20-West Longitude, our ETA remains solid. Both L-NAV and V-NAV are engaged. Our three altimeters are in agreement. Upcoming segment time, distance, and compass headings look good. Our fuel is within a reasonable variance from the flight plan. We note our pitch at 2.5 degrees nose-up, our power setting at 1.59 EPR, our winds at 230-degrees and 56 knots, and our heading of 097-degrees.

We build our post-position Howgozit at 0731Z, and we place it on our Navigation-Displays. Turning to the weather, we pull up the current and forecast weather for our destination London-Heathrow (EGLL) and our alternate Manchester (EGCC). There has been minimal change at either location: Overcast sky, light rain, light winds. As an added measure, Erica pulls up the weather for the three coast-in airports of Ireland: Shannon and Cork on the west coast, Dublin on the east coast. Dublin weather is similar to London and Manchester weather, no issues. Shannon and Cork, on the other hand, are experiencing low ceilings, equally low visibility and rather strong and gusty winds. We do not want to go to Shannon or Cork.

My Earl Grey arrives, along with Erica's coffee and her properly-topped ice-cream sundae, all provided by Garrett; who, at my invitation, settles into the flight-deck jump-seat, as the jet rolls into a twenty-degree left bank, passing overhead 20-West Longitude. Next point: The Malot intersection.

I make our final HF report to Shanwick Oceanic Control. "Good morning, Shanwick, Flight 28, reports 52-North and 20-West at 0721 Zulu, FL370, estimating Malot at 0745 Zulu, Burak is next, fuel 24.9."

"Flight 28, Roger, Shanwick Oceanic copies 52-North and 20-West at 0721 Zulu, FL370, estimating Malot at 0745 Zulu, Burak is next, fuel 24.9. At Malot, contact Shannon Control on 132.855."

It is time for the sunglasses. With the morning sun low on the horizon, at our twelve o'clock, its rays reflecting off the solid deck of clouds beneath us, the flight-deck has taken on a brilliance that cries out for shade. Mindful that Garrett is without sunglasses, I adjust the flight-deck sun-shades for his comfort.

Garrett, much like Cherie, has taken a detour off his planned career-path, for one year as a flight attendant. Having earned a degree in applied mathematics (way over my head), and recalling his too-many-to-count international journeys as a child and young man, Garrett has opted to "see the world" before settling down for whatever it is that applied-mathematicians do. His father was an airline pilot. His mother was a flight attendant. The world was his oyster. By the time he graduated from college, he had flown the equivalent of thirty-two times around the Earth's circumference, roughly 800,000 miles. His passion? Fine wines and champagnes. His experience reminds me of my own two boys, now young men: They have seen the world, courtesy of the airline travel benefits.

Garrett shares two stories from his past. His father had taken him to San Francisco, and had secured a seat for him, in the First Class cabin, for the return journey. Midway through the flight, the lead flight attendant had called the flight-deck, and asked his father (the Captain), "How old is your son?" His father, knowing where the question was headed, had replied "He is old enough for a glass of champagne." After a brief pause, the flight attendant had asked: "Is he old enough for a bottle and a half of champagne?"

His second story? While enroute to Hawaii, on vacation, his father had awakened Jason from a deep sleep, simply to ask how to turn on the overhead light. His father could fly a Boeing to Beijing, but he could not turn on his overhead light. Either way, Garrett is living the life. With a smile.

The sun, now flooding our flight-deck with brilliance, is casting an equally bright light upon a half dozen contrails, above and below us, some on track, some offset by one or two miles. Garrett asks the question: Where do contrails come from?

Gazed upon, the world over, through the eyes of children and adults alike; white contrails, slicing across the backdrop of a clear blue sky, often strike at the heart of our imaginations. The origins of contrails can be found in the very word "contrails." The "trails" portion is rather straight-forward, as contrails appear as trails in the sky. As for the "con" portion: Contrails are simply con-densation-trails. Put another way, contrails are nothing more than artificially-produced clouds. Recall for a moment the three pre-requisites for cloud formation: Water vapor, temperatures sufficiently cool (so as to produce saturation and condensation), and condensation nuclei (the surface upon which condensation may occur).

There are generally two types of contrails. *Exhaust-contrails* are most frequently formed in air which is sufficiently cool, but which lacks sufficient water vapor and/or sufficient condensation nuclei. Engine exhaust provides both the added water vapor and the required condensation nuclei. All three cloud elements are therefore present: The original cool temperature and the added water vapor and condensation nuclei. A con-densation-trail is thus formed.

By contrast, *aerodynamic-contrails* generally develop in air possessing both sufficient water vapor, and sufficient condensation nuclei, but which is not yet sufficiently cool. However, the mere passage of an aircraft's wing through the air may trigger the additional cooling necessary for condensation to occur.

How does the passage of an aircraft's wing, trigger the cooling necessary for condensation? We turn to two laws of nature. First: Lift results from a pressure reduction along the upper surface of the wing. Second: As per the $PV = nRT$ equation, whenever we decrease pressure (P) on a substance, we decrease temperature (T).

Combine the two laws: Lift stems from a decrease in pressure, that decrease in pressure leads to a drop in temperature, that drop in temperature cools the surrounding air, in which water vapor and condensation nuclei are already present. The three required elements are now present (the original water vapor, the original condensation nuclei and the now-added cooling). A con-densation-trail is thus formed.

A thousand feet above, paralleling our flight-path, we note the spiraling vortices trailing from the wingtips of an aircraft five miles ahead, at our eleven o'clock: A clockwise rotation off the left wingtip and a counter-clockwise rotation off the right wingtip. With near-perfect clarity, we observe the two vortices, as they merge in the wake of the generating aircraft, creating "wake-turbulence."

Descending to roughly 1000-feet below, and up to twenty-five miles behind the generating aircraft, wake-turbulence has sufficient energy to flip an aircraft. The most powerful wake-turbulence is generated by heavy, slow aircraft, with high angle-of-attack; most particularly in the takeoff and landing phases of flight; often leaving relatively little altitude in which trailing aircraft may successfully recover from a wake-turbulence encounter.

On 30 May 1972, while maneuvering to land at Fort Worth, Texas, a McDonnell Douglas DC-9 encountered wake-turbulence while following a heavier McDonnell Douglas DC-10. Tragic consequence followed.

As a corrective action following that accident, heavy and super-heavy aircraft are now required to include, in every radio transmission with approach and departure controllers, the applicable suffix following their call-sign: Flight 28-Heavy or Flight 28-Super. Air traffic controllers utilize the applicable suffix to customize in-trail separation standards: A Heavy following a Heavy might require a 4-mile separation, while a Small following a Heavy might require a 6-mile separation.

Wake-turbulence on departures and arrivals remains a threat, as a handful of accidents following the Fort Worth accident have made clear. However, in each of the wake-turbulence accidents following the Fort Worth accident, the required in-trail separation had not been maintained. Do the right thing. Every time. As an added element of caution, while approaching an airport for landing, flight-crews will often remain slightly above the flight-path flown by a preceding Heavy or Super aircraft, touching down just beyond the Heavy or Super aircraft's touch-down point, thereby avoiding a wake-turbulence encounter. Similarly, when departing an airport, flight-crews will often attempt to rotate prior to a preceding Heavy or Super rotation point, thereby remaining above that aircraft's flight path; again, avoiding a wake-turbulence encounter.

In our earlier discussion of the Strategic Lateral Offset Program (SLOP), we noted the requirement for aircraft to randomly offset, right of course, by one or two nautical miles; thereby mitigating the "too close" scenario of increased GPS accuracy. The avoidance of wake-turbulence is an additional SLOP inducement. Wake-turbulence generally settles 1000-feet below the generating aircraft. With a standard 1000-foot altitude separation while over the North Atlantic, a SLOP offset helps to minimize the likelihood, or severity, of a wake-turbulence encounter.

Reflection

Listen to your crew. The life you save may be your own.

On 13 January 1982, a Boeing 737 departed Reagan National Airport in the midst of a snowstorm. Prior to the start of their takeoff roll, the flight-crew failed to activate their engine anti-icing systems (a checklist item). Several times, while on their takeoff roll, the First Officer expressed his belief that the engines were not properly accelerating, that the takeoff thrust was insufficient. The Captain dismissed the concerns. The First Officer was, indeed, correct. The aircraft was unflyable. An unpleasant, tragic scenario ensued. Had they rejected the takeoff, they, and many of their Window Seat Pilots, would be alive today. Listen to your crew.

On 19 February 1989, a Boeing 747 approached Kuala Lampur, in the dark of night. A last-minute change to the planned approach, placed the First Officer (pilot flying) in a very uncomfortable position. He made very clear his desire to discontinue the assigned non-precision approach (for which he was wholly unprepared, and for which no arrival briefing had been conducted), and instead fly the far easier precision (ILS) approach to a different runway. He stated, quite clearly, "I do not even have the [expletive] approach chart in front of me." The Captain disregarded the First Officer's concerns. The Minimum Descent Altitude for their approach was 2400-feet, a figure clearly displayed on the approach chart. Without the approach chart for reference, the First Officer descended to 400 feet, 2000-feet below the Minimum Descent Altitude. The perfectly good aircraft flew into a mountain, miles short of the runway. Had they switched to the First Officer's suggested ILS approach, they would have lived to fly another day. Listen to your crew.

On 6 August 1997, on a dark and stormy night, a Boeing 747 approached Guam. The ILS (Instrument Landing System) was out of service. The Captain, nonetheless, believed he had intercepted the ILS glide-slope. With that in mind, he began his descent. His Second Officer (Flight Engineer) protested, several times, that the ILS glide-slope was, indeed, out of service. The perfectly good aircraft flew into a mountain, miles short of the runway. Had they executed a missed approach, they, and their Window Seat Pilots, would be alive today. Listen to your crew.

On 4 February 2015, an ATR departed Taipei, Taiwan. Immediately after lift-off, the right engine lost power. The Captain immediately announced his (erroneous) intention to shut-down the operating left engine. His First Officer replied: "Wait, let us confirm." The Captain nonetheless shut down the sole operating (left) engine (without the First Officer's confirmation). The aircraft stopped flying. An unpleasant, tragic scenario ensued. Had the Captain respected his First Officer's input, they, and many of their Window Seat Pilots, would be alive today. Listen to your crew.

On 15 September 2015, a Boeing 777 departed Miami, with four pilots on the flight-deck. The flight-crew had briefed, and planned for, a departure utilizing the full length of the assigned runway. While taxiing for takeoff, the Captain made a spur of the moment, unilateral decision to depart from an intersection located 4500-feet down the runway length. The "relief crew" (Captain and First Officer), present on the flight-deck, raised concerns. The flying Captain dismissed those concerns. Given their takeoff weight (fully-fuel-loaded for a thirteen-hour flight) and given the much shorter length of available runway, the *aircraft did not become airborne until they were well beyond the departure end of the runway, taking out the runway approach lighting, located 60 meters beyond the departure end of the runway. Listen to your crew.*

In life, as in flight: Listen to your crew.

The Approach

Most airports offer a number of approach options. The simplest option is the Visual Approach. In this scenario, the approach controller simply asks the pilot if she has the runway in sight. The pilot replies "runway in sight." The controller follows up with "cleared visual approach to runway two-seven-right." The pilot then simply maneuvers her aircraft to the runway for landing.

The Visual Approach comes with a handful of caveats. First, the pilot must keep other aircraft in sight (see and avoid). Second, the pilot the pilot must be aware of airspace restrictions. Third, the pilot must maintain in-trail separation and avoid wake turbulence.

While flying any other type approach, the air traffic controller retains responsibility for all three: Traffic separation, airspace restrictions, and wake turbulence. Why, then, would a pilot choose to fly a Visual Approach, having to assume those three responsibilities? What is the upside to the Visual Approach? Answer: Increased volume, increased through-put and expedited arrivals.

Are there potential downsides to a Visual Approach, beyond assuming responsibility for traffic, wake turbulence, and airspace restrictions? Absolutely. Those potential downsides include a handful of far more embarrassing, and potentially far more serious, issues: Landing at the wrong airport, landing on the wrong runway, and landing on the parallel taxiway (instead of the runway).

All of the above have happened, with men and women I have known and respected, at the controls. Such instances serve as a humbling reminder of the ever-present potential for human error.

How do we mitigate the chance for such errors while conducting a Visual Approach? First, following the air traffic control "Do you have the runway in sight?" query, we do not call the field and/or the runway in sight, until all pilots on the flight-deck are absolutely certain they have visual contact with the correct airport, and the correct runway. Second, we always attempt to augment the Visual Approach with a coinciding instrument-approach (for example, an ILS approach), thereby ensuring course-guidance to supplement the visual guidance.

Recently, while flying a night, Visual Approach into San Francisco, having been cleared to land on Runway 28-Right; an aircraft mistakenly aligned itself with the parallel taxiway, on which four fully-loaded aircraft had been lined up, awaiting take-off clearance. The errant, arriving aircraft initiated a missed-approach approximately eighty-five feet above the ground, mere seconds prior to touch-down, descending to within fourteen feet (vertically) of the four fully-loaded aircraft on the taxiway; narrowly averting the greatest disaster in aviation history, involving five aircraft and well over a thousand passengers. The flight-crew on the errant aircraft had opted *not* to augment their Visual Approach with the *available* ILS instrument-approach guidance to Runway 28-Right.

Not every approach can be a Visual Approach. Visual Approaches require visual conditions, generally defined as a ceiling of at least 1000-feet above the surface, and visibility of at least 3-miles. When those visual conditions are not present, as was the case in Newark, earlier this evening; and as will likely be the case in London-Heathrow; we must turn to instrument approaches.

There are generally two types of instrument approaches: Precision-approaches and non-precision approaches.

I have many fond memories of flying non-precision approaches in the pre-INS, pre-GPS era; at night, after long duty-days, in mountainous terrain, with spotty radar coverage, and marginal support from air traffic control. Those approaches (NDB approaches and VOR approaches) are largely just that: Fond memories. I cannot recall the last time I flew an NDB approach. As for VOR approaches, I have flown perhaps a half dozen, over the last half dozen years.

While flying those non-precision approaches; at night, in the weather, surrounded by terrain; without the benefit of today's flight-deck displays, auto-flight systems, inertial or satellite guidance; pilots had to be at the top of their game and the crew coordination had to be hitting on all cylinders, for the margin for error was often slim.

As for precision approaches, two forms have been around for quite some time. The Instrument Landing System (ILS) approach we anticipate using this morning, underwent initial development in 1929, and was first operated in Berlin, Germany in 1932. The Precision Approach Radar (PAR) approach was developed a few years later, during World War Two. These two approaches have recently been joined by the GPS family of approaches.

The mechanics of a PAR approach are rather straightforward. A radar controller faces a split-screen radar display. The upper display depicts a three-degree glide-path, extending from fifty feet over the runway threshold (standard threshold crossing height) to ten miles out from the runway threshold. The lower display depicts a runway centerline extending a similar ten miles out from the runway threshold. Both displays include the pilot's radar-return.

The controller's role is to interpret the two radar displays (centerline and glide-path); interpret the pilot, the aircraft and the winds; and provide proper guidance commands; placing the pilot's radar-return on her glide-path and centerline depictions. She does so by "talking the pilot down" the glide-path and along the extended runway centerline, with an every-five-seconds radio-update in both axes: "On glide-path, well-below glide-path, slightly-above glide-path" and "On course, well-right of course, slightly-left of course."

The pilot's role is to interpret the slightly-above and well-left commentary; to maintain a steady roll-rate into turns and a steady roll-rate out of turns; to finesse the rate of throttle-up and the rate of throttle-back for glide-path correction; and to eventually harmonize with the controller; all while maintaining a sharp eye on airspeed and altitude; as she descends ever-closer to the unforgiving, and unseen terrain.

The challenge, and the beauty, of the PAR merge-of-effort, rests in the ability of the two players (controller and pilot) to discern the subtleties unique to each controller, each pilot, each aircraft, and each approach, all in the span of a three-minute, ten-mile approach. Unlike sports teams, dance troupes, or orchestras; the two have likely never trained, danced, or performed together; much less traveled, dined, or shared a room together: Yet, they make it happen.

While correcting to course, while rolling into a standard-rate turn; some pilots may favor closer to thirty degrees of bank, while others may favor closer to twenty degrees of bank; some may execute with a rapid roll-rate, while others may execute with a more relaxed roll-rate. When above or below glide-path, one pilot may correct more rapidly, while the next pilot may correct less rapidly. Lighter and more agile aircraft may be quicker to correct to course and glide-path, while heavier and less agile aircraft may require a bit more time per correction.

Crosswinds have a considerable impact on the controller's course guidance commands, while headwinds and tailwinds have a similar impact on the pilot's glide-path adherence. Crosswinds can lead to an under-correction or an over-correction to centerline. Tailwinds will require more than the standard 700-foot per minute rate of descent, while headwinds will require less than the standard 700-foot per minute rate of descent. Again, all of the above subtleties must be recognized, accounted for, and mastered over the span of a three-minute approach; with all factors in constant flux; as no headwind, tailwind, or crosswind, remains an unwavering constant.

When the pilot and controller reach a state of harmony, with the pilot descending through the weather, blindly approaching the terrain; the sweetest words in the pilot's headset are "on course, on glide-path, on course, on glide-path" wrapping up with "at decision height, take over visually."

Breaking out with a 200-foot ceiling, and a half-mile visibility, with the runway lights at twelve o'clock, is a very sweet and satisfying end-game, after an in-the-soup PAR approach, with nothing but a controller's voice guiding you down.

The Instrument Landing System (ILS) operates much like the Precision Approach Radar. Except there is no radar screen, no controller and no dialogue. Smile.

Two ground-based transmitters, and two aircraft-mounted receivers, play the role of the PAR controller and the PAR pilot. One transmitter provides glide-slope guidance, while the second transmitter provides centerline guidance. The two aircraft-mounted receivers provide the pilot with a visual display of aircraft position relative to centerline (left, right, centered) and glide-slope (above, below, centered). The pilot's job is simple: Climb or descend to glide-slope, bank left or right to centerline.

As was the case with the PAR approach; crosswinds, headwinds and tailwinds complicate an otherwise simple exercise, for each wind element requires a particular correction. Moreover, what may be wind-corrected now, may not be wind-corrected thirty-seconds from now, as the winds are rarely, if ever, stable.

The ILS poses one additional challenge. ILS signal sensitivity increases markedly as the aircraft approaches the runway. A displacement from centerline or glide-slope, may require "this much" correction, ten miles from the runway. However, the same correction, one mile from the runway, would be wildly inappropriate, causing the aircraft to cross through the centerline or the glide-slope. Due to the increased ILS signal sensitivity as we approach the runway, any centerline or glide-slope corrections must become increasingly narrow, as in "small corrections." A failure to temper the corrections as we approach the runway, may place us out of position to make a safe landing, thereby requiring a missed-approach. The "small correction" imperative is the greatest challenge in learning to fly an ILS approach.

ILS approaches have become increasingly accurate with the passage of time. A Category-One ILS system, may bring an aircraft down to a surface visibility of 1800 feet, and a decision altitude of 200-feet above the surface. A Category-Two ILS system, may bring an aircraft down to a surface visibility of 1000 feet, and a decision height of 100-feet above the surface. A Category-Three ILS system may bring an aircraft down to a surface visibility of 300 feet, and a decision height of 50-feet above the surface.

The Category-Three, Land-Three approach allows an aircraft to land without any visual reference. Utilizing this option, our jet, carrying one hundred and eighty-four Window Seat Pilots and flight-crew members, may touchdown without ever seeing the ground.

The beauty of the Category-Three, Land-Three approach, is the ability to get the Window Seat Pilots to their destinations; when other, not-so-well-equipped (and trained) flight-crews must divert to their alternate. The Window Seat Pilots aboard those jets, will miss their connections, miss their sales meetings and miss their dinners with family.

What distinguishes Category-One, Category-Two, Category-Three ILS systems? The accuracy of the ground-based transmitters (some airfields make the investment, others do not), the accuracy of the aircraft-mounted receivers and the redundancy of auto-flight systems (some airlines make the investment, others do not), and the level of flight-crew training (some airlines make the investment, others do not). This evening, we are flying a "Category-Three, Land-Three" aircraft. Every nine months, as part of our simulator training, we routinely fly "Category-Three, Land-Three" approaches.

Comparing the PAR and ILS approaches, the ILS approach provides a direct, intuitive, visual depiction of aircraft position relative to glide-slope and course centerline. Armed with that direct, intuitive, visual depiction, the pilot can place the aircraft where it needs to be. The PAR, on the other hand, places fate in the hands of another person; while denying the pilot any direct, intuitive, visual depiction of aircraft position, with respect to glide-path and course centerline; while descending blind (at night, or in the weather), toward unforgiving terrain. Given the choice, this pilot will take the ILS over the PAR.

With just under ninety minutes of flight-time remaining, Erica and I turn our attention to our London-Heathrow arrival. We are expecting the Ockham-Two-Foxtrot (OCK-2F) Standard Terminal Arrival Route (STAR), with a transition to the Instrument Landing System (ILS) Approach to Runway 27-Right. We flip through our eighteen Heathrow STAR charts, until we find the OCK-2F.

With the charts in hand, we begin our review. Mindful that STAR headings, altitudes and courses are often constructed to ensure terrain avoidance and/or traffic-deconfliction; mindful that those headings, altitudes and courses may occasionally be modified; Erica and I confirm our charts are current, as of the most recent issue-date, ten days ago.

Turning to the Flight Management Computer (FMC), we confirm all STAR waypoints, courses and headings (lateral plane); and all STAR altitude and airspeed restrictions (vertical plane); are properly programmed into the FMC Legs-Page. All good.

We will begin the OCK-2F arrival by passing overhead the BEDEK waypoint at 14,000-feet, proceeding outbound on the 106-degree course; crossing our next waypoint, NIGIT, 15 miles later. We will depart NIGIT on a 093-degree course, slowing to 250-knots when 15 miles out of NIGIT. Twelve miles later, we will cross OCK at 7000-feet and 220-knots. From OCK we will descend to 6000-feet on a 077-degree course, slowing to 180-knots. We will level at at 6000-feet, sixteen miles out of OCK.

One possible variation: Upon reaching OCK, if we have not received further clearance, we will make a right turn over OCK, and enter the holding pattern (right-hand turns, one-minute legs, on the 329-degree course inbound to OCK). We will remain in the holding pattern until we receive further clearance.

Recalling our Newark Standard Instrument Departure (SID) discussion, the OCK-2F (STAR) allows us to load the arrival routing into our FMC, review all points and restrictions, and plan for speed reductions, descent points, and flap-slat extensions. The STAR allows us to do so, well before we begin our descent; thereby allowing us to focus (while in the descent) on flight-path adherence and aircraft performance, rather than on STAR planning and FMC programming.

Moreover, as was the case with the Newark SID, the London-Heathrow STAR will allow us to dispense with a multitude of air traffic control instructions, and the required radio read-backs, for each altitude change (14,000-feet, 7000-feet, 6000-feet), each speed restriction (250-knots, 220-knots, 180-knots), and each course change (106-degrees, 093-degrees, 329-degrees, 077-degrees). The radio-frequency congestion that would result, if each air traffic control instruction required a radio transmission, and a required radio read-back, at the "world's busiest two-runway airport," would be untenable.

With the STAR review complete, we turn our attention to the ILS (Instrument Landing System) Approach for Runway 27-Right. As was the case with the STAR review, with charts in hand, we note our chart issue dates, roughly ten days ago. We are current.

The STAR-chart and the approach-chart are two of the thousands of pages we are required to carry, accounting for roughly thirty of the forty pounds packed into our flight-bags. They are updated every two weeks, entailing hours of tedious, mind-numbing work: Rip the old one out, slip the new one in. We are all eagerly awaiting the advent of the electronic-device and the digital download.

Each approach chart is a roughly five-by-seven inch sheet of paper, providing the pilots with both a lateral (birds-eye) depiction and a vertical (profile) depiction, for a particular approach, to a particular runway, at a particular airport.

Each approach chart provides radio frequencies for the ATIS (Automatic Terminal Information Service), radar approach control, the control tower, and the ground control. The Minimum Safe Altitude (MSA) is likewise depicted. The MSA ensures 1000-foot clearance above the highest terrain or obstacle within 25 miles of the London VOR-DME, providing a quick reference altitude for terrain/obstruction avoidance for any approach or missed approach. London's 2200-foot MSA is a mandatory briefing item.

The lateral (birds-eye) view, displays the position of the two parallel runways, navigation aids, courses, headings, distances, terrain, obstacles, approach paths and missed-approach paths. The vertical (profile) view displays minimum, maximum and mandatory altitudes; minimum and maximum airspeeds; and, on occasion, a required angle-of-bank. Why airspeed restrictions? Why angle-of-bank restrictions? Two reasons. First, turn radius is a function of airspeed and bank-angle. When terrain is a factor, adherence to depicted mandatory airspeeds and bank-angles, will ensure proper turn radius, thereby helping to ensure terrain clearance. Second, traffic separation: If all aircraft are flying in accordance with the depicted airspeed-restrictions, traffic separation is a far more manageable challenge for the air traffic controller, thereby enhancing flight safety.

Every instrument approach has but one objective: Bring the aircraft and the flight-crew to a decision point, referred to as "minimums" and labeled as either a Minimum-Descent-Altitude, a Decision-Altitude, or a Decision-Height. Why is every decision point defined by altitude or height? While in the descent, in close proximity to the terrain, while lacking visual contact with the terrain; altitude and height are synonymous with life.

Upon reaching minimums, the decision is to either continue the approach and descend below minimums; or, execute a missed-approach. A decision to continue the approach requires the aircraft to be in a position to (1) make a safe landing, (2) within the touchdown zone, and (3) the crew has sufficient visual reference with the runway environment. Descending below minimums without satisfying all three of the above conditions is prohibited, for it can place the aircraft, and all aboard, in extreme jeopardy. Indeed, as has been the case with much of our discussion, the industry literature is rife with instances in which flight-crews have descended below minimums, without sufficient visual reference. Unpleasant outcomes.

On 14 August 2013, an Airbus A-300 approached Birmingham, Alabama in the pre-dawn hours, while in the weather, with limited visibility. Despite the clear FAA prohibition against doing so, taught to every entry-level student pilot, the flight-crew descended below the published Minimum Descent Altitude, while in the weather, with no visual reference of the runway environment. An unpleasant, tragic scenario ensued.

There is one exception to the above-described decision rule. In a "Category-Three-Land-Three" ILS approach, we are trusting proper operation of the auto-flight systems to place us safely on the runway, with no requirement for the flight-crew to see the runway. The decision, upon arrival at minimums, is based on the answer to the question: Are all auto-flight systems good? If yes, we continue the approach. If not, we execute a missed-approach.

One further comment regarding the decision: The decision to descend below minimums, is not a commitment to land. Rather, it is merely a decision to continue the approach. The flight-crew is not committed to land until selection of reverse-thrust following touchdown. At any point prior to the selection of reverse-thrust, to include following touchdown, the flight-crew may execute a missed-approach.

Back to our charts. There is much to review. As noted earlier, the OCK-2F STAR will bring us to a point 16 miles along the 077-degree course, level at 6000-feet, at an airspeed of 180-knots.

From that point, we will transition from the STAR to the ILS approach, rolling into a left turn, to a heading of 360-degrees, while descending to 3500-feet. Upon reaching 3500-feet, we will roll into a second left turn, to a heading of 300-degrees, placing us on a 30-degree intercept to the final approach course of 270-degrees. Following our intercept of the final approach course, we will slow to 160 knots.

Once established on the glide-slope, we will descend to our Decision Altitude of 278-feet (roughly 200-feet above the 78-

foot runway elevation). Four miles from the runway, we will slow to our target airspeed. Upon reaching the Decision Altitude, we will decide to either descend below minimums or execute the published missed-approach.

Each approach has a corresponding missed-approach. This morning, in the event of a missed-approach, we will climb straight ahead to 1580-feet. We will then roll into a climbing right turn to 3000-feet, while tracking outbound on the 318-degree course. Missed approaches provide guidance to a safe altitude, ensuring terrain and obstacle clearance, as well as deconfliction with arriving and departing aircraft.

An airport may have additional, engine-out missed-approach procedures, for those occasions in which a missed-approach is required with an inoperative engine. London-Heathrow has no engine-out missed-approach procedures. Both missed-approach procedures (all-engine and engine-out) must be reviewed, and briefed, prior to any approach.

Lastly, the approach chart provides an airfield diagram, depicting Heathrow's two parallel runways, taxiways, ramps and gate positions. Mindful of our earlier discussion regarding ground collisions, we take a moment to review our anticipated taxi route, from runway to arrival gate: We will exit the runway to the left, taxi east on taxiway Alpha or Bravo, hang a right turn on taxiway Kilo, and pop into gate 231.

Back to our flight: "Good morning, Shannon Control, Flight 28, is approaching Malot, Flight Level Three-Seven-Zero."

"Roger, Flight 28, Squawk 6108. Proceed direct Burak intersection."

Once again, we are heads-down over the Flight Management Computer (FMC): We place Burak at the top of the FMC Legs-Page, we note a dashed white line direct to Burak. I *verbalize* and *verify*: "Does this look good to you?" With Erica's concurrence, I hit the Execute key. We both *monitor* as the dashed white line morphs to solid magenta, and as the aircraft rolls into a shallow left turn for Burak. *Verbalize, verify, monitor.*

We set 6108 in our radar transponder. Moments later, we hear the comforting, "Flight 28, you are radar contact."

We are inbound to Burak. It is time to wrap up the London-Heathrow preparations. We go heads-down over the Flight Management Computer (FMC), and submit a datalink request for the forecast descent winds. Turning to the FMC Descent-Page, and with Erica's concurrence, I enter a descent speed of .80 Mach, with a transition to 280 knots. Utilizing the forecasted winds, the FMC will work the geometry of (1) "We are at 37,000-feet, and .80 Mach; (2) we want to go to 2500-feet, and arrive there at 160-knots; (3) we want to do so while descending at .80 Mach and 280 knots." Having worked the geometry, the FMC will calculate a Top-Of-Descent point. At that point, we will begin our...

Time To Earn The Pay Check

For the second time this evening, the aural Caution-Alert chime, and the flashing Caution-Alert light mounted on the instrument panel at our twelve o'clock, interrupt our flight.

Maintain aircraft control, analyze the situation, take proper corrective action. The first words for any inflight emergency: "You have the aircraft. I have the checklist." Erica will fly. I will work the checklist.

First step: Maintain aircraft control. We confirm we are stable, in straight and level flight, with auto-flight systems engaged. I reach out, and silence the mind-numbing Caution-Alert chime. *Second step: Analyze the situation.* Our EICAS (Engine Instrument and Crew Alert System) is displaying the amber "Cargo Fire-Fwd" message.

Anticipating the adrenaline rush of emergency situations, wanting to have a clear mind in the midst of that adrenaline rush, many pilots have given prior thought to their decision-matrices, to include the question: When to divert, when not to divert? A Cargo-Fire (any on-board fire, for that matter) is one of my previously-identified, divert-now scenarios. Several real-world episodes come to mind, to include the earlier-discussed ValuJet-Everglades and UPS-Dubai.

With that in mind, the "Cargo Fire-Fwd" alert calls for an immediate divert. We will run the applicable checklists, while diverting, and while descending. We cannot evacuate an aircraft at thirty-seven thousand feet, nor can we evacuate an aircraft at one thousand feet. We must be on the ground or on the water, to evacuate a jet. Hence, an immediate descent is key. I turn to

Erica, and advise her of my preference to execute an immediate descent and divert. I seek her concurrence. She concurs. Dublin is our target. She is in full agreement. The leadership role of setting the tone serves a worthy purpose, when all is going well. The task becomes ever more critical under emergency circumstances. When things begin to fall apart, people often look to the parent, the coach, the manager, the sergeant, the lieutenant. In this case, they will look to the Captain.

The words of the Captain who successfully guided the earlier discussed crippled DC-10, to Sioux City, following a total hydraulic failure, resonate: *"You must maintain your composure in the airplane, or you will die. You learn that from your first day of flight training."* Composure. Set the tone. Here. Now.

Erica has the jet. She will be responsible for flying, while I run the applicable checklist, work the emergency, and deal with the big-picture scenario. I reach out and select Code-7700 on our transponder. That transponder-code will inform/alert air traffic control that we are now an Emergency-Aircraft. We are now a flashing red read-out on our air traffic controller's radar screen. We are now an alarm bell in the Shannon Air Traffic Control Center.

Next up: "Shannon Control, Flight 28, we are declaring an emergency, Cargo-Fire warning, one hundred and eighty-four souls on board, 20,400 pounds, three hours and thirty minutes of fuel remaining. We are requesting immediate vectors to, and an immediate descent for, a Dublin divert. Please provide the latest weather observations, and approach status for Dublin, Shannon, and Cork."

Shannon replies with "Roger Flight 28, Shannon Control copies emergency aircraft, cleared present position direct to Dublin airport, cleared immediate cruise-descent to 5000-feet, standby for weather and approach status. Do you require any further assistance?"

"Negative further assistance. Proceeding direct Dublin. Leaving flight level three-seven-zero for 5000-feet. Say Dublin altimeter setting and transition level. Standing by for weather and approach status." Shannon replies: "Dublin altimeter setting 1007 hectopascals, transition level seven-zero."

We have placed Dublin at the top of the FMC Legs-Page, *verified* the dashed white line on the Nav-Display, and *verbalized* agreement. We have hit the Execute button, *verified* the solid magenta line on the Nav Display, and *monitored* the change of aircraft heading. We have placed 5000-feet in the Altitude Select Window, *verbalized* and *verified* the setting, punched the Flight Level Change switch, and *monitored* the power reduction and the start of our descent. *Verbalize, verify, monitor.* We are on our way to Dublin. We are descending. We are expediting. We have increased our descent speed to .82 Mach, transitioning to 330 knots. We will dive and drive.

Maintain aircraft control. Done. *Analyze the situation.* Done. *Take proper corrective action.* I reach for the checklist. Step-by-step, I work my way through the Cargo Fire–Fwd Emergency Procedure.

Step One: "Cargo Fire Arm Switch (FWD or AFT), Confirm and Push."

With Erica's confirmation, I push the "FWD Cargo Fire Arm" Switch.

Step Two: "Cargo Fire Bottle 1 Discharge Switch, Push And Hold (For One Second)."

With Erica's confirmation, I push and hold the "Bottle 1 Discharge" Switch.

Step Three: "Pack Control Selector (Either), OFF."

With Erica's confirmation, I reach up and select the "Forward Pack Control" to OFF.

Step Four: "Land as soon as practicable."

We have fired the first of two fire-extinguishing bottles into the forward cargo hold. We will fire the second/final bottle while on final approach to Dublin. Next step, I reach for the interphone handset, and hit the Crew-Alert button. Within moments, I have all flight attendants on the phone. I advise Cherie, along with her cabin team: We have indications of a forward cargo fire. We will not be landing in London-Heathrow. We are diverting to Dublin. I will have further information shortly. Please do not conduct a cabin breakfast service, or alert the passengers at this time. I will make a PA shortly. Please wake Fran from his crew-rest break, and send him to the flight-deck. If we have an additional pilot on board, please ask him, or her, to report to the flight-deck. Please advise me if you see or smell any smoke or fumes in the cabin.

Next, a quick datalink message to Dispatch: "Forward Cargo Fire warning. Diverting to Dublin. Have requested latest weather and approach status from ATC. Do you have anything for us?".

We are joined by Fran, and Jason, a Boeing 787 pilot on vacation with his family. After bringing them up to speed, I ask Fran to assist Erica with the jet and the radio, I ask Jason to assist me with the big-picture duties.

Both Shannon Control and Dispatch have provided us with the latest weather and approach status information for our three requested airports. Dublin looks good, with a broken cloud deck

1800-feet above the surface, visibility at eight miles, light rain, light winds, landing on Runway-28, all approaches are operational. Shannon does not look good, with an overcast deck 600-feet above the surface, visibility less than a mile, moderate rain, winds out of the southwest at 15-20 knots, landing on Runway-24. Cork weather looks much like Shannon, with an overcast deck 400-feet above the surface, visibility of a half mile, moderate rain, southwest winds at 20 knots, landing on Runway-35. Our initial divert choice looks solid. With the concurrence of the flight-deck team, Dublin remains a "Go."

Recalling the hazardous materials in our forward cargo compartment, now the subject of a fire warning, I send a quick note to Dispatch, seeking further information on the nature of the hazardous materials.

We are just a bit under 200 miles from Dublin. Accounting for approach vectors, we should be on the ground within twenty-five minutes. While Erica and Fran build the Dublin ILS approach to Runway-28 in our Flight Management Computer (FMC), I turn my attention to the T-E-S-T briefing. I once again reach for the Interphone handset, and hit Crew-Alert. Cherie and her team check-in. I give them the brief.

T-Type of Emergency: We have an indication of a cargo-fire in the forward cargo compartment.

E-Evacuation: May be necessary, depending upon the visual report from the Dublin Crash-Fire-Rescue team when we come to a stop on the runway. If an Evacuation is necessary, please use the left exits, as all cargo compartment doors open on the right side of the aircraft, and all fire-fighting vehicles will likely be on the right side. We do not want passengers evacuating into a fire-fighting situation. If we must evacuate, I will issue the standard evacuation commands. Please assemble all passengers to the left side of the aircraft, off the tarmac, on the grass. We do not want a successful evacuation to be followed with death on the concrete, due to an impact with responding emergency vehicles. Yes, it has happened.

S-Special Instructions: Please review your evacuation drills, note the location of bull-horns, and make sure the PA system works from all flight attendant positions.

T-Time Remaining: We should be on the ground within twenty-five minutes.

There is much to do in the remaining twenty-five minutes. I take the pulse of the flight-deck. Have we covered all the bases? Have we maintained aircraft control? Have we properly analyzed the situation? Have we taken proper corrective action? Have we missed anything? We have declared an Emergency. We are squawking the proper transponder code. We have begun our divert to Dublin. We are direct. We are descending. We are at max speed. We are expediting. We have coordinated with Dispatch and Shannon. We have accomplished the applicable emergency checklist. We have briefed the cabin crew. Inside, outside, backside. We have covered them all.

Remaining items: Build and brief the Dublin ILS approach. Brief the passengers. Determine the nature of our Hazardous Materials. Fire the remaining fire-extinguishing bottle. Put it on the ground. Hit Dublin Duty-Free. Call it a day. Buy the first round.

First up, the Dublin ILS approach. As an emergency aircraft, we will not be flying a Standard Terminal Arrival Route (STAR). Instead, as a time-saver, we will receive expedited vectors to intercept an abbreviated final approach course. Erica has tuned the Dublin ILS receiver, for Runway-28, frequency 111.35. She has set the ILS final approach course of 279-degrees. We have set the 402-foot Decision-Altitude on our altimeters. We have noted the high terrain to the south of the airport.

We have reviewed the published missed-approach procedure. However, as an emergency aircraft, with an eye toward simplicity, we will request, and we will likely be granted, a straight-ahead missed-approach procedure. That said, a missed approach is not something we want to do. We do not want to be airborne (unable to evacuate) any longer than necessary. We must nail the ILS approach. The first time.

We have noted our anticipated landing weight. Based on that anticipated weight, we have calculated our applicable approach speeds. We have entered those speeds on our airspeed indicators and within our Flight Management Computer (FMC). We have selected the maximum setting for our auto-brakes. Our fuel is balanced, and more than adequate. Erica will fly the approach, and make the landing. We will come to a stop on the runway, and allow the Dublin Crash-Fire-Rescue team to conduct a visual assessment. Based on their assessment, we will either evacuate, or we will taxi as directed by Dublin Ground Control.

With everything well in hand on the flight-deck, with Cherie's cabin team in the loop, it is time for the passenger announcement. I reach for the interphone handset, just as the printer begins to hum, and just as the Master-Caution aural alert and warning light annunciate once again. I replace the handset, and I silence the aural alert. Jason rips the message off the printer, and I note the latest EICAS message:

CARGO DETECT FWD (2)

Once again: *Maintain aircraft control, analyze the situation, take proper corrective action.* Erica and Fran have the jet under control. With Jason looking over my shoulder, I flip to the CARGO DETECT FWD (2) checklist. There are no action items. The checklist reads: "*Both detectors have failed and no fire detection remains for the forward compartment.*"

Referring to the printout, Jason advises me: The hazardous materials are a shipment of two dozen oxygen-generation canisters. There is not much need for discussion. We have a fire indication in the forward cargo compartment. With the loss of both cargo-fire detectors in that compartment, we have lost all ability to monitor that compartment. Hence, we do not know if the fire is still burning. More alarming: We have two dozen oxygen-generation canisters within that compartment. If a fire is present, the oxygen-generation canisters may simply feed the fire.

Four professionals, with roughly one hundred years of aviation experience, agree. We need to put the jet on the ground. Now. No delay. With that in mind, we shift our aim-point. Dublin is too distant, requiring too much time. Shannon is now our target. In the interest of time, despite the southwesterly winds, despite the Runway-24 operation, we want a straight-in, opposite-direction GPS-approach, to Runway-06.

"Shannon Center, Flight 28, change of plans. We require immediate vectors and immediate descent for the GPS-approach, opposite-direction, Runway-06, Shannon airport."

"Flight 28, cleared present position, direct Shannon airport, expect vectors for the ILS-approach to Runway-24. Descend to, and maintain, 3000-feet, altimeter setting 1016 Hectopascals."

"Negative, negative, negative. Flight 28 is exercising Captain's Emergency Authority. We are proceeding direct to Shannon airport, descending to 3000-feet, altimeter setting 1016 Hectopascals, for an opposite direction GPS-approach to Runway-06."

Regarding Captain's Emergency Authority, from the Federal Air Regulations: *"Each pilot in command has full control and authority in the operation of the aircraft ..."* That regulatory guidance wraps up with two pivotal words: *"... without limitation."*

The change in divert plans does not leave much time for discussion. We must each go into our respective roles, and operate at the speed of trust; an expression my son Ryan, a United States

Marine, shared with me, years ago, on a Southern California golf course.

Erica is mindful of the altered descent geometry (Shannon is far closer than Dublin), and the substantially increased energy-management challenge (less lateral distance in which to lose both the altitude-energy and the airspeed-energy). To assist in the energy-management challenge, she has deployed full speed-brakes (killing Lift on the upper surface of both wings) and she has selected maximum structural airspeed for our descent. With Fran's concurrence, she has programmed and executed the FMC for direct Shannon. She has set 1016 Hectopascals in her altimeter. I do the same. I hit the seat-belt sign. Erica hits the exterior lights.

Mindful of terrain, mindful of our potential for distraction, I select the Terrain option for my Navigation-Display. Erica does the same. Utilizing a global terrain database, factoring in our GPS lateral and vertical position, accounting for our ground-speed across the surface, and our rate of descent toward the surface; the Enhanced Ground Proximity Warning System (E-GPWS) will display green terrain, amber terrain, or red terrain on our respective Navigation-Displays. Green is safe. Amber is a warning. Red is an unpleasant scenario. If we were to find ourselves approaching a Red display, the E-GPWS would issue a "Terrain, Terrain, Pull-Up, Pull-Up" command. Upon hearing that command, Erica would execute the Terrain Escape Maneuver, reviewed ages ago, on the chair-fly drive to the airport.

"Max Thrust, Stow Speed-brake"
Thrust Levers To Mechanical Stops
Stow Speed-Brakes
Level Wings
Pitch To Stick-Shaker / Pitch Limit Indicator / Buffet
Auto-Throttle Off

Auto-Pilot Off
Ignore Flight Director

While I am heads-down building the GPS-approach to Shannon's Runway-06, while Erica is flying the jet, Jason and Fran have taken the initiative. Jason is on the Interphone with Cherie and her flight attendant team, updating my earlier T-E-S-T brief: Time to touchdown is less than ten minutes. Fran has begun running the Approach-Descent checklist. By doing so, he is ensuring, that despite the task-saturation and workload-management challenge, all the bases are covered.

Jason follows his updated T-E-S-T brief with a short and concise announcement to the passengers: We are diverting to Shannon. No need to be alarmed. We practice these scenarios, in the simulator, every nine months. We should be on the ground in less than ten minutes. Please follow the instructions of the cabin team. Your safety is their number one mission.

In many ways, the earlier-discussed ILS approach provides far superior service than that offered by a GPS-approach. An ILS approach can guide an aircraft to a landing, with far lower visibility readings, and to a far lower decision-height. The least accurate ILS, the Category-One ILS, requires a visibility of 1800 feet, and allows for a decision at 200-feet. By contrast, our Shannon GPS-approach requires 2400 feet of visibility, and requires a decision roughly 300-feet above the surface. Clearly, the ILS approach has its advantages.

With a superior ILS-approach available to Runway-24, why conduct an opposite-direction GPS-approach to Runway-06? Answer: With a Cargo Fire warning, with no means to monitor the cargo compartment (detector failures) and with oxygen-generating canisters present in the cargo compartment (may feed a fire); we must put the bird on the ground as soon as possible. We are currently on an easterly heading. Landing on an easterly heading (GPS Runway 06) will allow us to put the jet on the ground sooner. By contrast, flying an ILS approach to the active Runway 24 (a westerly heading) would require us to fly beyond the airport, then execute a 180-degree turn to land on a westerly heading. Added miles. Added time. Again, we cannot evacuate while airborne. We want to be on the ground. The sooner, the better. An opposite direction approach to Runway 06, gets us there sooner.

More broadly, putting aside our emergency scenario into Shannon, if an ILS system allows for lower visibility minimums, and lower decision-heights, why bother with GPS-approaches?

While an ILS system provides accurate lateral and vertical guidance along the final, straight-line portion of an approach; a GPS approach provides lateral and vertical guidance along an entire approach, to include curves, allowing an aircraft to weave its way through the terrain surrounding an airport, thereby allowing all-weather access to previously inaccessible airports.

The GPS approach has an added benefit, similar to our earlier-discussed SIDs and STARs: Once cleared for a GPS approach, a controller no longer needs to provide turns, headings, descents and speeds to an inbound aircraft. By way of example, having selected the GPS approach to Shannon's Runway-06, our Flight Management Computer (FMC) will populate a series of waypoints from an Initial Approach Fix through a series of intermediate waypoints, to a Final Approach Fix and onward to our Decision Altitude. Each of the GPS waypoints will be defined on both the lateral and vertical axes, and may be further defined with airspeed / bank angle restrictions.

Each GPS approach has a Required Navigation Performance (RNP) expressed in tenths of a mile. Throughout our approach, the Flight Management Computer (FMC) will continuously compare our Actual Navigation Performance (ANP) with our Required Navi-gation Performance (RNP). If ANP ever falls below RNP, the FMC will trigger an UNABLE RNP alert, requiring an immediate missed-approach, or reversion to a Visual-Approach.

I am heads-down, with Jason backing me up, comparing the GPS Runway-06 approach chart with the FMC Legs-Page. All waypoints, altitudes, airspeeds and bank angle requirements for the approach (and missed-approach) are in agreement. I set a Decision Altitude of 246-feet. Erica does the same. Our previously calculated landing speeds remain valid. Our previously selected, maximum auto-brake setting remains appropriate.

We are thirty-five miles out, proceeding direct to the final approach fix (ASGON) for the GPS Runway-06. We are passing through 10,000-feet, descending to 3000-feet, while slowing to 280 knots. We pass from clear-blue sky, to the opaqueness of cloud. I note our below-freezing outside air temperature. I flip the engine anti-ice switches. We do not want ice to accumulate in our engine nacelles, starve our engines of air, or break off and pass through our engine cores. We do not want to be a lawn-dart.

While the Dublin plan called for Erica to fly the approach and land the jet, given the added urgency of our changed circumstances (unable to monitor cargo fire status, and the possibility of oxygen-generation canisters feeding a fire), I have opted to fly the jet. My decision is not a reflection on Erica. Rather, it reflects my sense of responsibility, as the Captain: If anything should go wrong during the approach, I will want to be at the controls. The buck will stop with me. "I have the aircraft." Erica replies, "You have the aircraft."

I ask Erica to review my GPS approach set-up, checking for any errors. I likewise ask Jason and the Fran to look over both our shoulders. I re-confirm Approach-Descent checklist complete. I ensure all four of us are monitoring for UNABLE RNP alerts. I ask Fran to have the Evacuation Checklist available and open, immediately following touchdown. I ask both Jason and Fran to assist the flight attendants, should an evacuation be necessary;

with Jason remaining on board, and Fran deplaning with the passengers. Lastly, I ask Jason to inform Ground-Control (for relay to the Crash-Fire-Rescue team) of the nature and location of our hazardous materials in the forward cargo compartment, and of our two pets in the aft cargo compartment.

The term energy-management is a frequent element of debriefs. Under normal circumstances, it can often pose a challenge. Toss in weather and air traffic control, and the challenge can often become problematic. In an emergency scenario, such as ours, with the need to "put the jet on the ground now," energy-management can require pulling out all the stops. With that challenge in mind, I confirm full speed-brake extension, as we begin decelerating from our current 280 knots, to our clean-wing maneuvering speed of 205 knots.

"Flight-28, you are cleared for the GPS approach to Runway-06. Contact Tower at ASGON, on 121.80. Crash-Fire-Rescue trucks will be rolling."

Passing through 205-knots (our clean-wing speed), and while slowing to 185-knots (our Flaps-One speed), I retract our speed-brakes, and call for "Flaps-One." We are on a thirty-degree, dog-leg intercept heading to the final approach course. ASGON is at the top of our FMC Legs-Page, and properly displayed on our Navigation-Display. We are leveling at 3000-feet.

We are in the soup. We are in "instrument conditions." Our view to the front, is nothing but grey. A missed-approach will take us into rising terrain, with a Minimum Safe Altitude of 3400-feet. With that in mind, I reconfirm Terrain selected on the Navigation-Display.

Unlike our Newark instrument-departure, I have elected *not* to hand-fly this approach. The auto-pilot and the auto-throttles will get us from here-to-there, thereby allowing the four of us to monitor aircraft performance and the big-picture.

Approaching ASGON, I call "Set speed 170 knots" and "Flaps-Five." Erica makes it happen, spinning 170 knots into the Airspeed Select window, and selecting flaps-five. With my right hand riding the throttles, I note the thrust reduction for our 170-knot speed. The Flight Mode Annunciator (FMA) reads SPD, L-NAV, V-NAV, CMD, as we roll into a thirty-degree right bank, intercepting our final approach course of 058-degrees.

Passing overhead ASGON, I call "Flaps-Twenty, Gear Down, Landing Checklist." While extending the flaps to twenty, and while extending the gear, Erica flicks the radio transmitter select-switch to 121.80 and checks in with Tower: "Shannon Tower, Flight-28, emergency aircraft, is ASGON inbound, GPS-approach Runway-06."

Shannon Tower replies, "Flight-28, winds are 250-degrees, 15-knots, you are cleared to land, Runway-06, Crash-Fire-Rescue trucks are rolling."

Passing through 2000-feet, I call "Flaps-Thirty, Set Target Airspeed." My right hand rides the auto-throttles, as they reduce thrust, to capture our 145-knot target airspeed.

Jason has been busy. He chimes in with a reassuring "landing distance checks good." Of his own initiative, he has confirmed our 185,000-pound aircraft will "fit" into a 10,495-foot wet runway, with a touchdown speed of 145-knots and a 15-knot tailwind, with one brake deactivated, maximum reverse thrust, full speed-brakes and maximum auto-brakes.

Mindful of our wet runway and the tailwinds, we ask Tower for a final "wind check". They confirm: We have a steady 15-knot tailwind. We do *not* want to "land long" on a wet runway.

Every runway has a 3000-foot touch-down-zone. By contrast, an aircraft carrier touch-down-zone is roughly 122-feet, while the touch-down-zone for an Air Force assault-landing is 300 feet. FAA regulations require we touch-down within the 3000-foot touch-down-zone. Regulations further require we execute a go-around in the event we "land long" beyond the touch-down-zone. In pursuit of the super-smooth landing, eager to hear the passenger and flight-attendant compliments regarding a "nice landing," pilots will often "float" down the runway, "landing long," hoping and praying for that super-smooth landing. We will not do so this morning. A firm landing, at the 1000-foot marker, is our target. We will land firmly, on a spot. We will not float, for a smooth. Firm over float, spot over smooth.

Two minutes, and roughly 1500-feet above our Decision-Altitude, descending at roughly 700-feet per minute; four sets of eyes are inside, outside, inside, outside. We are alert for any UNABLE RNP message. We are monitoring our airspeed, steady at 145-knots. We are monitoring the lateral and vertical path. We are confirming gear-down, flaps-thirty, auto-speed-brakes armed, maximum auto-brakes selected. We are targeting our Decision-Altitude of 246-feet. We are scanning for any sufficient visual reference.

Passing through 1300-feet, Erica makes her required call: "One Thousand Feet, Landing Checklist Complete, Setting Missed Approach Altitude, 5000-feet." As per script, I visually and verbally confirm: "Set 5000-feet."

I click off the auto-throttles. I click off the auto-pilot. I am "hand-flying" the jet. There are two schools of thought regarding when to disengage the auto-flight systems in this scenario. The first school suggests delaying auto-flight disengagement until landing is assured, thereby ensuring auto-flight is available in the event a missed-approach is required.

The second school suggests early auto-flight disengagement, so as to become "one with the jet," allowing one to feel the jet: The pitch, the roll, the winds, the thrust. This school of thought is focused *not* on facilitating a smooth missed-approach; rather, it is focused on facilitating a successful landing (thereby negating the need for a possible missed-approach).

According to this latter school of thought, by becoming "one with the jet," sooner rather than later, a pilot is more likely to successfully manage the transition from instrument conditions to visual conditions, from inside to outside, in the brief interval between breaking out of the weather (a mere few hundred feet above the ground) and touch-down.

We pick our schools. I am a fan of the "one with the jet" school. The auto-flight systems are off. I am hand-flying the jet. As was the case hours ago, with our Newark departure, we are in the soup. The similarities end with that statement. Then, we were fresh. Now, we are in the midst of our "window of circadian low." Then, we were climbing away from the ground, which we could not see. Now, we are descending toward the ground, which we cannot see. Then, we had all the time in the world. Now, the fire-clock is ticking in the cargo compartment beneath our feet.

Passing through 346-feet, one hundred feet above our Decision-Altitude, Erica makes her required call: "Approaching Minimums." I silently review the missed-approach procedure, reviewed ages ago, on the chair-fly drive.

"Flaps 20, Check Thrust, Positive Rate, Gear Up, Set Missed Approach Altitude"

In order to descend below our minimums, we must have "sufficient visual reference with the runway environment." Over my right shoulder, Jason is the first to make the call: "Approach lights in sight." Flashing red lights are visible at our twelve o'clock. We have sufficient visual reference. We may descend below minimums.

At 246-feet, Erica makes her final required call: "Minimums." As per script, I reply with "Landing."

Mindful of the challenge in transitioning to visual conditions, I remain inside, outside, inside, outside. While inside, I am monitoring my artificial horizon, my airspeed, my altitude, my lateral and vertical path. While outside, I am monitoring the PAPI lights (Precision Approach Path Indicator) for my glide-path alignment, and the runway centerline lights for my runway alignment.

Two sets of PAPI lights, one set on each side of the runway, show two red lights, and two white lights. We are on glide-path. Three or more red lights, would indicate below glide-path, prompting me to add thrust. Three or more white lights, would indicate above glide-path, prompting me to reduce thrust.

Both off-glide-path scenarios pose their own particular danger. Below glide-path, might lead to landing short of the runway; in the water, on the grass, or in the airport parking lot; with obviously unpleasant consequences. Above glide-path, might have us "landing long," beyond the touch-down zone, leading to an unnecessary missed-approach. The PAPIs show two reds, and two whites. We are on glide-path.

As we cross the runway threshold, our radar altimeter calls out "Fifty-Feet." Half the landing challenge is nailed if we cross the threshold stable, on speed, on centerline, at fifty feet. We have done so. We are not correcting in the vertical. We are not correcting in the lateral. We are not throttling up. We are not throttling back. We are not banking left. We are not banking right. We are stable. We have but one variable to manage: The flare and the touch-down.

Passing through thirty feet, I slowly begin retarding the throttles to idle, while simultaneously easing back on the yoke. We are in the flare. We are in the round-out. My eyes are focused roughly three-quarters of the way down the runway. My peripheral vision is sub-consciously picking up the cues to my left and to my right. My seat-of-the-pants does not sense a sinking feeling (correct with added thrust), nor does it sense a floating feeling (correct with a bit more flare, and a bit more prayer). So far, so good. I am gingerly working my ailerons and my rudders to maintain alignment with the runway centerline. While doing so, my peripheral vision picks up the Crash-Fire-Rescue trucks, lights flashing, accelerating along the right side of the runway.

We touch down firmly, at the 1000-foot marker, well within the touchdown-zone, on runway centerline and on-speed. Textbook. I retard the throttles to idle. With the throttles at idle, and with main-gear touch-down, our Window Seat Pilots observe as the spoilers atop both wings deploy to their full extension (thereby spoiling Lift), ensuring the full weight of the aircraft is on the main gear, thereby enhancing brake effectiveness.

As I gently lower the nose-gear to the runway, I raise the reverse-thrust levers, and apply maximum reverse thrust to both engines. The Window Seat Pilots, having moments ago heard the relative quiet of Idle power at touch-down, now hear the roar of maximum reverse thrust, as the engines throttle-up and direct maximum thrust in the reverse direction, thereby assisting with our deceleration.

We have a problem. The aircraft nose is swinging to the left. The right reverser has failed to deploy. Erica calls out "Right Reverser."

I am wrestling with an asymmetric thrust condition, as the right engine is at idle forward thrust, while the left engine is at full-reverse thrust, pulling our nose to the left, on a wet and slippery runway. One with the jet, my right foot reflexively adds additional right rudder to counteract the thrust asymmetry. We maintain runway centerline. Mindful of the wet runway and our 15-knot tailwind, mindful that we have lost half of our reverse-thrust, not wanting to go off the far end of the runway; I choose to override the auto-brakes, and apply maximum manual braking. As the runway centerline lights transition from all white, to alternating red-and-white, marking the last 3000-feet of runway, and as we decelerate through eighty knots, Erica makes her required call-out: "Eighty-knots." I smoothly stow the thrust-reverse levers to their idle detent. I neutralize the rudders, and stow the wing-spoilers to their retracted position. As we decelerate through 60-knots, I smoothly reduce my brake pressure, bringing the aircraft to a full stop, on centerline.

Our job is not done. As we come to a stop on the runway centerline, with Crash-Fire-Rescue trucks in position to the right, I set the parking-brake, and Erica makes the required PA call: "Remain Seated, Remain Seated." Within the cabin, Cherie's flight-attendant team is repeating the "Remain Seated" command, as they scan out their windows, ensuring a clear path in the event an emergency evacuation is required.

As we await the call from Crash-Fire-Rescue, I call for the Evacuation Checklist. This checklist will; first, set us up for an evacuation; and, second, guide us through an actual evacuation.

"ATC Advise"	*"Done"*
"Parking-Brake"	*"Set"*
"Cabin Altitude Mode"	*"Manual"*
"Cabin Altitude Selector"	*"Hold In Climb, Until Open"*

We hold the checklist at that point. ATC has been advised, the parking-brake has been set, and we have ensured full depressurization (via manual placement of the outflow valve). Why do so? Any lingering positive cabin pressure, may have hindered the opening of the cabin doors, thereby posing an unwelcome complication during an emergency evacuation. Not wanting our Window Seat Pilots to evacuate directly into an operating engine, our next steps (should an emergency evacuation become necessary) will be:

"Fuel Control Switches (Both)"	*"Cut-Off"*
"Engine And APU Fire Handles (All)"	*"Pull"*
"Evacuation"	*"Announce"*

I reach for the Interphone handset, I hit the Crew-Alert, and I have Cherie on the phone: How is the cabin? How is your flight attendant team? How are the passengers? Her report: All is well.

Our flight-deck speakers come alive with the words "Flight-28, this is Shannon Crash-Fire-Rescue. Confirm engine shut-down. Confirm parking-brake set. We are approaching the forward cargo door."

I reply with a "Stand-By" as I direct Erica to shut-down both engines. She does so. Moments later, to Crash-Fire-Rescue: "Engines are shut-down, parking-brake is set." With that call, I surrender to the adrenaline-rush coursing through my body.

Ireland, Shannon International Airport, Gate 34

De-Brief, A Family Of Four

I have been in the habit of conducting a full crew-debrief since my earliest days as a Captain (airline gig) and Aircraft Commander (military gig). While the debrief often includes procedures and techniques, choices and judgments, my main focus has always been on the human-factor. How did we perform as a crew? What was the nature of our team-dynamic? As part of that query: What could I/we have done differently to better foster the all-important team-dynamic?

First up, Cherie and her flight-attendant team. They did an outstanding job with our Window Seat Pilots during the course of our lengthy Newark delay. They did an off-the-charts job with those same Window Seat Pilots during the course of our emergency. While an evacuation was not required, they had allayed passenger fears and anxieties with their calm, deliberate and professional demeanor. They had selected and briefed Able-Bodied-Assistants. They had conducted their evacuation-review drills.

How do I know such was the case? I stood at the cabin exit to thank each of our Window Seat Pilots as they deplaned. What did I hear from virtually every one of them? Cherie and her team had done an outstanding job.

Next up, the flight-deck team. First words out of my mouth: "Thank you. You made it easy." Recalling our earlier-discussed wingman lesson: Two was in. All the way. My three wingmen knew what had to be done: Put the bird on the ground. Now. Operating at the speed of trust, they had put all the pieces together, most frequently without my directing them to do so. They had made it happen. They had made my job easy. Two was in. My own self-assessment? Still on-going. I remain in the grip of the adrenaline rush. A bit unsteady on my feet. The shakes. I need a beer and a massage. I will settle for tea and a scone.

A handful of gotchas. We never fired the second fire-extinguishing bottle into the forward cargo compartment. We failed to recall the hazardous materials until our last-minute divert to Shannon. We failed to check the required landing distance until we were established on short-final. Kudos to Jason for taking the initiative to do so.

It is said "The exceptions prove the rule." So too, this morning. We were rushed. We committed a number of errors by omission. Mitigation strategy? Expect errors. Hope you have set the right tone. Never stop asking the right questions.

A handful of larger questions remain, many of which might make for some "Monday-morning quarterbacking." Should we have continued on to London? Should we have continued with our first divert option, and proceeded to Dublin? Was it necessary to divert into Shannon for an opposite-direction GPS approach, with a 15-knot tailwind?

As we learned shortly after landing, there was no fire in the forward cargo compartment. When Crash-Fire-Rescue opened the cargo door, all was good. Other than the residue from the fire extinguishing agent, the compartment looked no different, than it had looked hours earlier, in Newark. We could have continued on to London-Heathrow. False alarm.

Having said that, we *did* have a Cargo-Fire alert. We *did* lose all ability to detect any fire in that compartment. That compartment *did* contain oxygen-generating canisters, capable of feeding a fire. The checklist *did* direct us to "land as soon as practicable."

As professional pilots, we have made it a point to be familiar with the industry literature. On the matter of inflight fires, the literature is very clear. From the Department of Transportation: *"Studies and other experience indicate that flight-crew members should begin planning for an emergency landing as soon as possible after the first indication of fire. Delaying the aircraft's descent by only a couple of minutes might make the difference between a successful landing and evacuation, and the complete loss of an aircraft and its occupants."*

Hence, my single-minded focus on getting the jet down, within sight of the surface, prepared to put the jet on any patch of earth or water, thereby enabling evacuation. With that Department of Transportation quote in mind, I am at peace. I will not spend a moment pondering the alternative.

Following our deplanement at the terminal, our Shannon Airfield Operations team has gathered our Window Seat Pilots in the arrival hall auditorium, to lay out their options: A Shannon overnight on the company nickel, and the completion of their journey to London-Heathrow, tomorrow morning; or the continuation of their journey, today, on another air carrier.

As I stroll through the Shannon arrival hall, in search of my tea and scone, while awaiting flight-crew transportation, I spot the family of four; Mom and Dad, Ryan and Tessa, and the terrier in the kennel; as they listen to the Airport Operations team briefing. Both Tessa and Ryan, have spotted me, have tugged at Mom's skirt, and have whispered in Dad's ear. Thinking of my own two boys, grateful that I will see them again; recognizing my job is not yet complete; I put aside all thoughts of the tea and scone, and make a brief detour, to join the briefing.

With the permission of the Airport Operations team, I take a moment to brief our Window Seat Pilots. The operative (but false-alarm) smoke detector, and the inoperative smoke detector will both be replaced. The cargo fire extinguishing agent will be reserviced. The thrust-reverser will be repaired. Ditto the cabin pressure controller and the left transponder system. All corrective actions will be completed, and all systems will be tested, prior to the next flight. The flight-crew, and the flight-attendant crew, will both be well-rested for tomorrow's continuation of Flight 28 to London-Heathrow. We will not get them to London-Heathrow on time; however, we will get them there safely and comfortably. With an extra (Irish) stamp in their passport.

With my briefing complete, I drop to my knee, before Tessa and Ryan, hand each of them a set of Pilot Wings, a pair of Boeing 757 cards, and the crumpled copy of our flight-plan, a souvenir for a flight they are not likely to soon forget. I look them both in the eyes, and ask them: "Do you know what the best job in the world is?" They are silent. My answer: "Being a Mom, and being a Dad." Ryan's reply: "Come visit us in Estonia." I give both parents a wink. I give both children a sharp salute.

As I make my way out of the auditorium, both Marlena (our concerned-about-turbulence flyer) and Hannah (our nervous Anchorage flyer) approach me, with Marlena reaching out to grasp my hand. Again. Their message: They thank me for getting them on the ground safely. I accept their "Thank You" while making clear that I am doing so, on behalf of the entire crew, for it was indeed a team effort.

There will be further debriefs, both for the flight-deck crew, as well as for the flight attendant crew. Those debriefs will focus on lessons learned and "What could we have done better?" Despite our best efforts to avoid paperwork, we will be completing paperwork. Despite our best efforts to avoid come-see-me phone calls, we will receive those phone calls.

As I resume my stroll through the arrival terminal, in search of tea and scone, and postcards for my two boys, I glance to my right, through the floor-to-ceiling windows. I pause, and allow my eyes to track a jet as it rolls silently down the distant runway, accelerating from zero-to-rotate, twin rooster-tails of rainwater trailing in its wake. Smoothly and gracefully, the jet rotates and begins its silent, majestic, confident climb, corkscrew vortices spiraling off both wing-tips. A gentle thirty-degree bank, an effortless, climbing left turn. Cloud entry, and lost from sight.

I will slip the surly bonds of earth, and dance the skies on laughter-silvered wings. I will join the tumbling mirth of sun-split clouds, and chase the shouting wind along. I will top the windswept heights with easy grace, where never lark or even eagle flew.

Cherie interrupts my thoughts with the all-important question: "Will dinner be Thai or Indian?" Thai or Indian, Cherie will choose. Dinner will be on me. Erica will get her massage. Fran will have another story worthy of waving his hands. Evette will people-watch. Claire will enjoy her high-fructose corn syrup and lemon slices. Garrett will hit the liquor aisle in duty-free.

As the kids like to say: All good.

Epilogue

I first put pen to paper, and fingertips to keyboard, in 1990. Decades ago. My intent was to convey the wonder of flight, and answer the many questions I had been asked, after what was, at that time, ten years in the aviation business.

As I have raised my two boys, now two young men; as I have slipped the surly bonds with them on countless occasions, with each of them racking up over 900,000 miles; as I have answered their many questions; the dream of writing this book has never faded.

I dedicate this book to both of them. To Ryan. To Jason. Bob Hope was fond of saying, at the conclusion of each of his USO shows, "Thank you for the memories." Ryan and Jason, thank you for the memories. I treasure each of them, beyond measure.

Four forces act upon an aircraft while in flight: Lift and Weight, Thrust and Drag. In order for an aircraft to fly, Lift must exceed Weight, and Thrust must exceed Drag.

I dedicate this book, to all those who provided the Lift and the Thrust, without which, this bird may never have flown: The many, never forgotten, men and women, past and present, who have loved me, supported me, and believed in me; most particularly, my mother Anne, my father Robert, and my brother Duke-Man. You are with me, on each rotation, on each landing; and most powerfully, during those quiet moments at cruise altitude, in the dark of night, or the brilliance of day, when I reach out my hand, and touch the face of God.

Final Words

I salute the unseen men and women who toil, behind the scenes, day in and day out, to make the mission happen. I am reminded of a quote from an earlier life: "Logistics defines the possible." The unseen men and women make every flight possible. We would not "slip the surly bonds of Earth" without the flex of their mind and muscle.

Made in the USA
Las Vegas, NV
19 November 2024

11864707R00144